# The Message of the Buddha

# The Message of the Buddha

by K. N. JAYATILLEKE

*Late Professor of Philosophy, University of Ceylon*

a posthumous work

edited by Ninian Smart

*Professor of Religious Studies, University of Lancaster*

The Free Press

*A Division of Macmillan Publishing Co., Inc.*

NEW YORK

The Free Press
A Division of Macmillan Publishing Co., Inc.
866 Third Avenue, New York, N.Y. 10022

Free Press Edition 1975

Library of Congress Catalog Card Number: 75-15431

Printed in Great Britain

printing number
1 2 3 4 5 6 7 8 9 10

# Preface

It was for me a privilege that I was entrusted with editing the last writings of K. N. Jayatilleke. He was an esteemed friend and a great scholar. The present book is constituted of the manuscripts of lectures and talks given by him in 1969 (mainly), on the radio and elsewhere. He was working on these when he died so suddenly and tragically. His widow Mrs Pat Jayatilleke asked me to edit the extant manuscripts. I have done so with minimum violence to the original. Some parts I have cut out as repetitive – repetition being necessary in the original format but not in the present way of presenting the ideas.

As usual K.N. writes with clarity and economy. It was a labour of friendship and esteem for me to have performed this small service in memory of a considerable and important scholar and a good friend. The result is an excellent guide to the teachings of Theravada Buddhism.

I am very grateful to Mrs Geraldine Towers and Mr Martin Wiltshire for their excellent assistance in preparing the manuscript.

*Ninian Smart*
*Lancaster*
1974

# Abbreviations

Page and volume numbers refer to the Pali Text Society editions, for example, D. I. 84 = *Dīgha Nikāya.*

| | |
|---|---|
| A. | *Anguttara Nikāya* |
| D. | *Dīgha Nikāya* |
| D.A. | Commentary on the *Dīgha Nikāya*, i.e. *Sumaṅgalavilāsini* |
| Dh. | *Dhammapada* |
| It. | *Itivuttaka* |
| J. | *Jātaka* |
| M. | *Majjhima Nikāya* |
| Nid. I. | *Mahā-Niddesa* |
| S. | *Saṃyutta Nikāya* |
| Sn. | *Sutta-Nipāta* |
| Ud. | *Udāna* |
| Vin. | *Vinaya Piṭaka* |
| Ch. | *Chāndoyya Upanisad* |
| RV. | *Ṛg Veda* |
| P.T.S. | Pali Text Society |

# Contents


Preface *page* 7
Abbreviations 8
1 The Historical Context of the Rise of Buddhism 11
2 The Significance of Vesak 25
3 The Buddhist Conception of Truth 40
4 The Buddhist Attitude to Revelation 53
5 The Buddhist Conception of Matter and the Material World 65
6 The Buddhist Analysis of Mind 77
7 The Buddhist Conception of the Universe 90
8 The Buddhist Attitude to God 104
9 Nirvana 117
10 The Buddhist View of Survival 128
11 The Buddhist Doctrine of Karma 139
12 The Case for the Buddhist Theory of Karma and Survival 152
13 The Conditioned Genesis of the Individual 196
14 The Buddhist Ethical Ideal of the Ultimate Good 229
15 Buddhist Ethics 239
16 The Buddhist Conception of Evil 250
Index 261

I

# The Historical Context of the Rise of Buddhism

Tradition has it that the Buddha was born in a certain historical context, at a certain time and at a certain place when his doctrine was likely to be most needed, understood and appreciated. It was then that the aspirant to Buddhahood came down from the Tuṣita heaven to be born among men. Whatever the truth of this belief may be, there is no doubt that the appearance of the Buddha was preceded by the presence of a diversity of religious and philosophical beliefs about the nature and destiny of man in the universe. In fact, there is hardly any major religious or philosophical view prevalent today, or which has evolved in the course of human thought in the East or West, that was not represented then by some religious or philosophical teacher who had appeared on the scene.

## THEISTS, MATERIALISTS AND AGNOSTICS

These major views were in fact held by six outstanding religious or philosophical teachers, who are each said to have had a large following and who were the senior contemporaries of the Buddha. There was Makkhali Gosāla, the Theist (issara-kāranavādin), according to whom the world was created by a divine fiat and continues to unfold itself like a ball of thread that unwinds when flung on the ground.

Being under the impact of various evolutionary forces over which they have no control, beings gradually evolve under varying conditions of existence until they eventually attain final salvation. In the other extreme was Ajita Kesakambali, the Materialist, according to whom fools and the wise alike terminate their existence at death and there was no such thing as a 'good life', which religious men talk about.

Opposed to both these views was Sañjaya Belaṭṭhiputta, the Sceptic Agnostic or Positivist, who held that beliefs about an after-life, moral responsibility and ultimate salvation were beyond verification and that, therefore, one could not with reason hold any firm opinion about them. Many people are even today either Materialists, Theists or Sceptics. Their world-view or *Weltanschauung* is in fact basically not different from those put forward by these three leading philosophers at the time of the Buddha.

There are, however, three other leading thinkers referred to in the early Buddhist texts and they too represent certain types of thought met with (still) today as well as in the history of human speculation. There was Pūraṇa Kassapa, who was a Natural Determinist holding that everything was strictly determined by natural forces. As a corollary to his determinism he was, like the scientists who held a deterministic view of nature, an Amoralist who believed that there was nothing good or evil as such. Pakudha Kaccāyana, on the other hand, was, like Empedocles or Aristotle, a Categorialist, who tried to explain and comprehend man and the universe by classifying reality into discrete categories. Lastly, Nigaṇṭha Nātaputta, the historical founder of Jainism, was a Relativist in his theory of knowledge, holding that there was some truth in every point of view, and an Eclectic in his metaphysics, which tries to combine the truth of all these different, even contradictory standpoints.

All these teachers, it is said, who represent standard types of belief were held in great esteem and veneration by the people, and the religion and philosophy of Buddhism is distinguished from every one of them. Some of the disciples of the Buddha were in fact drawn from among those who adhered to their doctrines. Sāriputta, for instance, the chief disciple of the Buddha, was originally a follower of Sañjaya, the Sceptic.

Very often, however, the Buddha classified the teachers of his time into two categories, the Eternalists (sassata-vādā), who believed in the existence of an integral soul, which survived the death of the body, and the Annihilationists (uccheda-vādā) who asserted the total destruction of the human personality with the death and dissolution of the body. Among the Eternalists were various types of Theists and among the Annihilationists were various categories of Materialists. The views of these two schools of thought were the predominant views of the time and it is in opposition to both of them that the religion and philosophy of Buddhism is presented.

## VEDIC TRADITION

If we examine the non-Buddhist sources, we find that some of these theories are traceable to the Vedic tradition, while others can be traced to the non-Vedic. But these terms, Vedic and non-Vedic, are to some extent misleading. For it is possible or even probable that many of the views within the Vedic tradition evolved under the impact of the non-Vedic, while some of the non-Vedic teachings, on the other hand, can be shown to have branched off from the Vedic.

In this chapter, which concerns the historical context of the rise of Buddhism, we shall very briefly consider what is meant by the Vedic and the non-Vedic traditions and the general attitude of Buddhism to each of them, without going into details. It is generally agreed among scholars that Buddhism arose in the sixth century BC during or somewhat after the period when the Upaniṣadic doctrines were being formulated. The Upaniṣads are considered to form the tailend of the Vedic tradition and are hence known as the Vedānta or the end of the Vedas. But it is held to be the end of the Vedic tradition, not merely in a chronological sense, but because the Vedānta constituted the essence or consummation of the Vedic tradition. Even in the Buddhist texts we find the phrase, vedānta-gū-brahmacariyo, used to denote a person who has gained the heights of spiritual knowledge and as such has consummated his religious life. In an Upaniṣadic context, the phrase would denote one who has mastered the essence of the latter portion of the Vedic tradition and as such has realised the fruits of the religious life. This shows the close relationship between Upaniṣadic and early Buddhist thought.

The Upaniṣads, however, do not present a single view but a variety of views regarding the nature and destiny of man in the universe, although there is a certain homogeneity in the thought of the middle and later Upaniṣadic thinkers. These thinkers were historically separated and geographically isolated from each other and there is evidence that they built upon earlier theories and criticised each other. They are, however, all deemed to belong to the Vedic tradition by virtue of the fact that they owed a general allegiance to the Vedas. With the majority of the middle and later Upaniṣadic thinkers this allegiance was a very loose one, since they considered the earlier imaginative and discursive type of knowledge as a form of 'lower knowledge' (aparā vidyā), while their own knowledge was derived from an expansion of consciousness and extra-sensory powers of perception. This was due to the practice of Yoga and the intuitive knowledge thus gained was regarded by them as parā vidyā or the ultimate knowledge.

One important difference with Buddhism was the fact that it paid no special allegiance to the Vedas. The Buddha, it is said, studied under Yogic teachers presumably of the Vedic tradition, such as Alāra Kālāma and Uddaka Rāmaputta but, although he mastered their teachings, he is said to have gone away dissatisfied with them. However, immediately after his enlightenment, it is significant that he first thinks of preaching to these two teachers since he considered that they were very wise and would have soon profited from the Dhamma.

The recognition of the worth of these Upaniṣadic teachings in the Buddhist texts is embodied in the stanza with which Brahmā, the regent of the cosmos, invites the Buddha to preach the Dhamma to the world, which would otherwise be destroyed without it. It reads as follows: 'There arose in the past among the Magadhan peoples a Dhamma, which was not perfect and which was conceived by imperfect seers. Open now the door to immortality so that people may listen to the Dhamma, which has been fully comprehended by a Perfect One.'

A further recognition of the value of the intuitive insights of some of the Upaniṣadic seers is contained in the Buddhist concept of the Pacceka Buddha, which accepts the fact that one may attain salvation and a high degree of enlightenment by one's own efforts, without necessarily depending on the teaching of the Buddha himself. Even the teaching of the Buddha, it may be noted, is only a guide to understanding, 'for one has to put forth effort oneself, for the Transcendent Ones are only guides' (tumhehi kiccaṃ ātappaṃ akkhātāro Tathāgatā). In one place in the *Sutta Nipāta*, the Buddha recognises the fact that not all the recluses and brahmins are involved in decay and death (nā'haṃ bhikkhave sabbe samaṇa-brāhmaṇāse jāti-jarāya nivuttā ti brūmi).

## AN ANCIENT WAY

Of similar import is the conception of the Buddha or the Enlightened One as a discoverer of an 'ancient way' (purāṇaṃ añjasaṃ) already discovered in the past. But it is not clear whether the 'past' here referred to is the historical past of the present world-cycle or of a previous world-cycle. Buddhism upholds the cyclical oscillating theory of the universe, which expands and contracts during immense periods of time, called vivaṭṭa and saṃvaṭṭa-kappas, aeons of the expansion and contraction of the universe. One Sutta and a very early one states that the Buddha was the first in the history of the present world to break through the shell of ignorance and attain illumination. In another Sutta, however, which belongs to a later stratum, the historical Buddha is represented as the seventh Buddha of the current epoch, while still later in the tradition he becomes the twenty-fourth. It is possible that these latter views were developed under the impact of the Vedic and Jain traditions respectively. For the Vedas are traditionally revealed by seven seers, the saptarṣi, and Nigaṇṭha Nātaputta, the founder of Jainism, is held to be the twenty-fourth saviour or Tīrthaṅkara.

Yet the basic Buddhist concept is an inherently rational and plausible one. The Buddha merely discovers by his unaided efforts the truths about the nature and destiny of man in the universe and reveals them out of compassion for mankind. This has been done by countless Buddhas in the past. For according to the oscillating theory of the universe, the universe has no beginning in time, and the further we go back in time there is the possibility of going back still further, with successive and unending expansions and contractions of the universe. Likewise it is inferred that there would be such Buddhas in the future. As for the present, it is stated in the Mahāvastu, a work embodying some of the earliest views of Mahāyāna Buddhism, that there are galactic systems (loka-dhātu) in space in which Buddhas are presently preaching the Dhamma. This is not a conception that is wholly alien to the Theravāda tradition. For even today in Ceylon Buddhists recite the stanza, 'ye ca Buddhā atītā ca ye ca Buddhā anāgatā, paccuppannā ca ye Buddhā esaṃ vandāmi sabbada.' This means: 'I revere at all times the Buddhas in the past, the Buddhas in the future and *those in the present.*' It is not implausible to believe that, just as much as there are scientists in this earth who have discovered by experiment and observation certain laws operative in nature, there could be other similar beings who have similarly discovered these laws in an inhabited planet of our galactic system or in an alien galactic system.

To come back to earth and to history, we find that it was the convergence of the two traditions, the Vedic and the non-Vedic, which blossomed forth in Buddhism. And it is a remarkable fact, as we have observed, that towards the end of the Vedic tradition there emerged sincere seekers after truth and immortality, who devoted their entire lives to this quest, renouncing all else.

This quest begins in the Āraṇyakas or the early Upaniṣadic period, prior to about 800 BC, when we meet with the following prayer recorded in the Bṛhadārâṇyaka Upaniṣad:

> From the unreal, lead me to the real!
> From darkness, lead me to light!
> From death, lead me to immortality!
> (1.3.28)

It is in answer, as it were, to this quest that the Buddha *circa* 528 BC announced to the world: 'Open for them are doors to immortality' (Apārutā tesaṃ amatassa dvārā). And during the interval of time from 800 to 528 BC earnest seekers gave up everything for this quest.

### A NEW ERA

It marked a new stage in the development and evolution of the human mind, but mankind has still to learn the lessons from the discoveries made by this awakened human intellect about or somewhat prior to the sixth century BC. It is also at this time that we discover the world over a new awakening of the human race. In Greece, Pythagoras, perhaps influenced by Eastern thought, conceives of philosophy as a way of life, sets up a brotherhood and teaches the doctrine of rebirth, which later influenced Plato. Platonic ideas eventually had an impact on Plotinus, St Augustine and the modern Western world. In Israel, the prophet Isaiah dreams of a time to come when there shall be human brotherhood and all nations shall live in amity and friendship and wars shall be no more. In Persia, Zoroaster views the world as a battleground in which the forces of good and evil contend and is convinced of the eventual victory of good over evil. In India, as we have already seen, the Upaniṣadic seers achieve a breakthrough in human consciousness and one of them predicts that 'truth alone shall conquer and never untruth' (satyam eva jayate nānṛtam *Muṇḍaka Upaniṣad*, 3.1.6). In China, Confucius ethicises human relationships and Lao Tse speaks of the need for man to live in harmony with eternal values and principles.

This message of the sixth century BC which marks the spiritual awakening of man and the consequent faith in the possibility of harmonious living may appear to be antiquated to some, but it is likely to prove to be more relevant to the modern world than would seem at first sight. It was during this sixth century BC that the Buddha was born and spoke after his enlightenment in a modern idiom, which is becoming increasingly intelligible to man in the twentieth century.

Buddhist tradition, again, has it that the world at this time was eagerly awaiting the birth of an Enlightened One. The *Sutta Nipāta* says that the sage Asita predicted that the Buddha-child 'was born for the welfare and happiness of mankind' (manussa-loke hita-sukhatāya jāto). Certainly the Vedic tradition looked forward to someone, who would lead the people from darkness to light and from death to immortality. As H. G. Wells points out in his *A Short History of the World*, 'Gautama Buddha . . . taught his disciples at Benares in India about the same time that Isaiah was prophesying among the Jews in Babylon . . .' (Penguin Books, revised edn, September 1946, p. 90). Isaiah says that a people who walked in darkness have seen a great light and speaks of a child to be born at the time and who shall be called Wonderful, Counsellor, the Mighty God, the Everlasting Father and the Prince of Peace. Of the increase of his government and of peace, it is said, there will be no end.

It is a curious coincidence that all these epithets have been claimed by or for the Buddha either during his lifetime or a few centuries after his birth. For the Buddha says that he is the Acchariya-Puggala or the Wonderful Person and Satthā devamanussānam, the Counsellor of gods and men, while he has been called 'the God among gods' (Brahmātibrahma, Devātideva), the Eternal Father (Ādi Pitā) and the Sāntirāja or Sānti-nāyaka, the Prince of Peace. The Buddha himself says in the *Bhayabherava Sutta*: 'If anyone says that there is born in this world a perfectly enlightened being for the weal and welfare of mankind out of compassion for the world, for the weal welfare and happiness of gods and men, he may rightly say this of me.' In the *Ariyapariyesana Sutta*, the Buddha speaks of going to Kāsi to set up the Kingdom of Rule of Righteousness (Dhamma-cakkaṃ pavattetuṃ), which is elsewhere called Brahma-cakkaṃ or the Kingdom of God, but since Brahma here does not have a theistic connotation, it would mean the highest or the most sublime kingdom. And it is said that the gradual advance of this Rule of Righteousness cannot be prevented by any religious teacher, angel, Satan (Māra), God (Brahmā) or anyone in this cosmos. The *Mahāvastu* interprets this Rule of Righteousness in a political setting when it says that 'The Rule of Power ultimately depends on the Rule of Righteousness' (Balacakraṃ hi nisrāya Dharmacakram pravartate).

No one would say that the reference in Isaiah's prophecy is a Buddhist interpolation. But a similar statement attributed to Confucius in one of his classics is considered by scholars to be a Buddhist interpolation in the text, though the evidence is far from conclusive. It is said in the Chinese classical text, *Lieh-tẓu*, that when the chief minister of the state of Sung visited Confucius, he asked him the question, 'Are you a

Sage?' to which Confucius is said to have replied: 'How would I presume [to call myself] a Sage? In fact, I am only one who has extensively studied and who has [stored up] much knowledge.' The minister then asked Confucius whether various kings and emperors of China were Sages, to which he replied in the negative. Finally in exasperation he asked Confucius, 'Who then is a Sage?' It is said that Confucius changed countenance at this question and after a pause answered as follows: 'Among the people of the West there is a Sage. He does not speak and is yet spontaneously believed, he does not [consciously] convert people and yet [his doctrine] is spontaneously realised. How vast he is! There is none among the people who can find a name for it!' (See E. Zürcher, *The Buddhist Conquest of China*, E. J. Brill, Leiden, 1959, p. 274.) Some Chinese scholars have taken this to be a reference to Lao-tzu but the Buddhists of China have seen in it a reference to the Buddha for the Buddha was known as the Sākya-Muni or 'the Silent Sage of the Sākyans'. An ancient Chinese Buddhist scholar makes the following comment on this text: 'To judge from this [text], Confucius was fully aware of the fact that the Buddha was a great Sage. But at that time no opportunity had as yet arisen [to expound the doctrine], so he knew it but remained silent . . .' (ibid.).

## WAR OF IDEOLOGIES

Whatever the historicity of these texts, even if we judge the Buddha by our wordly standards, there is little doubt that the Buddha was a person with the keenest intellect and the kindest heart. He towers above the enlightened thinkers of his age for, in his Dhamma, we have an ideology which is claimed to put an end to all ideologies and which shall eventually be shown to be true when all other ideologies have in the light of reason and experience been shown to be false. The supreme victory in the battle of ideologies (anuttaro sangāma-vijayo), it is claimed shall be won by the Dhamma. It is for this reason among others that it has been claimed of the Buddha that he is the Enlightened One *par excellence* or the Anuttara Sammāsambuddha.

The doctrines of Buddhism can be better understood if we can see in them the impact of the different theories and practices enunciated in the Vedic and non-Vedic traditions. One of the basic principles of Buddhism has been that of accepting whatever it thinks is sound, good and true from whatever source it comes, and of rejecting what it believed to be unsound, evil and false. On this principle, we can observe that there are some things which are acceptable to Buddhism in the Vedic tradition and others which are rejected. It is the same with the theories of the Materialists, Sceptics, Ājīvikas and Jains in the non-Vedic tradition. A careful study of what is derived from each of these traditions as well as what is rejected will help us to comprehend the Dhamma with greater clarity and precision.

## CHRONOLOGY

We have already said that in the opinion of most scholars Buddhism arose during or after the Upaniṣadic period of Vedic thought. But this period stretches from about the eighth to the fourth century BC and the question as to what point in the chronological scale Buddhism comes into being is an important one.

For the question as to whether certain ideas in the Upaniṣads influenced or were influenced by Buddhism can be determined largely from such a chronological framework. For example, it has been surmised, though in my opinion not correctly, that Buddhism was not aware of the impersonal concept of Brahman as the ultimate reality to be realised by attaining union with it in this life itself. If so, then if Buddhism spoke of the ultimate reality beyond space, time and causation as the state of Nirvāṇa to be realised here and now, rather than as a Heaven of Brahmā or a Brahma-loka to be attained after death, someone may conclude that the conception of Brahman as an impersonal reality to be realised here and now was influenced by Buddhism. Such conclusions, however, should not be arrived at on the basis of our preconceptions, but on objective criteria, which can be accepted on the basis of their inherent plausibility in the light of reason and experience.

Traditionally, there are 108 Upaniṣads but in actual fact the number is about 200. Of these thirteen principal Upaniṣads were commented on by Śaṅkara and have been classified as early, middle and late. Thus *Chāndogya* is early, *Kaṭha* belongs to the middle period, while *Maitrāyaṇi* is late. Where does Buddhism take its rise? Is it contemporary with the early, middle or late Upaniṣads? Or does it appear long after the thirteen principal ones had come into being? All these views have been held by various scholars. But the theory that is most plausible and is consistent with the facts is the one that holds the rise of Buddhism is somewhat prior to the *Maitrāyaṇi Upaniṣad*, which is a late Upaniṣad. For there seems to be good evidence that this particular Upaniṣad refers to a rising Buddhist movement.

The Upaniṣad mentions a sect wearing a 'ruddy robe' (kaṣāya), which converts people by recourse to 'rational arguments and examples' (tarka-dṛṣtānta), denies the doctrine of the soul (nairātmyavāda), preaches a Dharma which is destructive of the Vedas and orthodox scriptures (Vedādi-śāstra – himsaka-Dharmābhidhyānam . . . ) and whose goal is the mere attainment of pleasure (ratimātram phalamasya).

It can be shown that all these descriptions could apply only to Buddhism in the historical context although some of them could have applied other movements. Thus, the Materialists may be said to have resorted to rational arguments and examples and posited the attainment of pleasure as their goal, but they did not teach Dharma or wear a ruddy robe. The Jains, on the other hand, had a Dharma but they did not deny the existence of the soul nor because of their ascetic way of life did they pursue pleasure. It was the Buddhists, who at this time were being criticised by other religious sects as being addicted to pleasure. Besides, they wore a ruddy robe, the kaṣāya-vastra. They used rational persuasion as the means of winning over others to their point of view. They taught a doctrine that denied the validity of the concepts of soul and substance and preached a Dharma, which was not based on, and in fact denied, the acceptance of the Vedic revelation.

Besides, the *Maitrāyaṇi Upaniṣad* shows evidence of the influence of Buddhism although it forbids the brahmins from studying what is not of the Veda.

So the rise of Buddhism, it may be presumed, is not far removed in time from the *Maitrāyaṇi Upaniṣad*, although it is somewhat prior to it. We may, therefore, regard the period from the *Ṛgveda* to the *Maitrāyaṇi Upaniṣad* as the Vedic tradition that could have had an impact on the rise of Buddhism.

But the non-Vedic tradition is equally important. The Materialists, Sceptics, the various speculations about time and change in the doctrines of the Ājīvikas and the ecelectic theories of the Jains have left their mark on Buddhism, which extracted what was true and valuable in each of these schools of thought leaving out the dross.

Predominant among these in the non-Vedic tradition were the Materialists. There are seven schools of such Materialists referred to in the *Brahmajāla Sutta* and the existence of several of them is independently attested in the non-Buddhist literature. The first maintained that the mind was identical with the living body and that there was no mind apart from the body that was alive. The second held that mind was an emergent by-product of the body, which disintegrated at death. There were also mystic Materialists, some of whom believed in the possibility of expansions of consciousness by the use of drugs and this was criticised by the Buddhists as micchā jhāna – trances attained by wrong means.

It is against the background largely of these two main schools of thought that Buddhism is presented. Buddhism accepted the fact there was some degree of truth in some of their doctrines but showed that the ultimate truth transcended them both. Referring to the bhava-diṭṭhi or 'the personal immortality view' and the vibhava-diṭṭhi or 'the annihilationist view', the Buddha says: 'These religious and philosophical teachers who fail to see how these two views arise and cease to be, their good points and their defects and how one transcends them both in accordance with the truth, are under the grip of greed, hate and ignorance . . . and will not attain final redemption from suffering' (*Majjhima Nikāya*, I. 65).

Besides these two main views, however, we must not forget the variety of views about the nature and destiny of man in the universe, prevalent at the time. These have been summarised in the *Brahmajāla Sutta*, which refers to sixty-two views and ways of life.

# 2

# The Significance of Vesak

Vesāk is traditionally associated with the birth, enlightenment and Parinirvāṇa of the Buddha, who renounced a life of luxury to solve the riddle of the universe and bring happiness to mankind as well as to other beings. As in the case of other religious teachers of antiquity, his birth is enshrouded in myth and legend, the later accounts found in the *Lalitavistara*, for instance, containing descriptions of more miraculous happenings than in the earliest accounts in the Pali Canon. As Buddhists, who have to believe only in things as they are, and therefore in verifiable historical truths, we are not obliged to believe in all these myths and legends. The truths of Buddhism stand or fall to the extent to which the Dhamma contains statements which can be verified as true, and the veracity of Buddhism, therefore, does not depend on the historical accuracy of legendary beliefs about the birth or death of the Buddha. Besides, the Buddha encouraged self-criticism as well as a critical examination of his own life on the part of his disciples. Even with regard to matters of doctrine or discipline, textual criticism was encouraged. For instance, a monk who claimed to have heard something from the Buddha himself was asked to examine its authenticity in the light of the Sutta and Vinaya (a collection of texts regarding doctrinal and disciplinary matters made during the time of the Buddha himself), since his personal recollections and interpretations may not have been altogether trustworthy.

## HISTORICAL FACTS

This does not mean that we need to dismiss all the statements associated with the birth, life and demise of the Buddha as mythical or legendary. Some of us may feel that if we were closer in time to the Buddha we would have had a better opportunity of apprehending the historical facts about him. But in a way we are better placed today, for we can study the historical development and expansion of Buddhism and also compare the life of the Buddha and contrast it with that of other great religious teachers and philosophers of mankind. Some of the legends may have a kernel of historical truth. Human imagination seems to have worked in a very similar way with regard to some of the heroes of history. At least a hundred years after the death of the Buddha we find in the *Mahāvastu* the statement that 'the Buddha's body was immaculately conceived' (na ca maithuna-sambhūtaṃ Sugatasya samucchritaṃ) or, in other words that the Buddha had a virgin birth, but if we trace the origin of this idea to the Pali Canonical texts, we find it stated that the mother of the Buddha had no thoughts of sex after the Buddha-child was conceived, which may quite possibly be historically true.

Some of the claims are certainly historically significant. Everyone would admit today that the Buddha was the first religious teacher in history with a universal message for all mankind and that he was the founder of the concept of a world religion. Asita's prophecy that the Buddha was 'born for the good and happiness of the human world' (manussaloke hita-sukhatāya jāto) may be seen today in all probability to be true although, at the time that it found its way into the text, it was a mere prophecy.

Let us now turn to the last days of the Buddha on earth, as reported in the *Mahāparinibbāna Sutta*. Here again we find fact with an occasional admixture of legend. Here again, it is difficult at times to distinguish the hard core of fact from legend. The Buddha, it is said, was transfigured just prior to his death. His robes, it is said, were aglow when touching the body. Is this fact or fiction? We do not know. But there are a number of significant statements about the Dhamma whose historicity is self-authenticated. It is said that the Buddha did not want to pass away until he had brought into existence a set of monks who were learned in the Dhamma, had realised its fruits and were competent to deal with any criticisms levelled against it.

When the sal flowers from the twin sal-trees under which he lay waved over his body, it seemed as though nature were paying him homage. Today we Buddhists worship the Buddha by offering flowers before his image. But the Buddha says that one does not really pay homage to the Transcendent One by such offerings. It is the disciple, whether he be man or woman, who follows in the footsteps of the Dhamma and lives in accordance with it who truly reveres and pays the highest homage to the Transcendent One. When Ananda is worried as to how the funeral rites should be performed, the Buddha asks him not to worry about these rituals but to 'strive hard to attain the good goal' (sadattha ghatatha), for Ananda had not as yet become an Arahant.

Most instructive is the Buddha's last sermon, which was to Subhadda, the wandering ascetic. The question he asked was very interesting. Did all the six outstanding teachers who were contemporaries of the Buddha understand the truth? Or is it the case that only some understood or none? In the order in which they are mentioned, there was Pūraṇa Kassapa, who was an Amoralist because he thought that everything was strictly determined by natural causes, Makkhali Gosāla who was a Theist who believed that everything happened in accordance with God's will, Ajita Kesakambali, the Materialist, who denied survival, moral values and the good life, Pakudha Kaccayana, the Categorialist, who tried to explain the world in terms of discrete categories, Sañjaya Belaṭṭhiputta, the Agnostic Sceptic or Positivist, who held that moral and religious propositions were unverifiable, and Nigaṇṭha

Nātaputta who was a Relativist and an Eclectic. The significance of the question comes to this. Are Amoralism, Theism, Materialism, Categorialism, Agnosticism and Eclecticism all true? Or is none true? Or are one or some of these theories true?

## THE TRUE RELIGION

Elsewhere, in the *Sandaka Sutta* there is a clear-cut answer to this question. There Ānanda says that in the opinion of the Buddha there are four false religions in the world and four religions which are unsatisfactory though not necessarily totally false, while Buddhism is distinguished from all of them. The word for religion here is used in a wide sense as in modern usage to denote theistic and non-theistic religions as well as pseudo-religions or religion-surrogates, i.e. substitutes for religions such as, say, Marxism, Existentialism, Humanism, etc. The four false religions or philosophies inculcating a way of life are: first, Materialism which denies survival, second, Amoralism which denies good and evil, third, any religion which asserts that man is miraculously saved or doomed and last, theistic evolutionism which holds that everything is preordained and everyone is destined to attain eventual salvation. The four unsatisfactory religions in some sense uphold survival, moral values, moral recompense as well as a relative freedom of the will. They are, first, any religion that claims that its teacher was omniscient all the time and knows the entirety of the future as well; second, any religion based on revelation, since revelations contradicted each other and were unreliable; third, any religion based on mere reasoning and speculation, since the reasoning may be unsound and the conclusions false; and fourth a pragmatic religion based on purely sceptical foundations which is, therefore, uncertain. On the other hand Buddhism is to be distinguished from all of them by virtue of the fact that it is realistic and verifiable. Its truths have been verified by the Buddha, and his disciples and are open to verification (ehipassika) by anyone who wishes to do so.

The answer to Subhadda's question, however, is different. There is no examination of the relative claims of Materialism, Theism, Scepticism, etc. Instead the Buddha says, leave aside the question as to whether these several religions and philosophies are all true or false or that some are true. In whatever religion the noble eightfold path is not found, in that religion one would not get the first, second, third or fourth stages of sainthood and in whatever religion the noble eightfold path is found, in that religion one would get the first, second, third and fourth stages: Finally, there is a very significant remark: 'If these monks lead the right kind of life, the world would never be devoid of Arahants' (ime ca bhikkhū sammā vihareyyuṃ asuñño loko arahantehi assa).

The Buddhist view is that any religion is true only to the extent to which it contains aspects of the noble eightfold path. Let us take one of the factors of the path – the necessity for cultivating right instead of wrong aspirations. Right aspirations consist in the cultivation of thoughts free from lust and sensuous craving and the cultivation of creative and compassionate thoughts. Wrong aspirations consist of the cultivation of lustful thoughts and sensuous craving as well as of destructive and malevolent thoughts. Now if any religion asserts that one may indulge in lustful, destructive and malevolent thoughts and yet be saved if one professes faith in the creed, then such a religion, according to the Buddha, is not to be trusted. It is the same with each of the other factors of the path. The net result is that there is no salvation outside the noble eightfold path. It is the one and only way for the salvation of beings and the overcoming of suffering.

## FIRST SAINT (SOTĀPANNA)

What kind of person is the 'first saint' spoken of here? It is none other than the person who attains the stream of spiritual development (sotāpanna) as a result of which his eventual salvation is assured and he does not fall into an existence below that of a human being. Such a person, it is said, sheds three fetters on attaining his spiritual insight. They are (1) the fetter of believing in a substantial ego somehow related to aspects or the whole of one's psycho-physical personality (sakkāya-diṭṭhi), (2) the fetter of doubting the veracity and validity of the Dhamma (vicikicchā) and (3) the fetter of clinging to the external forms of religion (sīlabbata-parāmāsa). The belief in an ego satisfies a deep-seated craving in us – the craving of our egoistic impulses (bhava-taṇhā). Misleading implications of language tend to make us believe that there is an 'I' and a 'me' (which is unchanging) when in fact there is only a constantly changing psycho-physical process. We certainly exercise a certain degree of control over ourselves, which makes us believe that there is an 'I' which controls, but such control is only an aspect of the conative functions of our conditioned psycho-physical process. A dispassionate analysis would ultimately expose the hollowness of this belief. Shedding our belief in such an ego does not, however, mean that we get rid of conceit (māna) altogether, for the 'conceited' view 'I shall try to attain the goal', it is said, is necessary to spur us on up to a point. He gets rid of this 'conceit' (māna) only in a later stage of his spiritual evolution. Doubt has to be got rid of in Buddhism not by blind belief but by critical inquiry and by living the Dhamma. Such inquiry and the personal experience of verifying aspects of the Dhamma gives us the inner conviction that we are treading on the right path. Overcoming such doubt through conviction does not, again, mean that we have totally got rid of ignorance (avijjā), which we can do only at a later stage in our spiritual evolution. Religion, likewise, becomes for such a person not a matter of conforming to external ritual and forms of worship, not a form of obsessional neurosis (to use Freudian terminology), but a matter of day-to-day living of the Dhamma. It is such a person who is said to have entered the stream of spiritual development, a state which is within the capacity of any of us to attain.

When we ponder over these admonitions of the Buddha in his last days on earth, we see how far the modern Theravāda tradition in Ceylon has strayed from the true path of the Dhamma. Are we not preserving the Dhamma in its pristine purity only in the books when we try to rationalise our belief in caste, for instance, with the help of opinions which go contrary to the teachings of the Buddha? Are we not rationalising our disinclination to live the Dhamma by fostering false beliefs that Arahantship is not possible today, when this is contrary to the assertions of the Buddha himself?

## ENLIGHTENMENT

If we turn from the birth and the last days of the Buddha to his enlightenment, it strikes us that it was not a revelation from above but an illumination from within. Part of the realisation was of the nature of causal laws operative in nature and in us.

When we come to the first sermon, we are again confronted with the noble eightfold path as the right path leading to emancipation, happiness and realisation. It is the straight and narrow road between indulgence of our desires and ascetic deprivation. The most obvious way to happiness appears to lie in the gratification of desires but unfortunately there is a law of diminishing returns which operates here. Gratification gives temporary satisfaction but continued gratification gives less and less of it. Besides, we become slaves of our passions and lose our freedom and self-control while our minds become unclear and confused. Ascetic deprivation on the other hand results in repression and self-inflicted suffering. It substitutes one kind of suffering for another. The way out or the way to transcend suffering is by a watchful self-control exercised by a person guided by the noble eightfold path.

Another significant fact about the first sermon is the claim of the Buddha that it was to set up the kingdom or rule of righteousness (dhammacakkaṃ pavattetuṃ), which shall in the fullness of time be established on earth and neither Brahmā (God), nor Māra (Satan), nor anyone else in the world could prevent this. In spite of many reverses, truth and justice shall win in the end. As one of the Upaniṣads puts it, 'Truth alone shall conquer and never untruth' (satyam eva jayate nānṛtam).

It is not possible to measure the enlightenment of the Buddha. As he said in the Siṃsapa forest taking a few leaves into his hand – what he knew but did not teach us was like the leaves in the forest, while what he taught amounted to the leaves in his hand. What he taught was only what pertained to man's emancipation, happiness and understanding.

Since the Buddha's ministry was spread over forty-five years, this teaching in itself is vast, as is evident from the Buddhist scriptures. If we take its essence we can see the immense worth of the Buddha's teaching and hence the true significance of Vesak, which mankind has yet to comprehend.

In these teachings we have a theory of knowledge, a theory of reality giving an account of the nature and destiny of man in the universe, an ethical system, a social and political philosophy and a philosophy of law.

Let us take the most significant teachings in each of these fields.

## THEORY OF KNOWLEDGE

Take the theory of knowledge. Nature is conceived as a causal system in which there are to be found non-deterministic causal correlations. The events of nature are not haphazard, nor are they due to the will of an omnipotent God nor again to rigid deterministic causal laws. The Buddhist theory of conditioned genesis (paṭicca-samuppāda) steers clear of the extremes of Indeterminism (adhicca-samuppada) on the one hand and of Strict Determinism (niyati), whether theistic or natural, on the other. Understanding, therefore, is the key to salvation and not blind belief in univerifiable dogmas. And for understanding we need an impartial outlook. We must not be influenced by our prejudices for or against (chandā dosā), by fear (bhayā) whether it be fear of nature or of the supernatural, nor by our erroneous beliefs (mohā). To gain personal knowledge, we must not rely on authority – whether it be revelation, tradition, hearsay, conformity with scripture, the views of experts or our revered teachers. We must not rely on pure reasoning alone, nor look at things from just one standpoint nor trust a superficial examination of things nor base our theories on preconceived opinions. Personal verification and realisation is the way to truth.

Here was man's charter of freedom, which makes Buddhism the most tolerant of religions and philosophies. It recommended an outlook which we today call the scientific outlook. So there have been no inquisitions, heresy trials or witch-hunts in Buddhism as in some theistic traditions and positively there has been the recognition of human dignity and freedom. The Buddha, again, was the earliest thinker in history to recognise the fact that language tends to distort in certain respects the nature of reality and to stress the importance of not being misled by linguistic forms and conventions. In this respect, he foreshadowed the modern linguistic or analytic philosophers. He was the first to distinguish meaningless questions and assertions from meaningful ones. As in science he recognised perception and inference as the twin sources of knowledge, but there was one difference. For perception, according to Buddhism, included extra-sensory forms as well, such as telepathy and clairvoyance. Science cannot ignore such phenomena and today there are Soviet as well as Western scientists, who have admitted the validity of extra-sensory perception in the light of experimental evidence.

THEORY OF REALITY

If we turn to the theory of reality, the Buddha's achievements were equally outstanding. Buddhism recognises the reality of the material world and its impact on experience. Conscious mental phenomena have a physical basis in one's body. Life (jīvitendriya) is a by-product (upādā-rūpa) of matter. The economic environment conditions human relationships and affects morality. Like modern psychologists, the Buddha discards the concept of a substantial soul and analyses the human personality into aspects of experience such as, impressions and ideas (saññā), feelings or hedonic tone (vedanā), conative activities (saṅkhārā) as well as cognitive or quasi-cognitive activities (viññaṇa). There is a dynamic conception of the mind and the stream of consciousness (viññaṇa-sota) is said to have two components, the conscious and the unconscious. The first explicit mention of unconscious mental processes and the unconscious (anusaya) motivation of human behaviour is in the Buddhist texts. The Buddhist theory of motivation may be compared with that of Freud although it is more adequate than the latter.

Man is motivated to act out of greed, which consists of the desire to gratify our senses and sex (kāma-taṇhā, comparable with the *libido* of Freud) as well as the desire to gratify our egoistic impulses (bhava-taṇhā, comparable with the *ego-instincts* and *super-ego* of Freud). He is also motivated to act out of hatred, which consists of the desire to destroy or eliminate what we dislike (vibhava-taṇhā, comparable with the *thanatos* or *death–instinct* of Freud) and also out of erroneous beliefs.

Both men and nature are in a stable of perpetual flux. As such, personal existence is insecure and there is no permanent soul or substance that we can cling to despite our strong desire to entertain such beliefs.

Owing to the causal factors that are operative, man is in a state of becoming and there is a continuity of individuality (bhava). Morally good and evil acts are correlated with pleasant and unpleasant consequences, as the case may be. Man is conditioned by his psychological past, going back into prior lives, by heredity and by the impact of his environment. But since he is not a creature of God's will or a victim of economic determinism, he can change his own nature as well as his environment.

There is no evidence that the world was created in time by an omniscient, omnipotent and infinitely good and compassionate God. In fact, the evidence clearly tells against the existence of such a God and the Buddhist texts mention two arguments in this connection. Although evil is logically compatible with the existence of a good God, there are certain evils (such as the suffering of animals and of little children, for instance), which are inexplicable on the assumption of the existence of a merciful God, who is also omniscient and omnipotent. Besides, the universe created by such a God would be a rigged universe in which human beings were mere puppets devoid of responsibility.

According to the Buddhist theory of the cosmos, it has no origin in time. This Buddhist conception of the cosmos, which is a product of clairvoyance, can only be compared with the modern theories of the universe. The smallest unit in it is said to be the minor world-system (cūlanikā lokadhātu), which contains thousands of suns, moons, inhabited and uninhabited planets. Today we call this a galaxy. The next unit is the middling world-system (majjhimikā lokadhātu), which consists of thousands of such galaxies, as we find in Virgo, for instance. The vast cosmos (mahālokadhātu) consists of thousands upon thousands of such clusters of galaxies. This cosmos is said to undergo periods of expansion (vivaṭṭamāna-kappa) and contraction (saṃvaṭṭamāna-kappa). So the universe is in a state of oscillation, continually expanding and contracting without beginning or end in time (anavarāgra).

Recent findings based on observations made from radio-telescopes have shown that the 'big-bang' theory (fancied by theists) and the oscillating theory are preferable to the steady-state theory. But of the 'big-bang' and oscillating theories, the latter is to be preferred on scientific and philosophical grounds. It does not involve the concept of the creation of the dense atom out of nothing and it does not have to face the problem of an infinitude of time prior to creation.

While the Buddhist conception of the cosmos foreshadows the modern astronomer's conception of it, it goes beyond the latter in speaking of a subtle-material world (rūpa-loka), which is not accessible to science.

Similarly, Buddhist atheism is not the same as materialistic atheism in that Buddhism speaks of the objectivity of moral and spiritual values and of a transcendent reality beyond space, time and causation. Neither the Buddha nor those who attain Nirvana cease to exist, according to Buddhist conceptions. When the Buddha was asked, whether the person who has attained Nirvana does not exist or exists eternally without defect, his answer was: 'The person who has attained the goal is without measure; he does not have that, whereby one may speak about him.'

## ETHICS

If we turn to Buddhist ethics and examine its system, we find that according to Buddhist notions, the propositions of ethics are significant. There can be no ethics without a concept of moral responsibility. But there cannot be moral responsibility unless (1) some of our actions are free (though conditioned) and not constrained, (2) morally good and evil actions are followed by pleasant and unpleasant consequences, as the case may be, and (3) there is human survival after death to make this possible with justice. Now the question as to whether these conditions are fulfilled or not, is a purely factual one. If there was no free will and human actions were strictly determined, there would be no sense in our talking about moral responsibility for our actions. According to

Buddhist conceptions, nature is such that all these conditions are fulfilled and, therefore, moral responsibility is a fact.

Buddhism considers human perfection or the attainment of arahantship as a good in itself and likewise the material and spiritual welfare of mankind. Whatever are good as a means in bringing about these good ends are instrumentally good and these are called right actions, defined as those which promote one's own welfare as well as that of others. Right actions consist in refraining from evil, doing what is good and cleansing the mind. The goal of perfection is also therapeutic in that only a perfect person, it is said, has a perfectly healthy mind. Hence the necessity for cleansing the mind, which consists in changing the basis of our motivation from greed, hatred and ignorance to selfless service, compassion and understanding. The Buddha emphatically pointed out that what he showed was a way, a way to achieve this change in motivation by a process of selfanalysis, meditation and self-development. Men and women are classified into different psychological types and different forms of meditation are prescribed for them to achieve this end. The aim of Buddhist ethics therefore is the attainment of personal happiness and social harmony.

The Buddhist theory of reality and its ethics are summed up in the four noble truths.

## SOCIETY, POLITY AND LAW

The social and political philosophy of Buddhism is equally relevant and enlightening. Again, the Buddha was the first thinker in history to preach the doctrine of equality. Man was one species and the division into social classes and castes was not a permanent or inevitable division of society, although it was given a divine sanction at the time. Historical and economic factors brought about, as the Buddha relates in the *Aggañña Sutta*, the division of people into occupational classes which later became castes. All men are capable of moral and spiritual development and should be afforded the opportunity for this. The doctrine of equality does not imply that all men are physically and psychologically alike for they are obviously not, but that there is a sufficient degree of homogeneity amongst men in terms of their capacities and potentialities as to warrant their being treated equally and with human dignity (samānattatā). It is a corollary of the doctrine of equality that there should be equality before the law, in educational opportunities and in the enjoyment of other human rights such as the right to employment, etc.

Society, according to the Buddhist, like every other process in nature was liable to change from time to time. The factors that determined this change were economic and ideological, for men were led to action by their desires and beliefs. It was the duty of the state to uphold justice and promote the material and spiritual welfare of its subjects. There is a social contract theory of society and government. Ultimate power, whether it be legislative, executive or judiciary, is vested with the people but delegated to the king or body of people elected to govern. If the contract of upholding law and order and promoting the good of the people is seriously violated, the people have a right to revolt and overthrow such a tyrannical government.

Sovereignty is subject to the necessity to conform to the rule of righteousness. The rule of power has to be dependent on the rule of righteousness (balacakraṃ hi nisrāya Dharmacakraṃ pravartate). Punishment has to be reformatory and only secondarily deterrent and never retributive. In international relations the necessity for subjecting sovereignty to the rule of righteousness requires that no nation be a power unto itself, while in its dealings with other nations it always has the good and happiness of mankind at heart. The ideal Just Society is both democratic and socialistic and ensures human rights as well as economic equity and the well-being of the people. It is likely to come into existence after a catastrophic world war, when the remnant who would be saved will set up a new order based on a change of heart and a change of system.

Such in brief is the message of the glorious religion and philosophy of the Buddha, whose value and full significance the world has yet to realise. Such is the message of Vesak.

# 3

# The Buddhist Conception of Truth

One of the five precepts that a Buddhist has to undertake to observe is that of 'refraining from saying what is false'. Stated in its negative as well as positive form he has to 'refrain from saying what is false, assert what is true (sacca-vādī), be devoted to the truth (sacca-sandha), be reliable (theta), trustworthy (paccayika) and not be one who deceives the world (avisaṃ-vādako lokassa)' (A. II. 209).

The necessity for speaking the truth is one of the Ten Virtues (dasa kusalā kammā) that one has to practise for one's own good as well as for the good of society. For it is held that a just social order requires that, among other things, the people in it be honest and speak the truth. In this context there is a social slant in the description given as to why one should speak the truth: 'Herein, a certain layman rejects falsehood and, refraining from saying what is false, asserts the truth whether he be in a formal assembly of people or in a crowd or at home among his relatives or in his office or when he is called to witness in a court of law – disclaiming to have known or seen what he did not know or see and claiming to have known or seen what he has known or seen. Thus, neither for his own sake nor for the sake of others, nor again for some material gain would he state a deliberate falsehood' (*Sāleyyaka Sutta*, M. I. 288).

Right speech, however, is not limited to the requirement

of speaking the truth. It is also necessary that (1) one avoids slander which causes divisions and dissensions among people and confines oneself to statements which bring about social harmony and understanding; (2) one refrains from harsh or foul language and is civil and courteous in one's speech, saying what is pleasant: and (3) one avoids gossip and vain speech and speaks at the right occasion and in accordance with the law what is profitable, righteous and true.

An exception is sometimes made in the case of (2), where it is held that our statements even when true, may be either pleasant or unpleasant. It is sometimes necessary to say what is true but unpleasant when it is useful, just as much as it is necessary to put one's finger in the throat of a child even when it causes a little pain in order to pull out something that has got stuck there. Thus in the *Abhayarājakumāra Sutta*, it is pointed out that statements may be true or false, useful or useless and pleasant or unpleasant. This results in eight possibilities as follows:

| | | | |
|---|---|---|---|
| 1. | True | useful | pleasant |
| 2. | True | useful | unpleasant |
| 3. | True | useless | pleasant |
| 4. | True | useless | unpleasant |
| 5. | False | useful | pleasant |
| 6. | False | useful | unpleasant |
| 7. | False | useless | pleasant |
| 8. | False | useless | unpleasant |

Of the eight possibilities, it is said, that the Transcendent One asserts (1) and (2) at the proper time. The text reads: 'He would assert at the proper time a statement which he knows to be true, factual, useful, agreeable and pleasant to others, i.e. (1) . . . He would assert at the proper time a statement which he knows to be true, factual, useful, disagreeable and unpleasant to others, i.e. (2). Lying is prohibited and the necessity to seek and speak the truth is emphasised because such action promotes one's personal happiness as well as social progress and harmony. Yet, one incurs moral blame only if there is an intention to deceive and cause disharmony, but negligence is also to be avoided so that a Buddhist must act with a high sense of responsibility with regard to what he says, considering its possible social repercussions.

## THE NATURE OF THE TRUTH

The statements of Buddhism or the Dhamma are claimed to be true. The central truths of Buddhism, pertaining to its theory of reality and ethics, are asserted in the form of 'the Four Noble Truths' (cattāri ariya-saccāni). Nirvāṇa is claimed to be 'the Truth' (Sacca), being the supreme truth (parama-sacca). It is also interesting to note that the two things which are claimed to be 'eternal values' (sanātana Dhamma) are Truth and Love. With regard to the former it is stated: 'Truth, indeed, is immortal speech – this is an eternal value' (saccaṃ ve amatā vācā – esa Dhammo sanātano). There is a tendency today to regard what is old as antiquated. This is a mistaken view, for all that is verified and established as true is forever modern irrespective of the age in which these truths were discovered.

What is the nature of truth? We use the words 'true' or 'false' normally of statements. We say that the statement, 'there is a harbour in Colombo' is true, while the statement, 'there is a harbour in Hambantota' is false. But we also speak of believing, conceiving of and knowing the truth and as such we have experience of truth. Knowledge of truth or even belief in it helps us to act efficiently in our environment without causing trouble to others. When we know the road to Kandy, it helps us to get there without difficulty and without the necessity for troubling others. Knowledge of causal laws operating in us or in nature helps us to control our selves or nature for our own good as well as that of others.

When we continue to think of any evil that somebody has

done to us, we tend to hate him, but if we continue to think of even some good that he has done to us, our hatred tends to disappear. So by understanding the psychology of mental phenomena, we can gradually get rid of our hatred and, thereby, make ourselves as well as others happy. This is why knowledge of the truth both with regard to ourselves as well as the environment is important, since it helps us to control ourselves as well as the environment for our own good as well as that of others. When we are aware of the truth, we have knowledge (or true beliefs.) Knowledge gives us control or power and this can help us develop our personal and social freedom and happiness.

What are the characteristics or criteria of truth? Philosophers have put forward about four main theories regarding this. Some hold that truth is what accords or corresponds with fact. This is called the Correspondence theory. Others hold that truth is what is consistent. This is called the Coherence theory. Yet others hold that what is true is useful and what is useful is true. This is called the Pragmatic theory. Others, again, hold that truth is verifiable in the light of experience. This is called the Verifiability theory of truth.

## CORRESPONDENCE AND COHERENCE

What is the Buddhist theory? Quite clearly, Buddhism maintains that truth is to be defined in terms of correspondence with fact. A theory or statement is true when it is 'in accordance with fact' (yathābhūtaṃ). It is the object of knowledge – 'one knows what is in accordance with fact' (yathābhūtaṃ pajānāti, D. I. 84). In contrast, a statement, theory, belief or conception would be false when it does not accord with fact. As the *Apaṇṇaka Sutta* states: 'When in fact there is a next world, the belief occurs to me that there is no next world, that would be a false belief. When in fact there is a next world, if one thinks that there is no next world, that would be a false conception. When in fact there is a next world, if one asserts that there is no next world, that would be a false statement...' (M. I. 402). On the other hand, true beliefs, conceptions or statements correspond with fact: 'When in fact there is a next world, if the belief occurs to me that there is a next world, that would be a true belief . . . ' (M. I. 403).

Although correspondence with fact is considered to be the essential characteristic of truth, consistency or coherence is also held to be a criterion. In contrast, inconsistency is a criterion of falsehood. In arguing with his opponents, the Buddha often shows that their theories lead to inconsistencies or contradictions, thereby demonstrating that they are false, using what is known as the Socratic method. In the debate with Saccaka, the Buddha points out at a certain stage in the discussion that 'his later statement is not compatible with a former statement nor the former with the later' (N. I. 232). Citta, one of the disciples of the Buddha, arguing with Nigaṇṭha Nātaputta, the founder of Jainism, says: 'If your former statement is true, your later statement is false and if your later statement is true, your former statement is false' (S. IV. 298).

This means that truth must be consistent. Therefore, when a number of theories with regard to the nature of man and his destiny in the universe contradict each other, they cannot all be true, though they could all be false if none of them corresponded with fact. So at a time when a number of different religious teachers and philosophers put forward a variety of theories about man and the universe, the *Sutta Nipāta* asks: 'Claiming to be experts, why do they put forward diverse theories – are truths many and various?' The answer given is: 'Truths, indeed, are not many and various . . . Truth is one without a second (ekaṃ hi saccaṃ na dutīyam atthi, Sn. 884). Consistency or the lack of contradiction is, therefore, a criterion of truth.' It is evident from this that if we take different theories such as Materialism, Theism, Scepticism, Buddhism, etc., not all can be true, though all may be false.

We must, however, distinguish consistency between

divergent theories and consistency within each theory. Two theories may be each internally consistent though mutually contradictory. So consistency is a necessary but not a sufficient criterion of truth. In other words, if a theory is internally inconsistent, it is false, but the fact that it is consistent is not sufficient for us to accept it as true. From the same shreds of evidence, two lawyers may concoct two mutually contradictory theories as to what happened. Each of these may be internally consistent but this alone is no criterion of their truth. This was why the Buddha rejected theories based on mere reasoning as unsatisfactory since the reasoning may be valid or invalid and even if valid (in the sense of being internally consistent), it may or may not correspond with fact (*Sandaka Sutta*, M. I. 520).

While internal theoretical consistency is a necessary but not a sufficient criterion of truth, Buddhism also holds that, with regard to theories which concern human behaviour, there must also be consistency between theory and practice. The Buddha claimed that 'he practised what he preached and preached what he practised' (It. 122). He expected his disciples also to follow his example. If I preach against the evils of taking liquor but take it myself, it may imply that I am not fully convinced of the truth of what I say. So if someone asserts a certain theory and acts as if he believes that at least part of it is false, his practice would be inconsistent with the theory he puts forward.

## PRAGMATISM

What does Buddhism have to say about Pragmatism? Does it uphold a pragmatic theory of truth? Evidently, it does not, since it does not maintain that all true statements are useful or that all useful statements are true. As we have seen above, there are useless truths and useful falsehoods according to Buddhism. The pragmatic theory of truth was put forward to accommodate thesistic beliefs, but Buddhism does not hold that a theory is true because people like to believe it and it is, therefore, of some use to them.

At the same time we have to stress the fact that the Buddha confined himself to asserting statements, which were true and *useful*, though pleasant or unpleasant, so that the Dhamma is pragmatic although it does not subscribe to a pragmatic theory of truth. This fact is well illustrated by two parables, those of the arrow and of the raft. The parable of the arrow states that a man struck with a poisoned arrow must be concerned with removing it and getting well rather than in purely theoretical questions (about the nature of the arrow, who shot it, etc.) which have no practical utility. Certain questions concerning matters beyond empirical verification were not categorically answered by the Buddha because this was 'not *useful*, not related to the fundamentals of religion, not conducive to dispassion, peace, higher knowledge, realisation and Nirvana' (M. I. 431).

Even the true statements in the Dhamma are not to be clung to. They are to be used for understanding the world and overcoming it. One should not identify oneself with it by forming a sentiment of attachment (upādāna) towards it and make it a basis for mere disputation. The parable states that a person intending to cross a river and get to the other bank, where it is safe and secure, makes a raft and with its help safely reaches the other bank, but however useful the raft may have been, he would throw it aside and go his way without carrying it on his shoulder. In the same way it is said 'those who realise the Dhamma to be like a raft should be prepared to discard even the Dhamma, not to speak of what is not Dhamma' (M. I. 135). The value of the Dhamma lies in its utility for gaining salvation. It ceases to have value to each individual though it does not cease to be true, when one's aims have been realised.

### VERIFIABILITY

The statements of the Dhamma are meaningful (sappāṭihāriyaṃ) and are supported by reason and experience (sanidāhaṃ) and are hence verifiable (ehipassika). It is the duty of each Buddhist to try and verify their truth in practice. The Buddhist starts with right beliefs in his sammādiṭṭhi endeavour gradually to eliminate greed and hatred and ends his quest for truth with right knowledge (sammāñānī) and emancipation of mind (sammāvimutti). In the process, each person has to verify the truths of Buddhism for himself. Verifiability in the light of reason and experience is thus a characteristic of the truths of Buddhism.

### MIDDLE PATH

Another characteristic of many of the important truths of Buddhism is that they happen to lie midway between two extreme points of view. Extreme realism, which says that 'everything exists' (sabbaṃ atthi) because everything comes into existence is one extreme, while extreme nihilism which asserts that 'nothing exists' (sabbaṃ natthi) since everything passes away is the other extreme – the truth is that everything is becoming. Similarly false extreme theories are the doctrines of the eternity of the soul and of annihilationism, the doctrines of the identity of the body and mind and of the duality of the body and mind. Strict Determinism (whether theistic or natural) and Indeterminism, the doctrine that we are entirely responsible personally for our own unhappiness and the doctrine that we are not at all responsible for our own unhappiness, extreme hedonism (kāmasukhallikānuyoga) and extreme asceticism (attakilamathānuyoga). In all these instances, it is said that the Buddha 'without falling into any of these two extremes, preaches the Dhamma *in the middle* (majjhena)'. The truth lies in the mean between two extreme views. The middle way (majjhimā paṭipadā) is thus a mean, both in the matter of *belief* as well as of conduct.

We have shown so far that, in the Buddhist texts, truth is defined as correspondence with fact, consistency is a necessary but not a sufficient criterion of truth, and the truths of Buddhism are pragmatic and verifiable.

## PARTIAL TRUTHS

As a result of the Correspondence theory, statements which strictly correspond with fact are considered to be 'true' and those which do not are considered to be 'false'. All statements would thus be true or false. Aristotelian logic is based on this assumption alone but modern logicians as well as ancient Indian thinkers have discovered that, without prejudice to our definition of truth, we can adopt other conventions.

We can consider statements which strictly correspond with fact (as those of the Dhamma are claimed to do) as absolutely true, while those which do not all correspond with fact would be absolutely false. In that case, those which correspond to some extent with facts would be 'partially true' (or partially false). According to this convention, all statements will be either true, false or partially true. Modern logicians have shown that a system of logic could be constructed on the basis of this fundamental assumption as well – namely that every statement is either true, false or partially true.

It is on the basis of this convention that the Buddha characterised certain theories held by individuals, religious teachers and philosophers as being 'partial truths' (pacceka sacca). It is in this connection that we have the parable of the blind men and the elephant (Ud. 68). The men who are born blind touch various parts of the elephant such as the tusks, ears, forehead, etc. and each reports, *mistaking the part for the whole*, that the elephant was like that part which was felt by him. In the same way, the various religious and philosophical theories contain aspects of truth and are based on the mis-described experiences of the individuals who propounded them, while the Buddha was able to understand how these theories arose as well as their limitations, since he had a total vision of reality with an unconditioned mind.

## THE CATUṢKOṬI

When a statement is characterised as 'true' or 'false', these characteristics (true, false) are called 'values' in logic. So a system of logic which is based on the fundamental assumption that all statements are either true or false is called a two-valued logic. Such a system may have two logical alternatives. We may illustrate this with an example:

| | |
|---|---|
| First Alternative | 1. This person is happy. |
| Second Alternative | 2. This person is *not* happy. |

We notice that in this two-valued logic of two alternatives, when the first alternative is true, the second has to be counted as necessarily false, while if the second alternative is true, the first would be false. But this system of logic would not do justice to the facts, if the person concerned was partly happy and partly unhappy.

In such a situation we cannot dogmatically assert that the first alternative was true because the person is partly unhappy and therefore not wholly happy. Nor can we say that the second alternative is true because the person is partly happy and therefore not wholly unhappy. But according to the laws of logic applicable within this system – namely the law of excluded middle – either the first alternative or the second must necessarily be true.

In order to have a better classification of the facts in situations such as this, the Buddhists adopted the logic of four alternatives, known as the catuṣkoṭi. This is a two-valued logic of four alternatives. According to it, statements can be made in the form of four logical alternatives of which only one will be necessarily true. Thus, speaking of the happiness or unhappiness of a person, we can say:

| | | |
|---|---|---|
| First Alternative | 1. | This person is (wholly) happy. |
| Second Alternative | 2. | This person is (wholly) unhappy. |
| Third Alternative | 3. | This person is (partly) happy and (partly) unhappy. |
| Fourth Alternative | 4. | This person is neither happy nor unhappy (e.g. if he experiences only neutral sensations of hedonic tone). |

This is one of the examples given in the texts. If we take another historical example, we may state the following four logically alternative possibilities with regard to the extent of the universe:

1. The universe is finite (in all dimensions).
2. The universe is infinite (in all dimensions).
3. The universe is finite (in some dimensions) and infinite (in other dimensions).
4. The universe is neither finite nor infinite (in any dimension). This last alternative would be the case if space or the universe was unreal. In such an eventuality, the universe cannot properly be described as either 'finite' or 'infinite'.)

Now, according to Aristotelian logic or the two-valued logic of two alternatives, the logical alternatives would have to be:

1. The universe is finite.
2. The universe is not finite.

Now if we explain 'the universe is finite' as 'the universe is finite in all dimensions', then the other alternative, 'the universe is not finite' can mean one of three things (as above).

The logical alternatives according to this system of logic, therefore, become vague, ambiguous and not clearly defined and distinguished. The logic of four alternatives, or the catuṣkoṭi, is thus employed in the Buddhist texts for purposes of classification or discussion, where the subject-matter requires it. Scholars like Poussin, who believed that Aristotelian logic represented the one and only system of logic, failed to understand its significance and thought that the Buddhists or the Indians did not know any logic. But the modern developments in the subject have shown that there could be different complementary systems of logic based on different conventions and that they may be employed according to the needs of the subject-matter to be discussed. Thus the early Buddhist conception of logic was far in advance of its time.

## CONVENTIONAL AND ABSOLUTE TRUTH

Another distinction that is made in the Buddhist texts is that of absolute (paramattha) and conventional (sammuti) truth. This is because appearances are sometimes deceptive and reality is different from what appearances seem to suggest. In the everyday world of common sense, we not only observe hard objects like stones and tables, which do not seem to change their form and structure, but also different persons who seem to continue as self-identical entities being reckoned the 'same' persons at different times of their existence. But this appearance, and the reasoning based on it, is deceptive and is due partly to the failure to see reality as it is and partly to the failure to understand the limitations of language, which employs static concepts to describe dynamic processes.

One we see reality for what it is and the limitations of language, we can still employ the conventional terminology without being misled by the erroneous implications of language and the assumptions we make because of our distorted view of reality. So we realise that from a conventional point of view we may speak of persons, who in reality are dynamic processes which change constantly owing to the impact of the physical, social and ideological environment and the internal changes which take place. But from an absolute point of view, there are no such persons, who are self-identical entities or souls which persist without change.

In the same way, modern science finds it necessary to distinguish between the conventional conception of stones and tables as hard, inert objects, which undergo no change, with the scientific conception of them as composed of atoms and molecules, whose inner content consists largely of empty space and whose fundamental elements have such a tenuous existence that they may be regarded as particles in some respects and waves in other respects, if at all it is possible to conceptualise their existence. Still, from a conventional standpoint we need to talk of stones and tables and there is no harm in doing so, provided we are aware of the false assumptions and misleading implications. As the Buddha would say, 'They are expressions, turns of speech, designations in common use in the world which the Tathāgata (the Transcendent One) makes use of without being led astray by them' (D. I. 202).

# 4

# The Buddhist Attitude to Revelation

In the *Saṅgārava Sutta*, the Buddha states that there are three types of religious and philosophical teachers, considering the basis of their knowledge, who prescribe divergent ways of life. First, there are the Revelationists (anussavikā) who claim final knowledge on the basis of revelation, such as, for instance, the brahmins of the Vedic tradition. Secondly, there are the rational metaphysicians (takkī vinaṃsī) who claim final knowledge on the basis of their faith in reason and speculation. Thirdly, there are those who claim final knowledge of things not found in the traditional revealed scriptures (ananussutesu dhammesu), based on a personal understanding derived from their extra-sensory powers of perception.

It is significant that the Buddha classifies himself as a member of the third group. Referring to this class of religious and philosophical teachers the Buddha says, 'I am one of them' (tesāhaṃ asmi, M. II. 211). It would surely be of interest to Buddhists to know something about this last class of religious and philosophical teachers with whom the Buddha identifies himself. It would also be important to note the difference between the Buddha and the other members of this class. But in order to do this, it would be necessary on the one hand to identify the Buddha's contemporaries and predecessors, who were presumed to belong to it. On the other hand, it is vital to examine the Buddhist attitude to the other two classes of religious and philosophical thinkers.

This would involve an analysis of the means of knowledge recognised in pre-Buddhist thought. For this purpose it would be necessary to look into both the Vedic and the non-Vedic traditions that preceded Buddhism. The pre-Buddhistic Vedic tradition comprises the thinkers who paid some sort of allegiance to the Vedas. From the evidence of the Buddhist scriptures and the Vedic texts, they consisted of the thinkers responsible for the literature from the Ṛgveda downwards up to about the *Maitrāyaṇi Upaniṣad.* The pre-Buddhistic non-Vedic tradition would comprise the Materialists, the Sceptics who are called amarā-vikkhepikā (i.e. eel wrigglers) in the Buddhist texts and ajñānavādins or agnostics in the Jain texts, the Ājīvikas who propounded theories about time and change, and the Jains who had Nigaṇṭha Nātaputta as their leader.

A careful study of the relevant texts of the Vedic and non-Vedic traditions shows that the thinkers who claimed a final knowledge of things not in the traditional revealed scriptures, based on a personal understanding derived from their extra-sensory powers of perception are to be found in both the Vedic and the non-Vedic traditions prior to Buddhism. They were none other than those who practised yoga and claimed to have acquired certain extrasensory faculties of perception and expansions of consciousness. We shall examine later the respects in which the Buddha may be compared and contrasted with them.

Here it is relevant to examine the claims of the authoritarian thinkers, who regarded the Vedas as revealed scriptures as well as of the Rationalists, who put forward metaphysical theories about the nature and destiny of man in the universe based on speculative reasoning. It is worth remembering at the same time that the authoritarian thinkers and the rationalists were by no means confined to the Vedic tradition. They are to be found in the pre-Buddhistic non-Vedic tradition as well. The *Sutta Nipāta* refers to 'the Vedas of the Samaṇas or recluses as well as to the Vedas of the brahmins' (Vedāni viceyya kevalāni samaṇānaṃ yāni p'atthi brāhmaṇānaṃ

*Sn.* 529) and there is evidence to show that some of the Ājīvikas had their own authoritative religious and philosophical texts handed down by tradition. Besides, there were Rationalists, perhaps the majority of them, in the non-Vedic tradition. The Materialists, Sceptics and many of the Ājīvikas were rationalists who based their findings on reasoning. So we find the authoritarian thinkers, the Rationalists as well as the Empiricists or Experientialists whose knowledge was derived from experience, represented in both the Vedic and the non-Vedic traditions prior to Buddhism.

We shall here examine the authoritarian thinkers of the Vedic tradition and the Buddhist attitude to them. For this attitude illustrates the Buddhist attitude to revelation. It was the belief of the majority of the thinkers of the Vedic tradition that the whole of it was the word uttered ot breathed forth by the Great Being, who is the ground of existence. A passage in the *Bṛhadāraṇyaka Upaniṣad* reads as follows: 'It is – as from a fire laid with damp fuel, clouds of smoke separately issue forth, so, lo, verily, from this Great Being has been breathed forth that which is Rgveda, Yajurveda, Sāmaveda, (Hymns) of the Atharvāns and Angirases, Legend, Ancient Lore, Sciences, Upaniṣads, Stanzas, Sūtras, explanations and commentaries. From it, indeed, are all these breathed forth' (2.4.10). Since this Great Being (Mahad Bhūtam) is conceived as the source of all knowledge and power, these scriptures were an infallible divine revelation. In a later passage in the same Upaniṣad, which adds to this list, the entire cosmos is said to be breathed forth by the Great Being. Both passages occur in a context in which the highest reality is said to be non-dual (advaitam). This impersonal conception is to be found in other works of this period, where the Vedas are said to be a product of the basic structure of the world (skambha), time (kāla) or logos (vāk).

Very much earlier in the Ṛgveda itself, though in a late hymn (RV. 10.90) the origin of the Vedas is traced to the sacrifice of the Cosmic Person (Puruṣa). This led in the

Brāhmaṇas to the theory that the Vedas are due to the creation of Prajāpati, the Lord of all creatures. This Prajāpati is often identified in the Brāhmaṇas with Brahmā, who according to the Buddhist texts is considered by the theistic brahmins to be creator of the cosmos. In the Upaniṣads, Prajāpati or the Lord of creation sometimes continues in his role as the creator of the Vedas (Ch. 4.17.1–2). But Brahmā often gains prominence as the creator of the Vedas, although they are actually revealed to mankind by Prajāpati. The *Chāndogya* says: 'This did Brahmā tell to Prajāpati, Prajāpati to Manu and Manu to human beings' (8.15). Very much later in the *Muṇḍaka Upaniṣad*, Brahmā is still 'the first of the gods and the maker of all', who eventually reveals both the higher and lower forms of Vedic knowledge to mankind.

On the internal evidence of the Vedic tradition itself, we find that the claim was made at a certain stage in its history that the texts of the Vedic tradition were divinely revealed. The later Vedic tradition, therefore, considers the ṛṣis who composed the Vedic hymns as 'seers' in the literal sense of the term, who 'see the Vedas by means of extra-sensory perception' (atīndriyārthadraṣṭaraḥ ṛṣayah . . .). Radhakrishnan gives expression to this traditional point of view when he says that 'the ṛṣi of the Vedic hymn calls himself not so much the composer of the hymns as the seer of them', but it is a theory that was put forward as early as the Brāhmaṇas.

It is because the Vedic thinkers believed their texts to have been divinely revealed that they looked down with scorn at the claims of certain religious and philosophical teachers to have personally verified the truths of their doctrines by developing their extra-sensory powers of perception. In the *Subha Sutta*, the Buddha criticises some of the ethical recommendations of the Upaniṣads on the ground that neither the brahmins at the time nor their teachers up to several generations nor even the original seers claimed to know the consequences of practising the virtues referred to by verifying the fact with their paranormal perception. Subbha, the brahmin student, is enraged at this and quoted the views of one of the senior brahmins, who treated such claims to verify these facts in the light of paranormal perception with contempt, considering them ridiculous (hassakaṃ), for it is impossible for *a mere human being* (manussa-bhūto) to claim such knowledge. The point here is that Vedic knowledge is divinely revealed in contrast with the knowledge of the Buddha, which was merely human and therefore of lesser worth.

It is the same criticism that is sometimes levelled against Buddhism by some of its theistic critics on the basis of theistic presuppositions. It is said that the knowledge of the Buddha was merely human, whereas the knowledge allegedly contained in their respective theistic traditions is divine, implying thereby that it was more reliable.

We may examine the value of this criticism. But let us first assess the value of the Buddhist criticisms of the Vedic tradition in their historical context. In the above context, the Buddha criticises the acceptance of certain statements merely on the ground that they are contained in an allegedly revealed text without their being verified as true. It may be stated here that verifiability in the light of experience is one of the central characteristics of truth according to Buddhist conceptions.

In the *Sandaka Sutta*, Buddhism is contrasted with four types of false religions, and four types of religions which are unsatisfactory though not necessarily false, by claiming that the statements of Buddhism have been verified by the Buddha and many of his disciples and were, therefore, verifiable in principle by anyone with the requisite competence. A statement can be reliably accepted as true only when it is repeatedly verified and not because it is dogmatically declared to be the truth on the grounds of revelation. In the *Cankī Sutta*, the Buddha says: 'There are five things which have a twofold result in this life. What five? A belief based on faith (saddhā), one's likes (ruci), on revelation (amussava), superficial reflection (ākāra-parivitakka) and agreement with one's preconceptions (diṭṭhi-nijjhāna-kkhanti) . . . For even what I learn to be the truth on the ground of it being a profound revelation may turn out to be empty, hollow and false, while what I do not hear to be a truth on the ground of it being a profound revelation may turn out to be factual, true and sound' (M. II. 170–1). The Buddha goes on to say that one safeguards the truth by accepting a statement from revelation as such without dogmatically claiming it to be true, which is unwarranted. This means that it is spurious to claim as knowledge the truth of a statement in a revealed text. It is different with a statement which has been reliably verified in the light of one's personal experience. It is noteworthy that the Buddha says that beliefs held on the grounds of faith, one's likes, revelation, etc., are likely to have a dual result, namely to be verified as either true or false in this life itself.

In the *Sandaka Sutta*, a similar conclusion is drawn. One of the reasons why a religion based on revelation is unconsoling or unsatisfactory (anassāsikaṃ) is that it may prove to be either true or false and one cannot say what it is for certain. It is said: 'Herein a certain religious teacher is a revelationist, who holds to the truth of revelation and preaches a doctrine according to revelation, according to what is traditionally handed down, according to the authority of scripture. Now a teacher who is a revelationist and holds to the truth of revelation may have well-heard it or ill-heard it and it may be true or false. At this, an intelligent person reflects thus – this venerable teacher is a revelationist, etc. . . . so seeing that his religion is unsatisfactory he loses interest and leaves it.' So even the fact that it has been clearly apprehended as a revelation is no guarantee of its truth, for revelation is no criterion of truth. For the statements of revealed scripture may turn out to be true or false.

This is one of the central criticisms of revealed religion as found in the Buddhist texts, which reappears in the context under discussion in the *Subha Sutta*. The second criticism that is made is that neither the brahmins living at that period, nor their teachers up to several generations, nor even the original seers claimed to know the consequence of practising these virtues after realising the fact with their higher knowledge, although the Buddha himself could do so.

While the Vedic tradition from the time of the Brāhmaṇas onwards, claimed that the composers of the Vedic hymns were in fact seers, who intuited the truths or saw the statements, which were revealed to them by their extra-sensory perception, the Buddhists not only denied any higher insight on the part of the seers but quite emphatically asserted that the hymns were in fact *composed* by them. The original seers (pubbakā isayo) are constantly described as 'the makers and the utterers of the hymns' (mantānaṃ kattāro, mantānaṃ pavattāro, D. I. 242). The internal evidence of the Ṛgvedic texts proves this for in them the Vedic poets merely claim to make (√kṛ), compose (√tak), produce (√jan) and utter (avadannṛtāñī) the hymns. The Vedic Anukramaṇī merely defines a ṛṣi as 'an author of a hymn' (yasya vākyaṃ sa ṛṣiḥ). So there is no historical justification for the claim that the original authors of the Ṛgveda had any extra-sensory vision. The Buddhist criticisms were, therefore, realistic and made in the light of objective facts as they saw them. What is true of the origins of the Vedic tradition is true of other revelational traditions, when their historical origins are objectively examined.

The idea that the Buddha was a 'mere human being' is also mistaken. For when the Buddha was asked whether he was a human being, a Brahmā (God) or Māra (Satan), he denied that he was any of them and claimed that he was Buddha, i.e. an Enlightened Being who had attained the Transcendent. This does not, however, make the Buddha unique for it is a status that any human being can aspire to attain. The significance of this claim is brought out in the *Brāhmaṇimantanika Sutta*, where it is shown that even a Brahmā eventually passes away while the Buddha, being one with the Transcendent Reality beyond space, time and causation, is not subject to such vicissitudes.

At the same time, the Buddhist criticism of revelation does not imply that revelations are impossible. According to the Buddhist conception of things, it is possible for beings more developed than us to exist in the cosmos and communicate their views about the nature and destiny of man in the universe through human beings. All that is said is that the fact that something is deemed to be a revelation is no criterion of its truth and revelation, therefore, cannot be considered an independent and valid means of knowledge. No book on scientific method today regards it as such and even theologians have begun to doubt the validity of such claims. According to Buddhist conceptions, revelations may come from different grades of higher beings with varying degrees of goodness and intelligence. They cannot all be true. This does not mean that they are all necessarily false. For they may contain aspects of truth although we cannot say what these are by merely giving ear to them. This is why Buddhism classifies religions based on revelation as unsatisfactory though not necessarily false.

It is a notorious fact that different revelational traditions and individual revelations contradict each other. If 'truth is one' (ekaṃ hi saccaṃ) as Buddhism believes to be the case, they cannot all be true though all may be false. There are diverse views on crucial matters even within the same revelational tradition. The Brāhmaṇas and the Upaniṣads, for instance, contain several creation-myths and divergent accounts as to how life came into existence on earth. The ideas they contain differ from those of the Babylonian myths with which the Western world is familiar.

One such creation myth, for instance, states that in the beginning the world was Soul (Ātman) alone in the form of a Person. Human beings are the offspring of Ātman, who first creates a wife to escape from anxiety and loneliness. Later the wife assumes the forms of various animals, while Ātman assumes their male forms in order to make love to her. It is thus that the various species of animals come into being. This account of creation is in a section of the *Bṛhadāraṇyaka Upaniṣad*. The creation-myth in the *Aitareya Upaniṣad* is quite different although this too starts with the story that in the beginning Soul or Ātman alone existed and there was no other thing whatsoever. Ātman creates the worlds by an act of will and then thinks of creating people to look after them. Then, it is said that 'right from the waters he drew forth and shaped a person' (I. 3). Here man is created not by an act of procreation, not out of clay, but out of the waters. The evolutionary account of the origin of life found in a section of the *Taittirīya Upaniṣad* is still different. It says that from the Ātman or the Soul there progressively emerged space, wind, fire, water, earth, plants, food, seed and then man.

If we compare and contrast the Materialist criticism of the Vedas with the Buddhist, we see the difference in approach. The Materialists condemned outright the whole of the Vedic tradition and saw no good in it at all. According to them, the Vedas were the work of 'fools and knaves' or in their own words, bhaṇḍa-dhūrta-nisācaraḥ i.e. buffoons, knaves and demons. On the other hand the Buddhists, while holding that the original seers who were the authors of the Vedas merely lacked a special insight with which they were later credited, in keeping with historical fact, praised them for their virtue and rectitude. The Materialists categorically repudiated the Vedas as false, self-contradictory and repetitive (anṛta-vyaghata-punarukta-doṣa). The Buddhists, while pointing out the contradictions and falsities and repudiating the claims to revelation, did not consider all the traditional beliefs in the Vedic tradition to be wholly false. Among the false beliefs the Materialists would point to the belief in sacrifices, in a soul, in survival, in moral values and moral retribution. The Buddhists, however, criticised the Vedic conception of the sacrifice and denied the necessity for the concept of a soul, but agreed with the Vedas in asserting survival, moral values and moral recompense, and retribution, which are among the beliefs which formed part of the right philosophy of life or sammā diṭṭhi in Buddhism.

Even with regard to the sacrifice, the Materialists saw nothing but deception and fraud in it. The Buddhists, while condemning sacrifices as involving a waste of resources and the needless destruction of animals, were not averse to the simple sacrificial offerings made in good faith by the earliest brahmins who killed no animals for the occasion. Just as much as some of the Upaniṣads re-interpret sacrifice or yajña as the religious life, Buddhism conceives of yajña at its best to be the highest religious life as advocated in Buddhism.

The difference between the attitude of the Upaniṣads and Buddhism towards sacrifices, despite the similarities indicated, may be described as follows. The Upaniṣads as the jñāna-mārga or 'the way of knowledge' tended to regard the earlier Vedic tradition in the Brāhmaṇas, advocating the karma-mārga or 'the way of ritual' and the associated learning as a lower form of knowledge (aparāvidyā), while the thought of the Upaniṣads was a higher form of knowledge (parāvidyā). But even as a lower form of knowledge, it was not discarded. For us to do so would be to deny the authority of the injunctive assertions of the Vedas, which advocated sacrifices, and thereby question and undermine the belief in Vedic revelation. So even where the Upaniṣads urge the cultivation of compassion, an exception is made with regard to the sacrifice. Paradoxically, it is said that one should not harm any creatures except at the sacrificial altars (ahiṃsan sarvabhūtany anyatra tīrthebhyaḥ, Ch. 8.15.1). So it was the belief in revelation, which is ultimately the basis for the belief in animal sacrifices.

The Materialists, likewise, saw no basis for a belief in revelation since they counted as real only the observable material world. Buddhism on the other hand, did not question the basis of the belief in revelation except for its denial of a personal creator God. It criticised particular claims to revelation and the attempt to regard revelation as a separate valid means of knowledge. In the *Tevijja Sutta*, the brahmins claim to have a diversity of paths for attaining fellowship with Brahmā or God. The Buddha criticises these claims on the ground that not one of them has 'seen Brahmā face to face' (Brahmā sakkhidiṭṭho, D. I. 238). This was true of the brahmins present at the time right up to the original composers of the Vedas. So the claim to revelation is without basis. Although Brahmā is believed to be the creator of the cosmos, he is none other than a temporary regent of the cosmos, an office to which any being within the cosmos could aspire. The knowledge of the Buddha, who has attained the Transcendent excels that of Brahmā, who is morally perfect (asaṅkiliṭṭha-citto) but is neither omniscient nor omnipotent. The Buddha, who has held this office in the past and has verified in the light of his extra-sensory powers of perception the conditions required for attaining fellowship with God or Brahmā, could state that there are not a diversity of paths all leading to such a state but the one and only path consisting in acquiring purity of mind, cultivating compassion and being selfless or without possessions. What is verifiably true is more reliable than a blind belief in a claim to revelation.

The Buddhist attitude to any such revelation would be that of accepting what is true, good and sound and rejecting what is false, evil and unsound after a dispassionate analysis of its contents without giving way to prejudice, hatred, fear or ignorance. The Buddhist criticism of religions based on authoritarian claims is not limited to a criticism of a claim to revelation. An analysis of the sermon addressed to the Kālāmas shows that it is only the first of the grounds for an authoritarian claim, although it was undoubtedly the most important and, therefore, the one to be examined and criticised in detail. The different kinds of claims to knowledge based on authority are seen in the classification of such claims in the *Kālāma Sutta*, which mentions besides revelation claims made on the grounds of tradition (paramparā), common sense, wide acceptance of hearsay (itikirā), conformity with scripture (piṭaka-sampadā) and on the ground of something being a testimony of an expert (bhavyarūpatā) or the view of a revered teacher (samaṇo me garu). They could not be deemed to be valid means of knowledge and the requirement of safeguarding the truth (saccānurakkhaṇā) demands that beliefs held on such a basis be admitted as such instead of dogmatically claiming them to be true. Such dogmatism leads to undesirable consequences for oneself and society – to intolerance, conflict and violence and is a departure from sincerity and truth.

# 5

# The Buddhist Conception of Matter and the Material World

We are all familiar with the visible and tangible world around us which we call the material world. We contrast it with what is mental and consider it to exist independently of our thoughts. We have learnt much about it from science during the last few decades but hope to learn much more about it in the future. A knowledgeable scientist who sums up the modern conception of matter in the light of the recent findings of science, says:

'Matter *is* the world around us; it is everything we see and feel and touch. It seems thoroughly familiar – until we read in the following pages what the scientists have discovered about it within the last fifty years, the last twenty, the last two. The diamond, for example, seems on the face of it resplendently substantial. But as we read on, we find that the diamond is a patterned arrangement of atoms which are themselves mainly empty space, with infinitesimal dabs of electrons whirling around infinitesimal dabs of protons and neutrons. All this we now know to be matter, but we are by no means sure the picture is complete. Within the minuscule heart of the atom – the nucleus – have been found no fewer than thirty kinds of elementary particle, and no one can say what more will emerge under nuclear bombardment. The further scientists analyse, the less obvious the answers become.' (See *Matter*, LIFE Science Library, Time-Life International, 1963, p. 7.)

## BUDDHIST VIEW

The conception of matter that is generally found in the Buddhist tradition, except in the extreme idealist schools of thought (Vijñāna-vāda), is essentially the same. The objectivity of the material world is affirmed. It is said that rūpa or matter is not mental (acetasikaṃ) and is independent of thought (citta-vippayuttaṃ).

Such matter is classified into three categories. First, there is the category of matter or material qualities, which are visible (sanidassanaṃ) and can be apprehended by the senses (sappaṭighaṃ) – such as colours and shapes. Secondly, there is matter which is not visible (anidassana) but reacts to stimuli (such as the five senses), as well as the objects of sense which can come into contact with the appropriate sense organs (excluding the visual objects which fall into the first category). Thirdly, there is matter which is neither visible to the naked eye nor apprehensible by the senses but whose existence can either be inferred or observed by paranormal vision. Such, for example, are the essences (ojā) of edible food (kabalinkārāhāra), which are absorbed by our bodies and sustain it. Today we call them proteins, carbohydrates, vitamins, etc. but in the *Dhammasaṅgani* the essences (ojā) of edible food are classified as subtle (sukhuma) matter, which is not directly observed or apprehended by the sense-organs. The subtle matter of 'the realm of attenuated matter' (rūpa-dhātu) would also fall into this last category.

In this same category one would also have to include the atom (paramāṇu), which is said to be so small that it occupies only a minute portion of space (ākāsa-koṭṭhāsika) as the Commentary to the *Vibhaṅga* (p. 343) states. The subcommentary to the *Visuddhimagga* observes that the atom 'cannot be observed by the naked eye but only comes within the range of clairvoyant vision' (maṃsacakkhussa āpathaṃ nāgacchati, dibba-cakkhuss'eva āgacchati, p. 286). If this is so, then the Buddhist and some of the Indian atomic theories are not the product of pure rational speculation (like those of the Greeks) but are partly the result of extra-sensory perception as well.

Yet what is remarkable about the Buddhist atomic theories as against the other Indian and Western classical atomic theories, is that they were able to conceive of the atom as existing in a dynamic state. As one scholar (Professor A. L. Basham) puts it, 'The atom of Buddhism is not eternal as in the other three systems since Buddhism dogmatically asserts the impermanence of all things.' (*History and Doctrines of the Ājīvikas*, Luzac & Co., London, 1951, p. 267). Another scholar (Sir Arthur Berriedale Keith) brought out the essentially dynamic conception of the Buddhist theory of the atom when he said that the atom is conceived as 'flashing into being; its essential feature is action or function and, therefore, it may be compared to a focus of energy' (*Buddhist Philosophy*, Oxford, 1923, p. 161). We may compare with it what a modern physicist says of the atom: 'The old view of it as simple discrete particles and precise planetary orbits is gone. The physicist now prefers to view the atom as a ball of energetic and uncertain fluff'. (*Matter*, LIFE Science Library, p. 158). We may recall that even the early Buddhist texts compared matter to a 'lump of foam' (phena-piṇḍa).

## ATOMIC THEORY

The atomic theories developed only in the schools of Buddhism which, apart from the general notions that they shared, did not always agree among themselves about the nature of atoms. For example, one school (Sautrāntikas) held that atoms have spatial dimensions (dig-bhāga-bheda), while their opponents (Vaibhāṣikas) denied this, arguing that the atom has no parts and no extension. This dialectical opposition led to a situation in which the Idealists argued that the conception of the atom leads to contradictions. If the atom has some finite dimension, however small this may be, it is further divisible and therefore it is not an indivisible unit or an atom. On the other hand if the atom had no spatial dimension at all, it is a non-entity and material objects having a spatial dimension cannot be composed of them. So the Idealists argued that the atom was a self-contradictory concept and as such could not exist. Since atoms did not exist, there was no material world. So they concluded that the material world was an appearance created by our own minds, like some of the objects in the mind of a hypnotised subject.

The mistake that all these schools committed was to try and prove or disprove the existence of atoms by pure reasoning. As the Buddha pointed out in the *Kālāma Sutta*, we cannot discover or discern the nature of things as they are by pure speculative reasoning (takka). It is only when reasoning is closely tied up with experience that there is a discovery of facts in the objective world. For this reason we have either to follow the method of experimental science, which is a matter of controlled observation guided by reasoning, or of developing our extra-sensory powers of perception by meditation, if we are to understand things as they are.

Judging by results the Theravādins seem to have kept their speculations close to the findings of jhānic or extra-sensory observation. The Vaibhāṣikas spoke of the ultimate element of matter as the dravya-paramāṇu or the 'unitary atom' and contrasted with this the sanghāta-paramāṇu or the aggregate atom, which we today call a 'molecule'. It is significant that the Theravādins conceived of even the atom (dravya-paramāṇu) as a complex (rūpa-kalāpa) and spoke even of 'the constituents of this complex atom' (kalāpaṅga), at the same time considering such an atom to be in a dynamic state of continuous flux.

A table given in the Commentary to the *Vibhaṅga* makes it possible to compare the size of an atom as conceived of in medieval Buddhism with modern conceptions. If we follow this table an average of thirty-six paramāṇus equal one aṇu, thirty-six aṇus equal one tajjāri and thirty-six tajjāris equal one ratha-reṇu. A ratha-reṇu is a minute speck of dust, which we can barely appreciate with the human eye. According to this calculation there are 46,656 atoms in such a minute speck of dust. Now modern scientists think that an average of about 100 million atoms placed side by side in a row would amount to about an inch in length. If so, there would be ten million atoms in a tenth of an inch and a two hundredth portion of this would have fifty thousand atoms. Although the comparison is to some extent arbitrary, the figures given in the *Vibhaṅgaṭṭhakathā* do not appear to be far divorced from reality.

## ORIGINAL BUDDHISM

At the same time we must not forget that it was not the intention of the Buddha to give a detailed account of the nature of the physical world. As the Buddha pointed out in the Siṃsapa forest, taking a few leaves into his hand, what he taught amounted to the leaves in his hand while what he knew but did not teach was comparable in extent to the leaves in the forest.

If there are priorities in the accumulation of knowledge, man should first and foremost learn more about his own nature and his destiny in the universe rather than about the nature and origin of the universe.

Nevertheless, a general understanding of the nature of the physical world is also useful in that it helps us in knowing the nature of things as they are.

The Buddha himself did not disclose any details of an atomic theory but there are passages in which he points out unmistakably that the minutest portion of matter in the world is in a state of constant flux. On one occasion a monk asks the Buddha whether there was any form or kind of matter (rūpaṃ) which was eternal, stable, lasting, not subject to constant change and everlasting. The Buddha replies that there is no such matter. He then takes a grain of sand on to the tip of his nail and says, 'Even such a minute bit of matter is not eternal, stable or lasting, it is subject to constant change and is not everlasting.'

What we claim to know with regard to the physical world would not amount to knowledge if it does not reflect the state of things as they are, but such knowledge, once acquired, is to be made use of for one's moral and spiritual development. The significance of the above statement is that even existence in a subtle-material world is not everlasting and that we cannot hope to attain final salvation by attachment even to such an ethereal body. So while early Buddhism gives a realistic account of the essential nature of the physical world, this is done mindful of the psychological and ethical impact of these teachings.

## DEFINITION

The totality of matter is classified in the Buddhist texts with reference to time as past, present and future; with reference to the individual as internal and external; with reference to the nature of matter as gross and subtle; with reference to the value of matter as base and ethereal and with reference to space as near and distant (M. III. 16).

At the same time the matter spoken of is not just dead matter but living matter as well. The concept includes both the organic as well as the inorganic realms of matter. In this respect, we must not forget that according to Buddhist conceptions, life (jīvitendriya) is a by-product of matter (upādārūpa).

In the *Abhidhamma*, too, we notice in the *Dhammasaṅgaṇi* that regarding the nature of the totality of matter there are references to the psychological and ethical aspects of its impact. Matter is causally conditioned (sappaccayaṃ), impermanent and subject to decay (aniccam eva jarābhibhūtaṃ). It is to be found in the gross world of sensuous gratification (kāmāvacara) as well as the subtle-material world (rūpāvacara). In itself it is morally neutral, being neither good nor evil (avyākata). But it can be cognised by the six kinds of cognition, (i.e. by means of the senses and the understanding) and it is the kind of thing around which sentiments can be formed (upādāniya). It is also the kind of thing that can act as a fetter (saññojaniya) although the fetter does not lie in matter as such but in the attachment to matter.

In the earliest texts rūpa, in its widest sense of 'matter' as including the organic body as well as the external physical world, is defined as 'what undergoes change' (ruppati) under the impact of temperature (such as heat and cold), atmospheric changes (such as wind and heat), organic affections such as hunger which is defined as 'heat inside the belly' (udaraggisantāpa), as well as thirst and the changes effected by the sting and bite of gnats and snakes, etc. The general definition that is adopted in the commentaries is that matter (rūpa) is so called because 'it undergoes change, i.e. becomes subject to modifications under the impact of cold and heat, etc.' (ruppatīti sītauṇhādīhi vikāraṃ āpajjati).

## PRIMARY MATERIAL FORCES

If we apply the definition at the level of sense-observation or the empirically observable world, matter is what undergoes change under the impact of temperature, i.e. heat or cold. Since there is no metaphysical substance called 'matter' apart from the observable objective states, the primary forms would be the states of matter themselves manifested under the impact of temperature changes.

Water when cooled would eventually become frozen and solid. If the frozen ice is heated, it turns into water and the water, if heated, boils and turns into steam or a gaseous state. All elements or forms of matter subjected to changes of temperature are to be found in the solid, liquid or gaseous states. Until the third decade of the twentieth century, physicists concerned themselves only with these three states of matter. But it was realised that with the further application of heat to matter in the gaseous state a further state of matter can be brought into being. This is today called the plasma state. If very great heat is applied to steam, the movement of the water molecules becomes so violent that they start smashing themselves into electrically charged ions. This ionisation is the passage to the fourth state of matter or plasma described as a 'swarming mass of hot electrically charged particles'. The blazing mass of the sun is considered to be in this plasma state.

The conception of matter as what undergoes changes of state under the impact of temperature is therefore logically and empirically sound. Although there is no mention of the plasma state as such in the Buddhist texts, the primary forms of matter are held to be the solid (paṭhavī), the liquid (āpo), the gaseous (vāyo) and the fiery (tejo), such as lightning.

We can make use of these notions to classify the material of the body as well as the external world. There are solid states of matter in our own body such as the teeth, nails, hair, flesh, etc. The blood, sweat, tears, bile, pus, etc., would be in a liquid state. The air we breathe in inhaling and exhaling, the wind in the abdomen, etc., would be in a gaseous state. The heat in the body which transmutes food and drink in digestion comes under the fiery state of matter.

While in a general sense the four states are referred to in the above manner, it was observed that the specific characteristic of each state was to be found in some degree in the other states. Thus the specific characteristic of what is solid is *extension.* It is solid in the sense that it extends or spreads out (pattharatiti paṭhavī). The characteristic of the liquid state is that of *cohesiveness* (bandhanatta, saṃgaha), while that of the gaseous state is vibration or *mobility* (samudīraṇa, chambhitatta, thambhitatta). The fiery state is said to have the characteristic of causing changes of temperature or *maturation* (paripācana).

These characteristics, it is argued, are not exclusive of the different states of matter but are their most prominent characteristics. As general characteristics they are to be found in all the states of matter. What is solid is most obviously extended but liquids, gases and fires do not lack extension, or occupancy of space. Similarly, the matter of what is solid has a certain degree of cohesiveness. It has also a certain degree of dynamism or mobility and has a certain temperature. Extension, cohesiveness, mobility and temperature are thus held to be inseparable but distinguishable characteristics of all material things right down to atoms.

Different kinds of material objects, therefore, all have these several characteristics in varying degrees. When it comes to atomic theory, Buddhism would have to say that atoms differ from each other according to the presence of these characteristics in varying degrees.

## DERIVATIVES

The four characteristic qualities of extension, cohesiveness, mobility and temperature, which co-exist (aññamañña-sahajata) are the four great material forces or forms of energy. In a gross state the qualities of extension, mobility and temperature can be directly appreciated by the sense of touch, but cohesiveness has to be inferred. When we put our hand in water, we can apprehend its resistance or extension, its pressure or mobility as well as its temperature, but its characteristic of cohesiveness eludes us, and the most prominent characteristic of water has therefore to be inferred from observation.

All material things, whether organic or inorganic, and certain material concepts like space are said to be dependent on or derived from these primary material forces. But the senses in which they are derived are different. In the case of 'space' the derivation is purely logical in the sense that ākāsa or vacuous space (not ether) is untouched by the four material forces and is in fact to be apprehended as the place in which they are absent. In the case of jīvitendriya or life, however, it is a derivation in the sense of being a by-product of the primary material forces. Other characteristics of matter such as weight, plasticity, wieldiness, growth, continuity, decay and impermanence are also by-products of the primary manifestations of energy.

## REALISM

The sense-organs as well as the objects of sense are also made up of them. The matter forming the sensitive parts of the eye (pasāda), which react to stimuli (sappaṭigha), is intimately bound up with our entire psycho-physical personality (attabhāva-paryāpanna) and is again a by-product of the primary material forces.

The sense of sight, for example, is defined in various ways: (1) It is itself invisible though reacting to stimuli, but it is the means by which what is visible and impinges on the eye has been seen, is being seen, will be seen or would be seen; (2) it is the organ on which visible objects which are capable of stimulating it have impinged, are impinging, will impinge or would impinge; (3) it is the organ which has been focused, is being focused, will be focused or would be focused on visible objects capable of stimulating it; (4) it is the organ on account of which visual impressions as well as ideas, feelings, conative and cognitive activities aroused by these impressions have arisen, are arising, will arise or would arise. The accounts given in some respects foreshadow and in other respects are not in conflict with the modern finding regarding the psychology or physiology of perception.

In some respects one feels that the modern accounts need to be re-examined in the light of observations made in these texts. For example, textbooks in modern psychology tell us that the primary tastes are the sweet, sour, salt and bitter. But the *Dhammasangani*, while mentioning the tastes sweet (sādu), sour (ambila), salt (lonika) and bitter (tittaka) also refer to other tastes such as the astringent (kasāva) and pungent (kaṭuka). Although what we identify as tastes are partly due to what we appreciate through the skin senses as well as taste in the interior of the mouth, and also partly to odour, it is a moot point as to whether the astringent taste (kahaṭa raha) is a by-product of these or is a separate taste altogether.

It is quite evident from the descriptions given of the objects of sense as well as the general theory of matter that original Buddhism upheld the reality of the physical world. What we apprehend through the senses by way of colours or shapes, sounds, smells, tastes, etc., are all by-products of the four primary material forces, which exist in the objective physical world independently of our perceiving them.

The physical movements of our bodies (kāyaviññatti) and our verbal activity (vacīīviññatti), which are due to our volitional actions, are also due to the operations of material factors, though they are concurrently occasioned and accompanied (citta-samuṭṭhāna, citta-sahabhū) by mental activity. It is also significant that none of the books of the *Abhidhamma Piṭṭaka* included in the Canon mention the heart as the physical basis of mental activity. The *Paṭṭhāna*, while recounting the role of the organ of vision in generating visual cognition, makes specific mention of 'the physical basis of perceptual and conceptual activity' (yaṃ rūpaṃ nissāya manodhātu ca manoviññaṇadhātu ca vattati) and ignores the cardiac theory of the seat of mental activity, which was widely prevalent at this time (Anuruddha, *Compendium of Philosophy*, P.T.S., London, 1963, pp. 277–9).

### PHYSICAL AND SOCIAL ENVIRONMENT

While conscious mental activity had a physical basis, what we call a person's mind is also conditioned by the physical environment, according to Buddhist conceptions. The physical objects of the external world among other factors stimulate the senses, generate mental activity, feed the mind and motivate one's behaviour. The mind continues to be conditioned by these impacts, which form part and parcel of one's accumulated mental experiences.

It is also the teaching of Buddhism that the economic and social environment also conditions our behaviour. In the *Cakkavattisīhanāda Sutta*, it is stated that the maldistribution of goods in society produces poverty. This eventually leads to the growth of crime and loss of faith in moral values which, along with a sound economic basis, are necessary to sustain a well-ordered society. However, Buddhism does not teach a theory of physical or economic determinism for, despite the fact that man is conditioned by these factors, they do not totally determine his behaviour. Man has an element of freedom, which when exercised with understanding makes it possible for him to change his own nature as well as his physical, economic and social environment for the good and happiness of himself as well as of society.

NOTE: One of the best books written recently about the Buddhist conception of Matter is Y. Karunadasa, *Buddhist Analysis of Matter*, Department of Cultural Affairs, Colombo, 1967. I do not, however, agree with some of the conclusions that the author has come to.

# 6

# The Buddhist Analysis of Mind

The present concise account of the Buddhist theory of mind is based on the early Buddhist texts, and leaves out for the most part the elaborations to be found in the later books of the Theravāda tradition such as the *Abhidhammattha-saṅgaha*. The main reason for doing so is that otherwise there is a danger of losing sight of the wood for the trees.

Another reason for this is that some of the later traditions of Buddhism developed only certain aspects of the original teaching, exaggerating their importance to such an extent as to distort other aspects. Such seems to have been the case with the Idealist (Vijñāna-vāda) schools of Buddhism, which spoke of a universal mind as a vast reservoir in which the individuals' minds were waves or ripples. In such a universe both the individual minds of various beings as well as the external material world were illusions created by the mind. The entire universe is a creation of the mind (sarvaṃ buddhimāyaṃ jagat) and physical objects do not exist outside our perceptions of them. In some of the Mahāyāna schools of thought this universal mind was conceived as the ultimate reality or the eternal Buddha, though never as a creator God.

## REALISM

Some Western scholars also tried to give an idealistic interpretation to early Buddhism by translating the first verse of the

*Dhammapada* to mean 'All things are preceded by mind, governed by mind and are the creations of the mind' (mano-pubbangamā dhammā mano-seṭṭhā mano-māyā). But the correct interpretation of this stanza, which is also supported by the commentary (*Dhammapadaṭṭhakatha*) is 'Conscious states of mind are led by will, are governed by will and are the products of will; so if one speaks or acts with an evil will, suffering comes after one like the wheel that follows the beast of burden who draws the cart.'

Besides, it is clear from the early Buddhist texts that original Buddhism was realistic and held that the world of matter existed independent of our mind (citta-vippayuttaṃ) and was not an illusion produced by it. Though our perceptions and our language distorted the nature of reality, this was only to the extent that a dynamic material world in a continual state of flux was perceived as permanent, solid and substantial.

### ATTITUDE TO TRADITION

The Theravāda tradition, in my opinion, has on the other hand to some extent ignored the conception of the transcendent mind to be found in the early Buddhist texts. This has led to misconceptions on the part of scholars and, perhaps, some Buddhists that Nirvana was a state of oblivion or annihilation. It is, I think, important that Buddhists who have been asked by the Buddha not to accept things merely because they are to be found in tradition (mā paramparāya) should be prepared to examine their own traditions.

We must not forget that even in the time of the Buddha, some concise statements made by him regarding matters of doctrine were elaborated and developed by monks and nuns. The Buddha very often commended these expositions of the Dhamma. On the other hand, there were others who made erroneous expositions and came to false conclusions in interpreting the statements of the Buddha. There was Sāti, for instance, who thought that 'the consciousness of a person ran along and fared on without change of identity' (viññānaṃ . . . sandhāvati saṃsarati anaññaṃ) like a permanent soul, whereas the Buddha points out that consciousness is causally conditioned (paṭicca-samuppāda) and changes under the impact of environment, etc.*

Then there is the case of the monk who argued that the doctrine of anattā (no-soul) implies the denial of personal responsibility. It is said that 'a certain monk entertained the thought that since body, feelings, strivings (conative acts) and intellect are without self, what self can deeds not done by a self affect?' (M. III. 19). The Buddha thought that this was an unwarranted corollary of his teaching since there was the continuity of the 'stream of consciousness' (viññāna-sota) without identity in re-becoming from existence to existence and this was called 'the dynamic or evolving consciousness' (saṃvattanika-viññāna).* Individuality continues though the person is 'neither the same' (na ca so) 'nor another' (naca añño).

## CHARACTERISTICS

One of the main features of the Buddhist theory of mind is that barring the mind in the Nirvāṇic state, all mental phenomena are causally conditioned (paṭicca-samuppanna). According to Buddhist tradition causal laws operate not only in the physical realm (utu-niyāma) or biological realm (bīja-niyāma), but in the psychological realm (citta-niyāma) as well.* Likewise, mental events are more fleeting than the material events of the body, although as a stream of events they outlast the body, whereas the body disintegrates at death. Yet while past phenomena continue to influence and condition the ever-changing present, there is no substratum which can be called a permanent soul. Nor does it make sense to say that the phenomena are in any way associated with or related to such a soul.

The present is conditioned not merely by the past but also by the factors of heredity and environment. Also, conscious mental phenomena have a physical basis. The *Paṭṭhāna* speaks of 'the physical basis of perceptual and conceptual activity'. There is mutual interaction between the physical basis and the mental activity. The mental phenomena are not mere accompaniments of neural or brain phenomena. The nature of the causal relations that hold among mental phenomena and their relations to the body, the physical, social and ideological environment are also analysed and the correlations explained in terms of them. In short we have the earliest historical account of a naturalistic view of the mind.

This knowledge with regard to the mind is to be had by observation and introspection. Introspection is considered to be an unreliable instrument for the study of mental phenomena, according to Western psychologists. This is partly because introspection can only tell us about our private mental experience, and since these cannot be checked by others, they cannot be trusted. The Buddhist theory is that introspection can be refined and developed by the culture of the mind. Besides, such mental development results in the emergence of extra-sensory powers of perception such as telepathy, clairvoyance, etc. This development of the mind is said to sharpen our observation and widen its range since with the development of telepathy, direct and indirect, the minds of others become amenable to public observation like physical objects. The elimination of personal bias makes one's observations objective. Jhānic introspection is described as follows: 'Just as one person should objectively observe another, a person standing should observe a person seated or a person seated a person lying down, even so, should one's object of introspection be well-apprehended, well-reflected upon, well-contemplated and well-penetrated with one's knowledge' (A. III. 27).

## MODERN WESTERN PSYCHOLOGY

With regard to one's own person, it is true that with the growth of objectivity one's emotions tend to evaporate under the scrutiny of objective observation. As a modern textbook of psychology says: 'If affective states are immediately at hand to be observed, their description and interpretation are not easy to come by, for they prove to be remarkably elusive. Try to observe in yourself the turbulent feelings aroused in anger. Ask yourself, "What does anger consist of?" If you are able, when angry, to get yourself in the frame of mind to ask this question, you are also in a fair way toward dispelling the anger' (Frank A. Geldarad, *Fundamentals of Psychology*, John Wiley & Sons, New York, London, 1963, p. 38). It is true that watchfulness (sati) regarding one's own emotions tends to dissipate them but this too is an important psychological fact. It is a fact that can be made use of to make our minds more stable and serene.

Many modern textbooks of psychology with a behavioural bias have not only completely discarded concept of a soul but regard psychology as 'the science of human behaviour'. This is because human behaviour can be publicly observed and measured while human experience cannot. This orientation has its uses. We have learnt a lot about the physiological, biochemical and neural basis of what we call psychological behaviour. As a result we have learnt to some extent to control such behaviour by surgical or biochemical means. But despite these advances in psychology mental tensions and anxiety have been on the increase in societies in which the tempo and philosophies of life give no room for intelligent self-restraint, relaxation, self-analysis and meditation as a means to achieving a healthier mind.

Buddhist psychology, on the other hand, while giving a comprehensive account of the nature of human experience and behaviour also provides the means by which we can understand, control and develop ourselves by a process of self-analysis and meditation, which changes our natures and makes it possible to live happily ourselves and with others.

## PSYCHOPHYSICAL UNIT

Man, according to Buddhism, is a psychophysical unit (nāma-rūpa). This is made up of three components – the sperm and the ovum which go to make up the fertilised ovum or zygote along with the impact of the stream of consciousness of a discarnate spirit (gandhabba) or what is called the re-linking consciousness (paṭisandhi-viññāna).

The psychic and organis physical components grow and mature in a state of mutual interaction. There is reliable evidence that certain children are born with memories of a previous life, which correspond to those of a real life of a dead person and that they could not have acquired these memories by any social contact with the dead person's friends or relatives in this life (see Ian Stevenson, *Twenty Cases Suggestive of Reincarnation*, New York, 1966). There is also evidence that hypnotised subjects regressed to a prenatal period give accounts of prior lives which they claimed to have lived and which have been partly historically verified as factual (see Morey Bernstein, *The Search for Bridy Murphy*, New Edition, 1965; also Dr Jonathan Rodney, *Explorations of a Hypnotist*, Elek Books, London, 1959). The above theory can also be experimentally verified if identical twins brought up in the same environment show some marked differences of character. All the available evidence cannot be more plausibly accounted for than on the above theory, although it has not as yet merited the attention of psychologists as a whole.

The belief that the Buddhist doctrine of anattā implies a denial of any kind of survival after death rests on a misunderstanding of this doctrine. The doctrine denies a permanent entity or soul which runs through different existences without change of identity but does not deny the continuity of an evolving consciousness. Although the emotionally charged experiences are more fleeting than the changes in the body, their memories registered in the unconscious mind outlast the body and determine its state of re-becoming in different forms of cosmic existence. As the *Saṃyutta Nikāya* says in one place: 'Though his material body is devoured by crows and other animals, yet his mind (citta), if long-practised in faith, virtue, learning and renunciation, moves upward and goes to distinction' (S. V. 370).

## MENTAL FACTORS

The components of the mind are classified into four branches (khandhā) or groups (kāyā) namely (1) feeling or hedonic tone (vedanā), (2) sense-impressions, images or ideas and concepts (saññā), (3) conative activities and their concomitants (saṅkhārā) and (4) intellectual activity (viññāna).

Vedanā is the feeling-component, which accompanies our impressions and ideas. They range from the pleasant to the unpleasant through the neutral. Its source may be physical or psychological. When we cut our finger we feel physical pain. When we hear that a close friend or relative has died suddenly the anguish we experience has a psychological origin. These feelings are classified as six according as they originate in the five senses or in the mind with an idea or concept. Since these may be pleasant, unpleasant or neutral, there would be eighteen in all. As associated with one's family life or with a life of renunciation, there would be 36 and as past, present or future 108 in all. Likewise, pleasure may be material (āmisa) as being associated with the satisfactions of needs or wants, or spiritual (nirāmisa) as being associated with a life of selflessness, compassion and understanding. The pleasures experienced in the mystical states of consciousness, personal or impersonal (i.e. rūpa or arūpa jhānas) are classified in an ascending scale, each one being 'higher and more exquisite' (uttaritaraṃ panītataraṃ) than the lower. Nirvana is the 'highest happiness' (paramaṃ sukhaṃ) but the happiness in it is not conditioned. It is not subject to the presence of any conditioned vedanā although the happiness can be positive (vimuttisukhapaṭisaṃvedī).

The experience of conditioned pleasant, unpleasant and neutral hedonic tone is associated with the impressions and ideas we have as a result of sense-contacts or the conceptual activity of the mind in imagining, remembering, reasoning, listening to others, reading books, etc. These impressions, ideas and concepts constitute saññā.

The last on the list of mental factors is viññāna which covers knowledge and belief. Knowledge of moral and spiritual matters constitutes paññā. This involves greater depth of understanding regarding the nature of reality. The difference between saññā, viññāna and paññā is well illustrated in the *Visuddhimagga* by the simile of the coin. When a child sees a coin it is only the colour and shape that interests him. A peasant knows its value as a means of exchange. A master of the mint knows its exact value and nature since he can distinguish between a counterfeit coin and a genuine one. There is a wider sense in which the word viññāna is used, but we shall examine that below.

### SAṄKHĀRĀ

We have left out the word saṅkhārā, which in a psychological context is used in three senses. First, in the sense of volitions as in the sentence avijjā paccayā saṅkhara, which means that our volitions are conditioned by our true or false beliefs, which constitute ignorance. We sometimes think rightly and do good or think wrongly and commit evil. We tread in saṃsāra like a blind man with a stick, who sometimes goes on the right and sometimes on the wrong track in trying to reach his destination.

In the second sense, sankhārā is used to denote our conative or purposive activities. They may be bodily processes and may include reflex actions such as breathing (assāsa-passāsa) as well as conditioned behaviour such as habits. They may be verbal activities involving cognitative and discursive thinking in waking life or even in dreams. Finally, they may be purposive thinking or ideation involving impressions, ideas or concepts associated with feelings. These are called kāya-saṅkhārā, vac-saṅkhārā and citta-saṅkhārā respectively.

We may perform these actions or indulge in these activities aware that we are doing so (sampajāna) or unaware that we are doing so (asampajāna). We can walk, aware or unaware that we are walking. We can talk aware that we are talking or unaware as in sleep. We can think or have trains of thought aware or unaware of what we are doing. The latter would constitute unconscious mental processes.

Likewise, we perform these activities with varying degrees of control. Normally we have no control over our reflexes but it is said that the yogin who has attained the fourth jhāna has them under control. Lastly these activities may be initiated by an internal stimulus (sayaṃ-katam) or an external one (paraṃ-kataṃ).

The third sense of sañkhārā denotes all those factors which accompany conscious volitional activity. If, for example, we are bent on doing a good deed these may be right beliefs (sammā diṭṭhi), some degree of awareness (satīndriya), or a quantum of selflessness etc.

## RELATIONS

All these psychological states are causally conditioned. They may be conditioned by contact with one's physical, social or ideological environment, by the physiological state of the body which is itself a product of heredity, and by our psychological past consisting of our experiences and upbringing in this life or even by the potentialities of prior lives. At the same time we can decide our goals and ideals and direct our courses of action since, despite the conditioning, we have an element of free will which we can exercise in our decisions and effort.

The various relations holding between different types of psychological and physical states have also been analysed. Thus, as we have already stated, there is mutual interaction (aññamañña-paccaya) between body and mind. The relation between an appropriate stimulus and the sense-organ it can activate is called the object-condition (ārammaṇa-paccaya). A dominant purpose that we intend to achieve governs and controls all the subsidiary activity it involves; so the relation between such a purpose and the activity it governs becomes a dominant-condition (adhipati-paccaya). A gradual development of awareness (sati) about our own activity of body, speech or mind reveals to us these intricate relations.

## THE CONSCIOUS AND THE UNCONSCIOUS

While, as we have stated above, viññāna was used in the sense of intellectual activity in a specific sense, in the general sense it denoted the whole of our mental activity, conscious or unconscious.

We have already come across the concept of unconscious mental processes in speaking of ideational activity (citta-saṅkhārā) of which we are not aware. In one place it is said that a yogin by observing directly with his mind how 'the mental saṇkhārā which are disposed in the mind of a particular individual' presumably in his unconscious mind, can predict what he will think at the next moment (A. I. 171). It is also said of a living person that part of his 'stream of consciousness' (viññāna-sota) is present in this world (paraloke patiṭṭitam) and part in the world beyond (paraloke patiṭṭhitam) without a sharp division into two parts (ubhayato abbochinnaṃ, D. III. 105). This means that a man's stream of consciousness has a conscious and unconscious component. Our conscious mental activity gets into this unconscious and accumulates in it, continuing to influence our conscious behaviour.

In the unconscious are also the latent tendencies of the mind, called the anusayas – the desire to satisfy our senses and sex (kāmarāgānusaya), our egoistic impulses (bhavarāgānusaya), or aggression (patighānusaya), as well as the belief we cling to in the unconscious mind (diṭṭhānusaya), doubt (vicikicchānusaya), conceit (mānānusaya) and ignorance (avijjānusaya) (A. I. 9). The goal of the religious life, it is said, is not attained until they are completely eradicated.

There are also several levels of consciousness and the Nirvanic state is distinguished from all of them. There is the level of normal consciousness (sañña-saññī) if the average person. Then, it is possible that one is insane being either a neurotic (khitta-citta) or a psychotic (unmattaka) and, if so, one has an abnormal 'disjointed consciousness' (visañña-saññī). There is also the 'developed consciousness' (vibhūta-saññī) of a person who has cultivated the personal or impersonal forms of mystical consciousness. The Nirvanic mind is distinguished from all of them as well as from a state of coma or oblivion (asaññī). It is attained with the cessation of all conditioned forms of ideation.

## DREAMS

Dreams occur when the mind is not relatively quiescent in a state of deep sleep nor fully awake. The mind is in a dynamic state and the Buddha compares it to a fire which smokes by night and flares up during the day. According to the *Milindapañha*, dreams are of four types, (1) those due to physiological disturbances in the body, (2) those due to mental indulgence, i.e. wish-fulfilment (samudāciṇṇa), (3) those due to intervention of a discarnate angel's spirit (devatā) and (4) prophetic dreams.

## THE IDEAL

The Nirvanic state is the ideal to be attained by all being one of supreme perfection and happiness. Being a state beyond space, time and causation it cannot be conceptually apprehended, since all our concepts are derived from the framework of the space-time-cause world.

Yet in an analogical sense it is often described as a state of transcendent consciousness. In one place it is said that the conditioned saṃsāric consciousness ceases to be in a state of 'infinite omni-luminous consciousness without distinguishing mark' (viññānaṃ anidassanaṃ anantaṃ sabbato-pabham) (D.I. 223, M. I. 329). It is this 'luminous mind' which is said to be in the case of each one of us 'tainted by adventitious defilements' (pabhassaram idaṃ cittaṃ tañca āgantukehi upakkilisehi upakkiliṭṭham) (A. I. 10).)

Man is, therefore, compared to a piece of gold ore and just as, when the defilements of that ore (upakkilesā) are got rid of, it shines with its natural lustre, the mind, it is said, becomes resplendent (pabhassara) when its defilements are eliminated. In the case of the mind, the primary 'defilements of the mind which weaken intuitive insight' (cetaso upakkilese paññāya dubbalī-karaṇe) (M. I. 181) are passion and various forms of greed, ill-will, sloth and torpor, excitement, perplexity and doubt. It is when these and other more subtle defilements are got rid of that the mind becomes relatively perfect and pure (citte parisuddhe pariyodāte) (D. I. 76) and acquires its extra-sensory powers of perception and activity. It is the culmination of this process which results in the attainment of Nirvana, a state 'beyond measure' (atthaṃ gatassa na pamāṇaṃ atthi) (Sn. 1076), 'deep, immeasurable and unfathomable' (M. I. 487). This transcendent mind is not a soul because it is not personal and is not a self-identical entity. Nor is it a creator God.

## THEORY OF MOTIVATION

The ideal state is one in which 'the mind is divested of its strivings and has attained the destruction of all desires' (Dh. 153). It is also a state of perfect mental health. Man suffers from mental disease until he has attained Nirvana.

The goal of Buddhism is, therefore, therapeutic. We have to start with our present condition in which we are impelled to act out of greed, hatred and ignorance. Greed consists of the desire to gratify our senses and sex (kāma-taṇhā) as well as to satisfy our egoistic impulses (bhava-taṇhā), such as our desire for possessions, for power, for fame, for personal immortality, etc. Hatred consists of our aggressive tendencies (vibhava-taṇhā) or the desire to eliminate and get rid of what we dislike. Both greed and hatred are fed by ignorance (i.e. erroneous beliefs, illusions, rationalisations) and vice versa. Indulgence in these desires give temporary satisfaction, but there is a law of diminishing returns which operates in our attempt to find satisfaction through gratification. The process eventually makes us slaves of our desires as in the case of alcoholics, misers, sex-addicts, etc.

Our endeavour should be gradually to change the basis of our motivation from greed, hatred and ignorance to selflessness (cāga, alobha), compassion (mettā, alobha) and understanding (paññā, amoha).

## PSYCHOLOGICAL TYPES

To do this effectively, we must know what psychological types we are. The earliest historical classification of individuals into different types is in the book called *Puggala-Paññatti* (Human Types) of the *Abhidhamma Piṭaka.* In the later tradition classifications were based mainly on the degree to which people possessed the traits of greed, hatred and ignorance as well as their opposites. Different meditational exercises are recommended for them to get rid of the evil traits and develop the good traits they have.

There could, of course, be various sub-types. Some greed-types (rāgacarita) may have strong sex desires, others the desire for power, etc. The general formula applicable to all would be to sublimate greed by desiring to develop restraint and selflessness, compassion and understanding, to sublimate hate by endeavouring to remove greed, hatred and ignorance, and to aid this process to adopt right-beliefs (sammā-diṭṭhi) in place of erroneous ones about the nature and destiny of man in the universe.

# 7

# The Buddhist Conception of the Universe

The early Indians and Greeks speculated about the nature, origin and extent of the universe. Anaximander, a Greek thinker of the sixth century BC, is supposed to have contemplated the possibility of 'innumerable worlds' successively coming out of (and passing away) into an indefinite substance. About a century later, the Greek atomists, Leucippus and Democritus, who postulated the existence of innumerable atoms and an infinite void, conceived of worlds coming-to-be and passing away throughout the void. These speculations were the product of imagination and reason and the 'worlds' they talked of were mere reproductions of the earth and the heavenly bodies such as the sun, moon and the stars.

The contemporary Indian speculations prior to Buddhism were on the same lines, except for the fact that some of them were claimed to be based on extra-sensory perception as well. Here there appears to have been even a wider variety of views than to be found among the Greeks.

The early Buddhist texts summarise their views according to the Buddhist logic of four alternatives. With regard to the extent of the universe, the following four types of views were current: (1) those who held that the universe was finite in all dimensions, (2) that the universe was infinite in all dimensions, (3) that the universe was finite in some dimensions and infinite in others, and (4) those who rejected all the above three views and held that the universe was neither finite nor infinite.

This last view was held by thinkers who argued that the universe or space was unreal. If so, spatial epithets like 'finite' or 'infinite' cannot be applied to it. So the universe is neither finite nor infinite.

Similarly, with regard to the origin of the universe, there were thinkers who put forward all four possible views, viz. (1) some held that the universe had a beginning or origin in time; (2) others that it had no beginning in time; (3) still others that the universe had in one sense a beginning and in another sense no beginning in time. This would be so if the universe had relative origins, its substance being eternal, while it came into being and passed away from time to time; (4) finally, there were those who put forward the theory that since time was unreal it did not make sense to say that the universe was 'neither eternal nor not eternal'.

It is with original Buddhism that we get for the first time in the history of thought a conception of the universe, which can in any way be meaningfully compared with the modern picture as we know it in contemporary astronomy. This is all the more remarkable when we find no other such conception, which foreshadowed or forestalled modern discoveries in ancient or medieval thought of the East of West.

## 'THE UNIVERSE'

Before we describe the essential features of the Buddhist account of the universe or cosmos, it is necessary to clarify what today we mean by the term 'universe' for it did not mean this at all times.

The conception of the universe in the West until the end of the medieval period was geocentric. It was mainly Aristotelian in origin. The earth was deemed to be the fixed centre of the universe and the moon, the planets, the sun and the stars were believed to move with uniform circular velocity in crystalline spheres around it. The universe was also finite in spatial extent. Apollonius and Ptolemy made some minor adjustments in an attempt to account for some of the movements of the planets but the basic conceptions remained the same.

This finite geocentric universe was later considered to be the orthodox theological view of the cosmos and attempts on the part of thinkers to change it were treated as heresy. A change came with Copernicus who was led by observational findings and the suggestions of early Greek thinkers, like the Pythagorean Philolaus and Aristarchus of Samos, to conceive of the sun as the centre of the universe. The 'universe' was now the solar system (i.e. the sun with the planets going round it), encircled by the stars.

With the construction of larger telescopes since the time of Galileo, the next advance was made by Herschel in the late eighteenth century. His observations convinced him and others that the unit of the universe was not the solar system but the galaxy or galactic system composed of clusters of stars, the blazing sun that we see being only one among such stars. On the basis of his observations of stars and the calculation of their distances, he was the first to make a map of our galactic system or 'island universe' (as he called it), known as the Milky Way.

He too placed our sun at the centre of the disc, though today we know that it is about half-way between the centre and the edge of this huge galaxy. Astronomical distances are so large that they are measured not in terms of miles but in light-years. Light travels at the rate of about 186,000 miles per second. It is held that light, travelling at this speed, would take about 100,000 years to travel across the diameter of the Milky Way. In other words, our galactic system has a diameter of 100,000 years.

It was left to modern astronomy with its more powerful telescopes, aided by radio, to delve deeper into space and to make more accurate observations of the relative locations and shapes of these galaxies.

In the light of these findings we know that the ten billion galaxies in space are not found in isolation but in clusters. So when we survey the universe the units we have to deal with are the galaxies. They are now classified as regular and irregular on the grounds of shape, the regular ones being elliptical, round or spiral. The commonest of all galaxies (i.e. about three quarters of them) are spiral. The majority of them are called 'dwarf galaxies' because they contain about a million stars.

The progress of astronomy has thus resulted in a gradual development of the concept of the 'universe'. The earliest conception was the geocentric, the 'universe' being the earth and the celestial bodies around it. Next, the heliocentric conception concentrated on the solar system. The real advance was made in the next stage when the solar system was conceived as one of many such systems in an 'island universe' or galaxy. Following this there was the concept of thc cluster of galaxies and the present conception of the universe as consisting of a number of such clusters.

## BUDDHIST CONCEPTION

In the Buddhist texts the word used to denote the 'world', the 'cosmos' or the 'universe' is *loka*. Its uses are as various as the English word 'world'. It would be tedious to enumerate them here since we are concerned only with thc sense in which it is used to denote 'the world in space'. This is called akāsa-loka or the 'space-world' (i.e. the world in space) in the Commentaries, which illustrate this by reference to a relevant passage in the *Visuddhimagga* (204): 'As far as these suns and moons revolve, shining and shedding their light in space, so far extends the thousand-fold universe' (sahassadhā-loko) – here the word "loka" is used to denote 'the world in space'.

In another context of this passage, the universe is described in three tiers or stages. The smallest unit is here called sahassī cuḷanika loka-dhātu, i.e. the Thousand-fold Minor World-

System. This is defined as follows: 'As far as these suns and moons revolve, shining and shedding their light in space, so far extends the thousand-fold universe. In it are thousands of suns, thousands of moons . . . thousands of Jambudīpas, thousands of Aparagoyanas, thousands of Uttarakurus, thousands of Pubbavidehas . . .' (A. I. 227, V. 59). Jambudīpa, Aparagoyāna, Uttarakuru and Pubbavideha are the four inhabited regions or the continents known to the people of North India at the time. From descriptions given about them, it appears to have been believed that these peoples had different temperaments and ways of living.

So it is as if one were to say today that there were 'thousands of Indias, thousands of Arabias, thousands of Russias and thousands of Chinas'. Its significance is that there were thousands of inhabited places or planets since the earth was associated with one sun and one moon.

This Cūḷanikā Loka-dhātu or Minor World-System, which is the smallest unit in the universe though it contains thousands of suns, moons and inhabited planets, can only be compared with the modern conception of a galaxy, the majority of which have about a million suns.

Most modern astronomers believe that the chances are that there could be life of the form to be found on earth in planets of other solar systems in this as well as other galaxies. Professor Harlow Shapley says after making a most conservative estimate: 'We would still have after all that elimination, ten billion planets suitable for organic life something like that on earth' (*The View From a Distant Star*, New York, London, 1963, p. 64). Another well-known astronomer, Dr Ernst J. Opik states: 'Many planets may carry life on their surface. Even if there were only one inhabited system in every million, there would be 10,000 million million abodes of life in the universe. What a variety of forms and conditions this implies!' (*The Oscillating Universe*, New York, 1960, p. 114).

## CLUSTERS OF GALAXIES

The next unit in the universe, according to the early Buddhist texts, is described as consisting of thousands of Minor World-Systems. This is called a 'Twice-a-thousand Middling World-System' (dvisahassī majjhimikā loka-dhātu). It would correspond to a cluster of galaxies according to modern conceptions.

This notion of a cluster of galaxies is a fairly recent one in modern astronomy. As Professor A. C. B. Lovell, the Director of the Jodrell Bank Experimental Station, said in his BBC Reith Lectures in 1955:

'Some years ago we thought that these galaxies were isolated units in space, but now we believe that the galaxies exist in great groups or clusters. In the same way that the earth and planets are bound to the sun and move as a unit through space, so on an inconceivably vaster scale we think that the galaxies are contained in clusters as connected physical systems. The local group contains the Milky Way system, the Andromeda Nebula, and perhaps two dozen others. It is not very populated, compared, for example, with the Virgo cluster of galaxies, which contains at least a thousand visible galaxies, although occupying only about twice the space of the local group' (The Individual and the Universe, Oxford University Press, London, 1958, pp. 6–7).

In the opinion of Professor Bonnor: 'The Milky Way is one of a small cluster of galaxies called the Local Group, which includes all galaxies within about a million light-years from the Earth, and contains about twenty members. Beyond this distance one would have to travel about ten million light years before coming across another galaxy. Other galaxies, too, show a distinct tendency to cluster. The clusters may be small, like the Local Group, or may contain several hundreds or even thousands of galaxies' (William Bonnor, *The Mystery of the Expanding Universe*, New York, 1964, p. 32).

We find that here 'thousands' is practically the upper limit since many of the clusters of galaxies contain less. On the other with reference to the 'Thousand-fold Minor World-System', 'thousand' appeared to be too little. Since the Dhamma is summed up in stereotyped formulae (which recur in the Pali Canonical texts) for easy memorisation, it is possible that 'thousand' was selected as a convenient common number to describe the hierarchy of units. However, elsewhere in the Canon smaller numbers of such 'Thousand-fold Minor World-Systems' to be found in clusters are referred to.

In the *Saṅkhāruppati Sutta* of the *Majjhima Nikāya*, the basic unit is again the Thousand-fold World-System (sahassī lokadhatu) (M. III. 101). But there is a reference to two, three, four . . . up to hundred such world-systems grouped together (e.g. sata-sahassī-loka-dhātu) (ibid.).

Of frequent occurrence is the dasa sahassī-loka-dhātu, which should be translated as 'the ten thousand-fold world-systems'. It is used with reference to the Local Group of galaxies, which consists of about twenty in all, of which about ten cluster relatively close together. One text in fact refers to 'the ten nearest island universes' (Rudolf Thiel, *And There Was Light*, New York, 1957, p. 355).

## COSMOS

While the Middling World-Systems consisted of a few up to a hundred or even a thousand galaxies, the next unit is the whole cluster of Middling World-Systems. For it is said that thousands of Middling World-Systems (i.e. clusters of galaxies) go to form the vast universe or the Major World-System (Mahā Lokadhātu), which some texts on astronomy refer to as the Metagalaxy.

Although some astronomers wonder whether there is a hierarchy of clusters of galaxies within the universe, the general opinion is against this. As Professor Bonnor points out: 'One may ask whether clusters of galaxies are the last in the hierarchy. As stars aggregate into galaxies, and galaxies into clusters, do clusters aggregate into superclusters, and so on? Although astronomers are not quite unanimous, it seems that the clusters are the largest individual entities, and we should not be justified in speaking of clusters of clusters. Thus we have at last reached the unit of cosmology – the cluster of galaxies. In practice the galaxy is usually taken as the unit because galaxies can be recognised more easily than clusters' (Bonnor, op. cit., p. 32).

The modern astronomical descriptions of the universe as well as those of the early Buddhist texts stop here. The modern accounts stop because there is a limit to observability on the part of the telescopes. If, as is inferred to be the case, the galaxies further and further away are receding at greater and greater speeds from us, then as they approach the speed of light, they would pass beyond the range of theoretical observability. So the theoretically observable universe is also limited and what happens beyond this would have to be pure speculation even according to science.

The early Buddhist texts, too, do not state that the Major World-System is all there is in the universe, for the question as to whether the world is finite or infinite (ananto) in extent is left unanswered (avyākata).

The later commentarial tradition, however, goes a step further. One of the synonyms for a 'World-System' or Loka-Dhātu is Cakkavāla, a word of uncertain etymology meaning a 'wheel', 'circle' or 'sphere'. The Pali Society Dictionary commenting on Loka-dhātu (s.v.) says that it means 'constituent or unit of the Universe', 'a world, sphere' and adds that Loka-Dhātu is another name for Cakkavāla.

Calling a galaxy a 'sphere' or a 'wheel' is certainly appropriate, for as we know from modern astronomy a galaxy is like a huge catherine wheel revolving round a centre or hub. But the commentary states that these galaxies or spheres (cakkavāla) are infinite in number (anantāni cakkāvalāni) (*Manorathapūraṇi*, II, 342). This is certainly going beyond the standpoint of the early Buddhist texts, which is uncommitted on the question of the origin or extent of the universe. While the later traditions of the Sarvāstivāda and Theravāda suggest that the number of galaxies or world-systems is infinite in extent, the Mahāyāna texts hold that the universe is infinite in time, stating that 'the universe is without beginning or end' (anavarāgra).

Here again the standpoint of original Buddhism was merely to state that the universe was 'without a known beginning' (anamatagga). The Buddha, it is said, could see worlds without limit 'as far as he liked' (yātatā ākaṅkheyya) (Nid. I. Vol. II, 356). He could also probe into the past without limit, for the further back that he looked into the past, there was the possibility of going back still further. But to say that the world or universe is infinite in time and space is to go beyond the stand of early Buddhism and give an answer to an 'unanswered question' (avyākata).

While all schools of Buddhism retained the general picture of the universe as given in the early Buddhist texts, their detailed accounts and elaborations are not always to be trusted. The Sarvāstivada accounts given in the *Abhidharmakoṣa* differ from those of the Theravādins. The reason for this is that the simple but stupendous conceptions of the early Buddhist view of the universe got mixed up with popular mythological geography and cosmology in the commentarial traditions of the schools.

The Mahāyāna texts, for the most part, retain the early view of the galactic systems spread out through space. We only notice that 'thousand' is replaced by 'million'. The *Vajracchedikā*, for example, refers to the universe as 'this sphere of a million millions of world-systems' (XIX, XXIV, XXX).

## MYTH AND FACT

While the early Buddhist texts are, therefore, more reliable, we must not forget that the account given of the extent of the material universe exhausts the early Buddhist conception of the cosmos. The passage quoted above from the *Aṅguttara Nikāya* goes on to speak of the subtle-material worlds (rūpa-loka) or the worlds of higher spirits or gods (devā) as being associated with the material worlds or galaxies. They cannot, however, be observed by human vision.

Are we going to dismiss this aspect of the universe as belonging to the realm of mythology? Did the Buddha have grounds for belief in the existence of devas or was this only a popular belief at the time, to which he did not subscribe? We can see the real attitude of the Buddha by the answers he gives to the Brahmin youth Saṅgārava who questions him on this subject.

SAṄGĀRAVA: 'Tell me, Gotama, are there gods (devā)?'

BUDDHA: 'I know on good grounds (ṭhānaso) that there are gods.'

SAṄGĀRAVA: 'Why do you say when asked "whether there are gods" that you know on good grounds that there are gods. Does this not imply that your statement is utterly false?'

BUDDHA: 'When one is questioned as to whether there are gods, whether one replies that "there are gods" or that "one knows on good grounds that there are gods", then surely the deduction to be made by an intelligent person is indubitable, namely that there are gods.'

SAṄGĀRAVA: 'Then, why did not the venerable Gotama plainly say so from the very start?'

BUDDHA: 'Because it is commonly taken for granted in the world that there are gods.'

The significance of this reply is that the Buddha holds that there are devas not because of a popular or traditional belief, which he took for granted, but because he was personally convinced of their existence on good grounds.

On the other hand, the Buddha had to make use of some of

the traditional terms and coin others to describe the different types of worlds of these devas. There is other evidence to suggest that the Buddha did not take popular conceptions for granted. In one place he says that ignorant people believe that there is a 'hell' (pātāla) but asserts that this belief was false. 'Hell (pātāla),' the Buddha says, 'is a term for painful bodily sensations' (*Saṃyutta Nikāya*, IV. 206). 'Heavens' are better than human forms of existence, where what one experiences is pleasant (S. IV. 124) while 'hells' are subhuman forms of existence where everything one experiences is unpleasant. The Buddha claims to 'see' both these kinds of 'worlds' (ibid.). The danger of being born in these subhuman states of downfall (vinipāta) is that it is difficult to emerge to human level after that. The reason is given: 'Because there prevails no practice of the good life, no righteous living, no doing of good works, but just cannibalism, the stronger preying on weaker creatures' (S. V. 455).

## CLAIRVOYANCE

It is stated that the Buddha's ability to see these World-Systems and the beings in them is due to his clairvoyance. It is said: 'The Blessed One with his clairvoyant paranormal vision can see one world-system, two, three . . . fifty world-systems – the Thousand-fold Minor World-System, the Twice-a-Thousand Middling World-System and the Thrice-a-Thousand Major World System. He could see as far out into space as he liked. So clear is the clairvoyant vision of the Blessed One. In this way is the Blessed One with his clairvoyant vision one who has his eyes open (vivaṭacakkhu)' (Nid. I. Vol. II, 356).

The clairvoyant powers of the disciples both according to the texts and commentaries are not unlimited like that of the Buddha. Anuruddha who was considered the foremost of those who had attained the faculty of clairvoyant vision could see only as far as the 'Thousand-fold World-System':

'It is by the fact of cultivating and developing these four arisings of mindfulness that I have acquired the ability to see the Thousand-fold World-System' (S. V. 302).

## COSMIC PHENOMENA

Some of the casual statements made by the Buddha appear to come from one who has in fact observed aspects of cosmic space. In one place, the Buddha says: 'Monks, there is a darkness of intergalactic space [Woodward has "interstellar space"], an impenetrable gloom, such a murk of darkness as cannot enjoy the splendour of this sun and moon' (S. V. 455). Modern astronomy would agree with this verdict. We see so much light because we are fortunate enough to be close to a sun.

The uncertainty of life in some of these worlds is sometimes stressed with graphic descriptions of cosmic phenomena. The Buddha says that there comes a time after a lapse of hundreds of thousands of years; when it would cease to rain and vegetable and animal life in the planet would be destroyed (A. V. 102). He also speaks of times when seven suns would appear and the earth, including the biggest of mountains which appears so stable, would go up in smoke without leaving any ashes at all. He speaks as though he has witnessed some of these phenomena. He says: 'Who would think or believe that this earth or Sineru, the highest of mountains, would burn up and be destroyed except on the evidence of sight?' (A. V. 103). Today we know that suns or stars could become cosmic hydrogen bombs, flare up and explode, burning up their planets, if any, and even affecting neighbouring solar systems. A student of astronomy commenting on this possibility says: 'Humanity would at any rate enjoy a solemn and dramatic doom as the entire planet went up in a puff of smoke' (Rudolf Thiel, *And There Was Light*, p. 329). These phenomena are called *novae* and *supernovae*, which are observed from time to time in galaxies including our own.

Colliding galaxies, of which there is some evidence, also spell such disasters.

## TIME AND RELATIVITY

The destruction of the worlds, however, which will cause such phenomena to be manifested in all the world-systems comes only at the end of an epoch or aeon, called a kappa. Several similes are given to illustrate what an immensely long period an aeon is. One such passage reads as follows: 'Suppose there were a city of iron walls one yojana in length, one in width and one high filled up with mustard seed, from which a man were to take out at the end of every hundred years a mustard seed. That pile of mustard seed would in this way be sooner done away with and ended than an aeon, so very long is an aeon. And of aeons thus long more than one has passed, more than a hundred, more than a thousand, more than a hundred thousand' (S. II. 182).

The cosmos undergoes two major periods of change in time called the aeons of expansion and contraction. The aeon of expansion is the period in which the universe unfolds itself or opens out (vivaṭṭa-kappa). The other is the one in which the universe closes in and is destroyed (saṃvaṭṭa-kappa). Elsewhere they are described as the four stages of the universe: (1) the period of expansion, (2) the period in which the universe remains in a state of expansion, (3) the period of contraction and (4) the period in which the universe stays contracted.

There are several models according to which astronomers try to explain the movement within the universe in time. One of them is the cycloidal oscillating model according to which the universe expands and contracts until, as Professor Bonnor says, 'the contraction slows down, ceases and changes to expansion again'. The theory is currently favoured by many astronomers in the light of recent findings.

There is also a reference to the relativity of time in different parts of the universe. But this is a comparison of time on earth with time in the heavenly worlds. One day in one of these different worlds is equated with 50 years, 100 years, 200 years, 400 years and 1,600 years respectively on earth. Such in brief outline is the early Buddhist conception of the universe.

# 8

# The Buddhist Attitude to God

The word 'God' is used in so many different ways and so many different senses that it is not possible to define the Buddhist attitude to God without clarifying the meaning of this term. The Concise Oxford Dictionary defines its sense in a theistic context as: 'Supreme being, Creator and Ruler of the Universe'. A theistic text (The Book of Common Prayer) gives the following description: 'There is but one living and true God, everlasting, without body, parts or passions; of infinite power, wisdom and goodness, the Maker and Preserver of all things both visible and invisible . . .' I have left out the rest of the quotation since it concerns the specific dogmas of this particular school of theism.

In this form it would be a definition of the concept of a personal God, common to monotheistic belief with the proviso that the idea of creation varies according to different traditions. According to one tradition, God's creation consists in fashioning co-existent chaotic matter and making an ordered cosmos out of chaos. According to another tradition, God's matter in creation is an emanation or emission (sṛṣṭi) from the being of God, while according to yet another tradition, God creates matter out of nothing (*ex nihilo*).

Using the word in the above sense of a Personal Creator God, who is a Supreme being possessed of the characteristics of omniscience, omnipotence and infinite goodness, if we ask the question, 'Does God exist?', there are four possible answers. They are: (1) those theists who say 'yes' and affirm

God's existence, (2) those atheists who say 'no' and deny God's existence, (3) those sceptics or agnostics who say 'we do not know' or 'we cannot know' and (4) those positivists who say that the question is meaningless since the meaning of the term 'God' is not clear.

## ATHEISM

What is the Buddhist answer to this question? Was the Buddha a Theist, an Atheist, an Agnostic or a Positivist? The answer is fairly clear. Given the above definition of God in its usual interpretation, the Buddha is an atheist and Buddhism in both its Theravāda and Mahāyāna forms is atheism.

Some Western scholars have tried to make out that Mahāyāna Buddhism came into being about the beginning of the Christian era and that in it the Buddha is deified. Both these conclusions are false. Mahāyāna Buddhism came into being with the Mahāsaṅghika Council, when a group of liberals broke away from the conservative elders or the Theravādins about a hundred years after the death of the Buddha and in none of the Mahāyāna schools is the Buddha conceived of as a Creator God, though this does not mean that the Buddha was a mere human being in either the Theravāda or Mahāyāna schools of thought.

In denying that the universe is a product of a Personal God, who creates it in time and plans a consummation at the end of time, Buddhism is a form of atheism.

## GOSĀLA'S THEISM

That Buddhism is atheistic is also clear from its denunciation of the religion and philosophy of Theism put forward by Makkhali Gosāla, one of the six senior contemporaries of the Buddha. It is a remarkable fact that these six teachers put forward prototypes of religious or philosophical theories, which have become widely prevalent in the world. Makkhali was a Theist or an issara-nimmāna-vādin, i.e. one who posited the theory that the ultimate cause was God. The others consisted of a Materialist, an Agnostic, a Categorialist (who explained the universe in terms of discrete categories), a Natural Determinist and an Eclectic.

According to the Jain *Bhagavatī Sūtra* and the Commentary to the *Dīgha Nikāya*, Makkhali is called Gosāla because he was born in a cow-shed (go-sālā). In his teaching he denied moral causation and urged that human beings become corrupted or doomed or become purified or saved miraculously, presumably by the will or grace of God. Human beings lacked initiative or freedom and their future was entirely planned by the will of the creator. All beings evolved in various states of existence under the impact of destiny, circumstances or nature. Eventually fools and the wise alike completed their saṃsāric evolution and attained salvation, making an end of suffering.

It is called the theory of salvation through saṃsāric evolution (saṃsāra-suddhi) and in one place in the Buddhist texts it is described as follows: 'There is no short-cut to Heaven. Await thy destiny. Whether a man experiences joy or sorrow is due to his destiny. All beings will attain salvation through saṃsāric evolution, so do not be eager for that which is to come' (J. VI. 229). The same idea is expressed as follows in a theistic text: 'Beings originate in the Unmanifest, they evolve in a manifest condition and eventually come to rest in the Unmanifest. So why worry.'

Makkhali explicitly states that 'there is no question of a person attaining maturity of character by good deeds, vows, penances or a religious life' (D. I. 54). Man is merely a product of the creation and will of God and his future is laid out. As Makkhali says, 'Just as much as a ball of thread when flung on the ground unravels itself until it comes to an end, so the wise and the fools alike fare on in saṃsāra and eventually attain salvation.'

Makkhali's theism has several attractive features. First, it is logically consistent. As philosophers have pointed out, God's omniscience and omnipotence strictly imply a rigid deterministic universe. God being omniscient sees the entire future in all its aspects and details. It is like human foreknowledge, which is only probable. So the future of the creature is strictly mapped out and God can see it as in the reel of a film. God being omnipotent is entirely responsible for it as well, so that a belief in free-will on the part of his creatures is merely illusory. Secondly, God is impartial in that he treats all beings alike for, as Makkhali says, 'there are no high and low' (natthi ukkaṃsāvakkaṃse), since all go through the same course of evolution in various stages of existence. Thirdly, there are no eternal hells and beings do not have to burn in an everlasting hell-fire, for they all attain salvation. There are three hundred hells (tiṃse nirayasate), or rather purgatories, along with seven human worlds (satta-mānuse) and several heavens to pass through before attaining eventual release.

His theism relieves human beings of the burdens of responsibility, gives them security, solace and the joys of the heavens (mixed with the sorrows of purgatories) before assuring salvation. In this sense, it may be compared with many modern forms of theism, which try to equalise opportunities for all and are very apologetic about eternal hell-fires.

### PUPPET ARGUMENT

Yet the theism of Makkhali is severely criticised by the Buddha since it gave a false sense of security to the people and encouraged complacency by denying free-will and the value of human effort. The Buddha says that he knows of no other person than Makkhali born for the detriment and disadvantage of so many people, and compares him to a fisherman casting his net at the mouth of a river for the destruction of many fish (A. I. 33). Similarly in the *Sandaka Sutta*, the Buddha (as reported by Ānanda) says that there are four types of religion which are false in this world and four types which are unsatisfactory though not necessarily totally false, distinguishing Buddhism from all eight of them.

Two of the types condemned as false refer to two forms of theism. One is the doctrine that salvation is not due to human effort or the moral causation effected by good or evil deeds, but that people are miraculously saved or doomed presumably because of the grace or will of God. The other is the doctrine of predestination, theistic evolutionism.

It would be interesting to see the reasons given for this stand taken against certain forms of theism. There are two main arguments against theism presented in the early Canonical texts. The first may be called the Puppet Argument and is stated as follows: 'If God designs the life of the entire world – the glory and the misery, the good and the evil acts, man is but an instrument of his will (niddesa-kāri) and God (alone) is responsible' (J. V. 238).

Theists who do not take a predestinarian stand (which is logically consistent) try to evade this conclusion by saying that God has endowed man with free-will. But it can be shown that the concept of divine providence is not compatible with a notion of human freedom. To be consistent, one has either to give up the belief in theism or the belief in freedom or confess that this is a mystery that one cannot understand, which is a departure from reason.

Antony Flew who has made the most recent and most comprehensive analysis of the concept of theism, including the case for and against it, states one of his conclusions with regard to this matter as follows:

'The stock image is that of a Supreme Father showing long-suffering tolerance towards his often rebellious children: he has given us, it is said, our freedom; and we – wretched unworthy creatures that we are – too often take advantage to flout his wishes. If this image fitted there would be no problem. Obviously, it is possible for children to act against their parents' wishes. It is also possible for parents to grant to their children freedoms, which may be abused, be refusing to exercise powers of control which they do possess. But the case of Creator and creature must be utterly different. Here the appropriate images, in so far as any images could be appropriate, would be that of the Creator, either as the Supreme Puppetmaster with creatures whose every thought and move he arranges; or as the Great Hypnotist with subjects who always act out his irresistible suggestions. What makes the first image entirely inept and the other two much less so is crucially that God is supposed to be, not a manufacturer or a parent who may make or rear his product and then let it be, but the Creator. This precisely means that absolutely nothing happens save by his ultimate undetermined determination and with his consenting ontological support. Everything means everything; and that includes every human thought, every human action, and every human choice. For we too are indisputably parts of the universe, we are among the "all things both visible and invisible" of which he is supposed to be "the Maker, and Preserver"' (*God and Philosophy*, Hutchinson & Co., 1966, p. 44).

His final conclusion is the same as what I mentioned above. In his own words: 'For it is, as we have argued already, entirely inconsistent to maintain both that there is a Creator; and that there are other authentically autonomous beings' (ibid., p. 54). A careful study of the theistic texts of any tradition will show that often this is directly admitted in certain contexts, despite the contradictions in other places.

According to the Buddhist theory of causation, man's actions are not strictly determined. The Buddhist theory steers clear of both Natural and Theistic Determinism on the one hand and total Indeterminism on the other. Man has an element of free-will although his actions are conditioned but not determined by external and internal stimuli. By the exercise of this freedom along the right lines man can change his own condition from one of anxiety, unrest and suffering to one of serenity and happiness. This is effected not by invoking the grace of God but by human effort and the comprehension of human psychology. In the *Devadaha Sutta*, the Buddha uses the arguments of the theists against them, saying that if theists are suffering psychologically, then according to their own theories it must be because God has withheld his grace from them whereas in his own case (if theism were true), 'he must have been created by a good God' (bhaddakena issarena nimmito) (M. II. 227).

### ARGUMENT FROM EVIL

The second argument against theism found in the Canonical texts is the argument from evil. It proceeds on the presumption that if the world is created by God, then certain evils are inexplicable. It has several variants but let us take some of them together: 'If God (Brahmā) is Lord of the whole world and creator of the multitude of beings, then why (1) has he ordained misfortune in the world without making the whole world happy, or (2) for what purpose has he made the world full of injustice, deceit, falsehood, falsehood and conceit, or (3) the Lord of creation is evil in that he ordained injustice when there could have been justice' (J. VI. 208).

Here again, leading modern philosophers endorse the argument after showing that all the attempts to explain away evil are unsatisfactory. It will not do to say that evil is negative or unreal, for suffering, ignorance, poverty and ugliness are as real as their opposites. It will not do to say that evils (like wilful injury) are necessary for the existence of higher-order goods (like forgiveness), for there are still many evils unaccounted for in this fashion. Nor will it do to say that the evils in the world are due to the grant of free-will to human beings (quite apart from the difficulty of reconciling this with divine providence, as indicated above). For as Professor Flew has shown, 'There are many evils which it scarcely seems either are or could be redeemed in this way: animal suffering, for instance, especially that occurring before – or after – the human period' (Flew, op. cit., p. 54).

Here again the inability to give a rational explanation leads the theist to a confession that it is a mystery: 'The origin of moral evil lies forever concealed within the mystery of human freedom' (J. R. Hick, *Philosophy of Religion*, Prentice-Hall, 1963, p. 43). So there is the mystery or the incompatibility between divine providence and human freedom as well as the mystery or the contradiction between belief in divine goodness and the existence of certain evils.

The result is that while some of the Upaniṣads hold that 'the world is enveloped by God' (īṣāvasyam idaṃ sarvam), Buddhism held that 'the world was without a refuge and without God' (attāṇo loko anabhissaro).

## OTHER ARGUMENTS

I have stated only the two main arguments to be found in the Canonical texts, which may be attributed to the Buddha himself. But the later literature both of Theravāda and Mahāyāna provides an abundance of arguments against the concept of a Personal Creator God (Īsvara). While positive arguments are adduced to show the truth of atheism, there are others which show the fallacies of the theistic arguments for the existence of God.

Even when we take the arguments for theism in a modern context we find that the Ontological Argument was a mere definition, which mistakenly regarded existence as an attribute. The Cosmological Argument contradicted its own premise by speaking of an uncaused cause or using the word 'cause' in a non-significant sense. The argument from Design, which is superficially the most appealing flounders when we consider the waste and cruelty of evolution, with nature 'red in tooth and claw'. It is impossible to contemplate that a loving God could have created and watched the spectacle of dinosaurs tearing each other to pieces for millions of years on earth.

## INCONCEIVABLE OR MEANINGLESS?

In order to reconcile divine love with the apparent cruelty of nature, a move is often made by theists to say that God's love is inscrutable or is another mystery. A human parent would do whatever he could to relieve the suffering of his child who is in great pain. Would an omnipotent and omniscient being look on without intervention? To say that such a being exists is to equate his love with callousness or cruelty. In such a situation we would not know what meaning to attach to the concept of 'love' considered as an attribute of God. This has led theists to say that God's attributes as well as his nature are inconceivable. The *Bodhicaryāyatāra* makes a *reductio ad absurdum* of this contention arguing that in such a case the concept of a God or creator is meaningless: 'If, as theists say, God is too great for man to be able to comprehend him, then it follows that his qualities also surpass our range of thought, and that we neither know him nor attribute to him the quality of a creator.' It follows that if normal meanings are given to the words, all-knowing, all-powerful and infinitely good (or analogous meanings), the evidence points against God's existence, whereas if this is not done, the concept becomes meaningless.

## FRUIT TEST

Another test that Buddhism applies in gauging the validity of a belief is the 'fruit test', or the attempt to see what consequences a belief or set of beliefs, when acted upon, has led to. With regard to theism it may be held that it has given people a sense of security and inspired them to various kinds of activity. This does not prove that the belief is true but suggests that it may be useful. A realistic survey would show that while beliefs in theism has done some good, they have brought much evil in their train as well.

Wars have been fought between the main warring creeds of

theism and also among the sects within each in the name of God. In contrast we may quote the words of Edward Conze about Buddhism: 'All those who dwell in Asia can take pride in a religion which is not only five centuries older than that of the West, but has spread and maintained itself without recourse to violence, and has remained unstained by religious wars and crusades' (*A Short History of Buddhism*, p. 111). In addition, a careful study of the literature of theism will show that there is hardly a crime or vice which has not been committed or recommended in the name of God.

Hitler thought that he was merely carrying out the will of God and that he and his party were the instruments of Providence. The references are too many to quote and may be found in his speeches (Norman H. Baynes, *The Speeches of Adolf Hitler*, Oxford University Press, 1942, s.v. *God* in Index). For example, in 1938 Hitler says: 'I believe that it was God's will to send a boy from here into the Reich, to let him grow up, to raise him to be the leader of the nation so as to enable him to lead back his homeland into the Reich. There is a higher ordering and we all are nothing else than its agents' (ibid., p. 1,458). In 1939, he says: 'The National Socialist Movement has wrought this miracle. If Almighty God granted success to this work, then the Party was His instrument' (ibid., p. 406). In his *Mein Kampf* (My Struggle), he says: 'Thus did I now believe that I must act in the sense of the Almighty Creator. By defending myself against the Jews, I am doing the Lord's work' (London, 1938, p. 36). These thoughts may have greatly relieved his conscience when he ordered the extermination of six million Jews from the face of the earth.

Some have argued that the concept of the fatherland of God leads to the idea of the brotherhood of man. At the same time, human inequalities have also been sanctioned in God's name. Such are the concepts of chosen castes, chosen races, chosen nations, chosen classes, chosen creeds, a chosen sex or a chosen individual. As the Buddhist texts say, if God created the world, he would be responsible for the crime and suffering no less than the acts of goodness and self-sacrifice.

## BUDDHIST ATHEISM

While Buddhism is atheistic, we must not forget that Buddhist atheism has at the same time to be distinguished from materialistic atheism. Buddhism asserted the falsity of a materialistic philosophy which denied survival, recompense and responsibility as well as moral and spiritual values and obligations, no less than certain forms of theistic beliefs. In its thoroughly objective search for truth it was prepared to accept what was true and good in 'the personal immortality view' (bhava-diṭṭhi) of theism as well as 'the annihilationist view' (vibhava-diṭṭhi) of atheistic materialism: 'Those thinkers who do not see how these two views arise and cease to be, their good points as well as their defects and how one transcends them in accordance with the truth are under the grip of greed, hate and ignorance . . . and will not attain final deliverance' (M. I. 65).

## THE DIVINE LIFE

Buddhism recognises all that is true, good and valuable in certain forms of theistic doctrine. Among the four types of religions which were unsatisfactory but not necessarily false were those based on a revelational tradition (anussava). A religion which granted the truth of an element of free-will, of moral causation, of survival and responsibility and the non-inevitability of salvation had value in it.

Although there is no Personal God with the characteristics of omniscience, omnipotence and infinite goodness, there is the concept of a Mahā Brahmā (Mighty God) who is morally perfect and has very great knowledge and power but is not omniscient and omnipotent. Certain forms of theism, it is said, are put forward by teachers who are born on earth after dying from the world of such a being. Born here, they lead a homeless life of renunciation and meditation, see the heaven that they came from and teach a religion of fellowship with Brahmā (God). They believe that such a Brahmā is omnipotent (abhibhū anabhibhūto), omniscient (ãñnadatthudaso), the Mighty Lord (vasavatti issaro), Maker (kattā), Creator (nimmātā), the Most Perfect (seṭṭho), the Designer (sañjitā) and the creatures we are.

The Buddha does not deny the existence of such a being; he is morally perfect but not omniscient and omnipotent. He is the chief of the hierarchy of Brahmās who rule over galactic systems and clusters of galactic systems. He is the regent of the cosmos who requests the Buddha to preach the pure and perfect Dhamma to the world, which will otherwise be destroyed. But he too is subject to the judgment of karma. According to the Buddha as reported in the *Brāhmaṇimantanika Sutta* and elsewhere, Buddhahood is a state for exceeding the knowledge and power of any Brahmā. As the *Tevijja Sutta* points out, fellowship with Brahma is not to be attained by petitionary prayers but by cultivating the divine life: 'That those Brahmins versed in the Vedas and yet bearing anger and malice in their hearts, sinful and uncontrolled, should after death with the dissolution of the body attain fellowship with God who is free from anger and malice, pure in heart and has self-mastery – such a state of things can in no wise be' (D. I. 248).

It is said that the cultivation of compassion in its purest form is 'called the divine life in this world' (Brahmam etaṃ vihāraṃ idhamāhu). It is also said that when one lives the moral and spiritual life with faith in the Buddha, then 'one dwells with God' (Brahmunā saddhiṃ saṃvasati). The Buddha came to establish 'the rule of righteousness' or 'the kingdom of righteousness' (Dhamma-cakkaṃ pavattetuṃ) in this world, which is elsewhere called 'the kingdom of God' (Brahma-cakkaṃ). The Buddha and his disciples who have attained Nirvana are said 'to abide with self-become-God' (Brahmabhūtena viharati). One who has attained Nirvana, it is said, 'maẏ justifiably employ theological terminology' (dhammena so Brahma-vādaṃ vadeyya). The old theological terms are given a new meaning and significance in what is comparable to the modern death-of-God theology, which is currently gaining ground in the West with seekers after truth who can no longer with honesty and sincerity accept the old theology and the old dogmas.

### SUPERFLUOUS

Yet it is unnecessary and to some extent misleading to put Buddhism into a theological cast. Whatever we may mean by 'God' and whether we say 'God exists' or 'God does not exist', it is a fact that there is physical and mental illness. The right approach is to understand the nature of these illnesses, their causes, their cure and to apply the right remedies. Buddhism provides not palliatives but the right remedies for the gradual and complete eradication of all anxiety, insecurity and the mental illnesses we suffer from until we attain the completely healthy Nirvanic mind. If Nirvana is God in the sense of being the Transcendent Reality, then those who are using these remedies cannot still comprehend it, while those who attain it do not need to.

# 9

# Nirvana

Nirvana or Nibbāna is considered to be 'the reality' (sacca) or 'the ultimate reality' (parama-sacca) in Buddhism. It is also a state of perfection (pārisuddhi) or the highest good (parama-kusala), which, at least, a few can attain in this life itself. It is the *summum bonum*, which not only all human beings but all beings in the universe should seek to attain. For unless and until they attain it, they are subject to the unsatisfactoriness and insecurity of conditioned existence, however pleasant it may be for a short or even a long period of time.

As with some of the other Buddhist concepts, the term Nirvana has sometimes been misunderstood by scholars. It is also by no means clear that all Buddhists understand the meaning and significance of the term in the way in which it was understood in the early Buddhist texts. Some have considered Nirvana to be a state of annihilation. Others deem it to be identical with Divinity and identify Nirvana with the Brahman of the Upaniṣads. Yet others who regarded Buddha as an Agnostic thought that he had no clear conception about the nature of Nirvana or was, in fact, unconcerned about it, since what was important was to find a solution to the problem of human anxiety and suffering rather than be concerned with the nature of ultimate reality.

A knowledgeable Western psychologist, who recently made a careful and enlightening study of the psychology of Nirvana in the light of the statements of the Pali *Nikāyas*, arrived at the tentative conclusion that, 'The nibbāna of the *Nikāyas* is then a transformed state of personality and consciousness. In none of the innumerable cases where the attainment of nibbāna is referred to as the destruction of the obsessions, is it ever suggested that this transformation is not enough: the new state *is* "the end of suffering" ' (Rune Johansson, *The Psychology of Nirvana*, George Allen & Unwin, London, 1969, p. 111).

Finally, there are those who would assert that Nirvana is a transcendent state of reality, which the human mind, limited in its conceptions, cannot intellectually comprehend.

What then is the correct answer, if such an answer is possible? It is only a careful study of all the authentic texts, which can suggest an answer to this question.

The term Nirvana (Pali, Nibbāna) is claimed in the Buddhist texts to be pre-Buddhist in origin, although the term as such is not to be found in the extant pre-Buddhistic literature. The *Brahmajāla Sutta* refers to several schools of thought, which put forward different 'theories about Nirvana that could be attained in this life' (diṭṭhadhamma-nibbāna-vādā). The thinkers who posited these theories resembled in some respects the modern Existentialist philosophers, who are concerned about the solutions to the problems of human anxiety and suffering and have found various theories concerning the nature of authentic living, which gives inner satisfaction to people and makes it possible for them to escape their boredom and anxiety. In other respects, these thinkers resemble the mystics of the different traditions, such as the Christian or Islamic (e.g. the Sūfīs), who claim to have found ultimate happiness in some contemplative mystic experience.

What concerns us here is the meaning of the term Nirvana. The first school of thought held that the soul experiences the highest Nirvana in this life (parama-diṭṭhadhamma-nibbāna) when it is fully engrossed and immersed in the enjoyment of the pleasures of the five senses. Some of the other schools, however, held that sense-pleasures were not lasting and were a source of unhappiness and that the soul truly experiences the highest Nirvāna in a contemplative state in which one is detached from sense-pleasures and aloof from morally evil states of mind. In these contexts we find that the term Nirvana is used to denote a state of positive happiness conceived as the most desirable in the light of their respective philosophies.

On the other hand, when we examine the pure etymology of the term, we find that the word is formed of the components, the prefix nis- and the root √vā, meaning 'to blow'. The word would, therefore, mean 'blowing out' or 'extinction'. On the occasion on which the Buddha finally passed away into Nirvana Anuruddha described the Parinirvāna of the Buddha as, 'The final liberation of mind was like the *extinction of a lamp*' (pajjotass 'eva nibbānaṃ vimokho cetaso ahū ti) (D. II. 157).

In the word Nirvana, therefore, we have a term which means both 'extinction' as well as 'the highest positive experience of happiness'. Both these connotations are important for understanding the significance of the term as it is employed in the Buddhist texts.

## ANNIHILATION?

The meaning of 'extinction' easily lent itself to the annihilationist interpretation of Nirvana. 'The individual', according to Buddhism, is in fact a process or a 'stream of becoming' (bhava-sota) continuing from life to life, which in the human state was conditioned by heredity, environment and the psychological past of the individual. This process of conditioning was due to causal factors such as the operation of desires fed by beliefs. When the desires and beliefs ceased to operate, so it was argued, with the extinction of greed, hatred and ignorance, the individual was extinguished and ceased to exist for good. If the Buddha did not openly state this (so they say), it was because individuals being self-centred have a longing for life and personal immortality and would be frightened to hear of the truth.

There are some Buddhist scholars who virtually give the same explanation. They only object to the use of the word 'annihilation' to describe 'the ceasing of "the individual" for good'. They argue that 'annihilation' is possible only if there is a 'being' (satta) to be annihilated. But there is no such 'being'. If there is no such 'being' to be annihilated, there is no annihilation, for nothing or no one is annihilated. So what is wrong according to them is the use of the word 'annihilation' to describe this state of affairs. They would not deny that the saṃsāric individual ceases to be for ever. This seems to be a merely verbal difference because, for all practical purposes, 'the individual' is completely extinguished and if we are wrong (according to them) in saying so, it is because 'the individual' did not exist in the first instance.

Such an interpretation leaves a lot of material unexplained in the early Buddhist texts. The Buddha certainly denied the persistence of an unchanging substratum or entity in the process of the individual but did not deny the phenomenal reality of the individual. The Buddha approves the use of the following language to describe the nature of individual existence on one occasion: 'I did exist in the past, not that I did not, I will exist in the future, not that I will not and I do exist in the present, not that I do not' (. . . atthā haṃ etarahi nāhaṃ n'atthīti) (D. I. 200). We must not forget that the Buddha held the view that 'nothing exists' (sabbaṃ natthi) because everything passes away as one extreme point of view. The Buddhist criticism of the Materialist's position was that the Materialist posited without reason 'the destruction of an existent individual' (sato sattassa ucchedam).

When the Buddha himself was charged with being an Annihilationist with regard to his teaching about Nirvana, he counters it by saying that this was a gross misrepresentation of his teaching on the part of some of the other religious teachers (M. I. 140). In the same context, the Buddha gives his reasons for saying so. When a person's (bhikkhuṃ, i.e. monk's) mind becomes finally emancipated (vimutta-cittam), even the most powerful and intelligent Gods (sa-Brahmakā) of the cosmos are unable to trace where the consciousness of such a Transcendent One (tathāgata) is located (... anvesaṃ nādhigacchanti idaṃ nissitaṃ tathāgatassa viññānaṃ ti, ibid.). It is stated that this is so even while he is living. For, says the Buddha, such a Transcendent One cannot be probed (ananuvejjo) even in this life.

When one's mind is emancipated, it does not become a dormant nonentity. If so the Buddha and the Arahats should have been apathetic individuals unconcerned about anything after attaining liberation. Instead, when the mind is purged of greed, hatred and ignorance it is transformed and shines with its natural lustre. It can then act spontaneously out of selflessness (cāga), compassion (mettā) and understanding (paññā).

The Transcendent One or the Tathāgata (a word used both of the Buddha and the Arahats) cannot be measured by the conditioned constituents of his personality (khandhā) such as the body, the feelings, the ideas, the conative activities and the acts of cognition. Freed from reckoning in terms of these constituents of his personality, he is said to be 'deep, immeasurable and unfathomable like the great ocean' (gambhīro appameyyo duppariyogāho seyyathā pi mahāsamuddo, M. I. 487). Qualities like compassion (mettā) and the other divine modes of behaviour (Brahma-vihāra), we may note, are called 'the infinitudes' (appamaññāyo).

Such an emancipated person, the depths of whose mind cannot be plumbed, it is said, cannot be considered to continue to exist after death (uppajiati, hoti parammaraṇā) as an individual (whose existence is invariably self-centred and conditioned), nor to cease to exist or be annihilated at death (na uppajjati, na hoti parammaraṇā). Neither description was apt for these reasons as well as for others.

The question as to whether the liberated person continues to exist for ever in time as a distinct individual or is annihilated at death is clearly posed in the *Suttanipāta*, where the Buddha is asked the question: 'The person who has attained the goal – does he not exist or does he exist eternally without defect; explain this to me well, O Lord, as you understand it?' (1075). If annihilation was a fact or the person ceased to exist altogether, the answer would have been quite clear; it would have been, 'He does not exist', but this is expressly denied. The reason given is that, 'The person who has attained the goal is *beyond measure*' (. . . na pamāṇam atthi). Elsewhere, it is said that he does not come within time being beyond time (kappaṃ neti akappiyo) or that he does not come within reckoning (na upeti saṇkhaṃ). In other words, we do not have the concepts or words to describe adequately the state of the emancipated person, who has attained the transcendent reality, whether it be when he lives with the body and the other constituents of personality or after death.

We may describe this situation in yet another way. Our minds function in this conditioned manner because they have become self-centred and corrupted by adventitious defilements (upakkilesa) and involvements (upādāna) in the course of our saṃsāric history. The mind, it is said, is naturally resplendent though it has been corrupted by adventitious defilements (pabhassaram idaṃ cittaṃ tañ ca āgantukehi upakkilisehi upakkiliṭṭhaṃ). It is often compared in this respect to gold ore, which has the defilements of iron, copper, tin, lead and silver, but when it is purified it becomes pliant (mudu), flexible (kammanīya), resplendent (pabhassara) and not brittle (na pabhaṇgu).

So when the mind is cleansed of its defilements by meditative exercises and divested of its chief defilements, such as the obsessional attachment to sense-pleasures (kāma-chanda), aggressiveness (vyāpāda), apathy (thīna-middha), restlessness (uddhaccā-kukkucca) and scepticism about moral and spiritual values and their rationale (vicikicchā), then it acquires a high degree of freedom, happiness, stability, serenity and awareness. Such a nature is in fact called 'temporary Nirvana' (tadaṅga-nibbāna). When the mind is further purified, it acquires certain extra-sensory faculties such as telepathy, clairvoyance, etc., which are intrinsic to its nature. With the help of these faculties, it is possible to have an understanding of reality, which results in the mind being freed from the obsessions or inflowing impulses (āsavā). Such a mind attains liberation. In the verses of the Brethren and Sisters (*Thera* and *Therī-gāthā*) we find the testimonies of several monks and nuns, who by these methods have gained emancipation.

Such a person is said to abide with his mind, having transcended its bounds (vimariyādikatena cetasā). It is divested of personal strivings (visaṃkhāra-gataṃ cittaṃ), being wholly dominated with the greatest freedom and spontaneity by selflessness, compassion and understanding.

However, despite his liberation, since he is still limited by his conditioned psycho-physical individuality, it is called 'the Nirvāṇic state with limitations still remaining' (sa-upādisesa nibbāna-dhātu). Although his roots of greed, hatred and ignorance have been destroyed, he is still subject to pleasant and unpleasant experiences associated with his senses but not originating from his mind (It. 38).

## GOD OR BRAHMAN?

The question as to what happens to his psycho-physical personality (nāmarūpa) at his final death is sometimes posed. 'Where does the psycho-physical individuality cease to be without remainder?' The answer is given as follows: 'Consciousness, without distinguishing mark, infinite and shining everywhere – here the material elements do not penetrate . . . but here it is that the conditioned consciousness ceases to be' (D. I. 223). Even the Commentary identifies the 'infinite consciousness' with Nirvana, saying that 'it is a term for Nirvāṇa' (nibbānassa taṃ nāmaṃ) (D.A. II. 393), while the second occurrence of the term consciousness is described as 'the last stages of consciousness or conditioned consciousness' (tattha viññāṇaṃ ti carimaka-viññāṇaṃ pi abhisaṅkhāra-viññanaṃ pi) (D.A. II. 393, 394).

The *Brāhmaṇimantanika Sutta* further corroborates the above interpretation. Here there is a dialogue between Buddha and Brahmā, and it is shown that the reality that the Buddha attains to is the ultimate and is beyond the ken even of Brahmā. The Buddha says: 'Do not think that this is an empty or void state. There is this consciousness, without distinguishing mark, infinite and shining everywhere; it is untouched by the material elements and not subject to any power.' The Buddha, it is said, can become invisible in it without being seen by any of the most powerful beings in the cosmos. In other words, it is the ultimate reality. We may recall the statement of the *Brahmajāla Sutta* that after the death of the body of the Transcendent One, gods and men would not see him. In other words, the Transcendent One does not cease to exist though his existence is of a different order altogether. It is for this reason that the Mahāyāna texts represent this cosmic Buddha as an everlasting Father (see *Saddharmapuṇḍarīka Sūtra*).

However, all these phrases, 'exists', 'ceases to exist', etc. are misleading since they have a spatio-temporal connotation. Nirvana is not spatially located (na katthaci, na kuhiñci), nor located in time so that 'one cannot say of Nirvana that it is past, present or future'. It is also not causally conditioned (na paṭicca-samuppannaṃ). It is therefore not capable of conceptual formulation (asaṅkhiyo) or literal description.

So the explanations given to us who have not attained it are compared to the attempt to explain the nature of light or colour to a man born blind. To tell him that light or colour is not a sound, nor a taste, nor smell, nor touch, is literally true, but since he is only acquainted with sounds, tastes, smells and touches he may think that colours are nothing or cannot exist. The problem with Nirvāṇa is analogous. What we have to do with the blind man is to evolve a method of restoring his sight. When this is done, no explanation is necessary, but before that strictly no explanation was possible. So to explain Nirvāṇa by some form of rational demonstration is impossible – it falls beyond the pale of logic (atakkāvacara). So all one can do is to show the person who is anxious to attain Nirvāṇa the methods of doing so and then he is likely, if he carefully follows those methods, to have glimpses of it (e.g. tadaṅga-nibbāna) and perhaps eventually to attain it. At this stage no explanations would be necessary. This is precisely what the Buddha sets out to do and why he is averse to making detailed pronouncements about Nirvana. As a result of this, the questions pertaining to the existence of the Transcendent One after death are treated as 'unanswered questions' (avyākata).

However, certain brief indications are not lacking as we have seen from what we have stated above. In the *Udāna* we get some passages of this type. One of them reads as follows: 'There is that sphere (āyatanaṃ) wherein is neither earth nor water nor fire nor air; wherein are none of the stages reached by arūpa-jhāna (impersonal mystical consciousness), where there is neither this world nor a world beyond nor both together, nor sun or moon; this, I say, is free from coming or going, from duration, arising or passing away; it has no foundation, no beginning and no object – this is, indeed, the end of unsatisfactoriness' (80).

Again, it is said: 'There is, O monks, the Unborn, the Unoriginated, the Unmade, the Uncompounded and if it were not for this Unborn, Unoriginated . . . there would have been no salvation from the born, the originated, the made and the compounded' (80, 81).

These passages are sometimes interpreted as not having a positive connotation but as merely implying the possibility of attaining Nirvāṇa conceived as a state of nothingness, but such an interpretation would be incorrect in the light of what we have said.

Yet if we do so, it may be asked whether the Nirvana of the Buddhist texts is in any way different from the conception of Brahman or God in the Upaniṣadic or theistic traditions. Here again, some scholars have claimed that there is no difference between the ultimate reality, or the Brahman of the Upaniṣads, and the Nirvana of Buddhism. Some of the epithets used of Brahman such as śānta – (peaceful) (Pali, santa), śiva (beneficial) (Pali, siva) are the same. While Brahman is said to have the characteristics of sat (existent), cit (intelligent) and ānanda (blissful), Nirvana was called sacca (true or real), annanta viññāna (infinite consciousness) and parama sukha (final bliss).

One who has attained Brahman is known in the Upaniṣads as Brahma-prāpta (*Kaṭha*, 6.18), while the Buddha is called Brahma-patta (M. II. 386) in the Buddhist texts. The word Brahmapatti is also used of 'attaining Nirvāṇa' (majjhesitā brāhmaṇa Brahma-patti, S.I. 149). More frequently those who have attained Nirvana are called Brahmabhutena attanā viharati, i.e. 'abides with self become Brahman'. Again, while the term Nirvana is not found in the pre-Buddhist Upaniṣads, the *Bhagavadgītā* describes the ultimate reality as Brahma-nirvāṇam.

There is no doubt that Nirvana is a transcendent reality beyond space, time and causation but, despite the similarity between the two notions, an identification would be erroneous and misleading. Some of the final stages of jhānic attainment in Buddhism were achieved by Upaniṣadic seers and identified with Brahman, Buddhism points out their inadequacy and the necessity of going beyond. Besides, in some of the Upaniṣads we find a theistic interpretation of the ultimate experience and reality. For example, in the *Śvetāsvatara Upaniṣad* (6.10 = *Kaṭha*, 5.15 = *Muṇḍaka*, 2.2.10) we find the following description:

> The sun shines not there, nor the moon and stars,
> These lightings shine not, much less this (earthly) fire!
> After Him, as He shines, doth everything shine,
> This whole world is illuminated with His light.

In the *Udāna* we find a similar passage, which reads as follows:

Where earth, water, fire and air do not penetrate;
There the stars do not glitter, nor the sun shed its light;
The moon too shines not but there is no darkness there.

Here there is no theistic interpretation of the experience and we earlier explained why such an interpretation would be erroneous. Besides, many of the metaphysical ideas about soul (ātman) which are rejected in Buddhism are to be found in the Upaniṣads, so that it would be quite misleading to identify the two.

The Agnostic interpretation has also to be rejected. It was not that there was something that the Buddha did not know but that what he 'knew' in the transcendent sense could not be conveyed in words because of the limitations of our concepts and of language. Nirvana is, therefore, the Transcendent Reality, whose real nature we cannot grasp with our normal minds because of our self-imposed limitations. It is a state of freedom (vimutti), power (vasī), perfection (pārisuddhi), knowledge (aññā) and perfect happiness of a transcendent sort. It is also said to be a state of perfect mental health, which we should try to attain for our personal happiness as well as for harmonious living.

# 10

# The Buddhist View of Survival

It is necessary to have a clear and authentic formulation of the Buddhist view of survival as found in the early texts since there seem to be some misconceptions about this. We may briefly state some of these misconceptions.

## MISCONCEPTIONS

According to one view the Buddha lived in a society in which the doctrine of rebirth was universally (or widely) taken for granted from time immemorial. The Buddha himself saw no reason to question this belief which he accepted uncritically and dogmatically.

Another such misconception may be stated as follows. The Buddha's doctrine of anattā or no-soul was a denial of the existence of an animistic soul which survived the death of the body and transmigrated. Since nothing survived the death of the body, Buddhism is a form of materialism. The Buddha utilised the doctrines of rebirth and karma prevailing in his society (so they say) to impart ethical teachings but did not himself believe in these doctrines.

There is yet another misconception. According to this view, the Buddha was not interested or held no specific views about the question of human survival or life after death. He roundly decried speculation about the past or the future (i.e. about prior or future lives) as unprofitable or mistaken. He was only concerned with man's present state of anxiety, suffering and dissatisfaction, and the solution for it.

These misconceptions can be cleared only by making a careful study of the authentic texts of Buddhism. When we do so we find that the Buddha did assert (1) the continuity without identity of individuality due to the operation of causal factors, (2) the doctrine of anattā, which denied the existence of a physical, mental, psycho-physical or independent entity within or related to the psycho-physical aspects of personality and (3) that mere metaphysical speculation about prior or future lives which did not result in the verification of facts about them was useless.

## HISTORICAL BACKGROUND

In order to understand the Buddhist view of survival it is desirable to have some knowledge of the views presented by pre-Buddhist thinkers, since the Buddhist conceptions were often presented in contrast to them.

It is a remarkable fact that in no other age in the history of thought was a solution to the problem of survival sought with such intensity as in this period and nowhere else can we find such a variety of views put forward.

Logically there are four possible points of view that we can adopt with regard to the question of survival. We may say (1) that we survive death in the form of discarnate spirits, i.e. a single after-life theory; (2) that we are annihilated with death, i.e. a materialist theory; (3) that we are unable to discover a satisfactory answer to this question or there is no satisfactory answer, i.e. a sceptical or positivist theory; and (4) that we come back to subsequent earth-lives or lives on other similar planets, i.e. a rebirth theory.

The Buddhist texts record several variants of each of these four types of theories. Let us take the variants of single after-life or one-life-after-death theories.

SINGLE AFTER-LIFE THEORIES

There are thirty-two of them listed in the *Brahmajāla Sutta*. According to what the philosophers or religious teachers, who put these theories forward, assert, they are broadly classified into theories which posit that the soul after death is (A) conscious (saññī), (B) unconscious (asaññī) and (C) super-conscious (nevasaññīnāsaññī).

There are sixteen variants of (A) and eight of each of (B) and (C). The sixteen variants of (A) are due to

I Variations regarding the *material form* of the soul:
- i has a subtle material form
- ii has no such form
- iii has for some time a subtle material form and then has no such form
- iv has no such form but has the power of manifesting one

II Variations regarding the *duration* of the soul:
- i comes to an end
- ii is eternal
- iii changes its state after some time and becomes eternal
- iv does not exist in time

III Variations regarding the *nature and extent* of consciousness:
- i is conscious of unity
- ii is conscious of diversity
- iii is of limited consciousness
- iv is of unlimited consciousness

IV Variations regarding the *hedonic tone* of the experiences:
- i is extremely happy
- ii is extremely unhappy
- iii is partly happy and partly unhappy
- iv does not experience happiness or unhappiness, i.e. has a neutral hedonic tone.

Only variations I (i)–(iv) and II (i)–(iv) are considered applicable to those who hold that the soul was (B) unconscious or (C) superconscious after death.

The above classification appears to be a purely logical one, but the fact that many of these theories can be traced to pre-Buddhistic literature, proves that it is not just that.

Thus Prajapati held on the basis of rational and metaphysical speculation that the soul was 'conscious and having its own form after death' (Ch. 8.12) – i.e. (A) I (i). Uddālaka held that the soul was 'unconscious and without form' after death – i.e. (B) I (ii). The *Taittirīya Upaniṣad* holds that the soul has a subtle material form for some time after death and then ceases to have such a form – i.e. (A) I (iii). Yajñavalkya has tried to show that the soul is 'neither conscious nor unconscious after death and has no form' – i.e. (C) I (ii). The Brāhmaṇas often speak of a 'second death' after personal survival – i.e. (A) II (i).

The one-life-after death theories held by people in the West who subscribe to different forms of Theism or Spiritualism are also classifiable as permutations and combinations of the above alternatives. Thus, the views held by those who subscribe to the belief that the soul survives as a discarnate spirit for all eternity, or those who say that the soul goes to heaven or hell for eternity after death, or those who maintain that the soul sleeps with the body till a day of judgement when its state is changed, or those who believe that the soul goes to purgatory till a day of judgement – all these views are classifiable under the above scheme.

In sharp opposition to those who held dualist theories of body-and-soul and claimed that there was only a single life after death were the Materialists who denied a life after death altogether. Seven schools of such Materialists are referred to in the *Brahmajāla Sutta* and some of them are independently referred to in the non-Buddhist literature.

The most extreme of them held that there is no mind or soul apart from the body which was entirely a hereditary product of one's parents (mātāpettikasambhavo) and the material elements. What we call 'mind' is the patterns of movements in our bodies. The modern version of this is called Central State Materialism (see J. J. C. Smart, *Philosophy and Scientific Realism*, Routledge & Kegan Paul, 1963), which tries to do away with phenomenal factors such as 'experience', 'consciousness', etc. According to this theory, when we say that a person is happy, it refers not to a mental but to a physical state which has among its consequences that it causes a person to behave in a characteristically happy way.

Another school held that the mind is an emergent product which has a material basis and its condition is determined by the food we eat. They argued that, just as when we mix up certain chemicals in certain proportions, there emerges the intoxicating power of liquor, even so the material particles of the body and the food we eat go to form the mind, which is an emergent by-product. There were also schools of mystic materialists who by the use of drugs claimed the possibility of achieving expansions of consciousness (called micchā-jhāna in the texts).

All these schools of materialists were characterised by the fact that they did not hold that mind and body were two different entities but were one and the same entity, either denying the reality of mental phenomena altogether or asserting that they were epiphenomena or accompaniments of the state of the body (for modern versions, see 'The Identity Hypothesis – A Critique', in J. R. Smythies, *Brain and Mind*, Routledge & Kegan Paul, London, 1965).

The dialectical opposition between the dualistic soul-theorists who asserted the reality of survival and the monistic materialists, who denied survival, had already resulted prior to Buddhism in the rise of several sceptical schools of thought. The *Kaṭha Upaniṣad* states: 'This doubt is there with regard to a man deceased – "he exists" say some; "he exists not" say others' (1.20).

The four schools of Sceptics (amarāvikkhepikā) in the *Brahmajāla Sutta* adopted scepticism on the basis of various intellectual or pragmatic grounds. Some maintained that, in holding the view either that 'there is survival' or that 'there is no survival', there results an involvement or entanglement (upādāna) in a theory and this promotes mental unrest. Others argued that in holding or denying the theory of survival one is led by one's prejudices for (chanda, rāga) or against (dosa, paṭiggaha) and that, therefore, truth demands that we do not come to any definite conclusions. Yet others avoided making definite pronouncements from fear of being engaged in debate. Others again like Sañjaya argued that statements about an after-life, about moral responsibility, or transcendent existence were not verifiable and therefore it was not possible to discover their truth or falsity.

Among those who held a dualist hypothesis and asserted 'the eternity view' (sassatadiṭṭhi) were not only the single-after-life theorists but those who held several variants of rebirth-theories as well. It is important to bear in mind the fact that Buddhism was opposed to all these theories, including those on rebirth that had been propounded. The Buddha did not posit the existence of an unverifiable, unchanging entity to account for his theory of re-becoming and rebirth. Nor did he hold that the process of re-becoming was strictly determined by past karma, by natural causes, or by the will of God. Causal factors were operative, no doubt, but they were not deterministic. Besides, some rebirth theories held that beings could be reborn even as 'rice and barley, herbs and trees, sesame plants and trees' (Ch. 5.10.6). The Buddha did not subscribe to such a point of view. In fact, it is doubtful whether he held that there was rebirth at the lowest levels of life. The Buddha later recounts as a mistaken view some of the beliefs of Jainism, which he put to the test prior to his enlightenment. In one place he says: 'I used to walk up and down conscientiously extending my compassion even to a drop of water, praying that the dangerous bacteria in it may not come to harm' (yāva udabindumhi pi dayā paccupaṭṭhitā hoti: mā'haṃ khuddake pāṇe visamagate saṅghātaṃ āpādessanti) (M. I. 78).

## BUDDHIST SOLUTION

It is in the historical context, outlined above, that the Buddha appeared on the scene and sought a solution to the riddle of life. It is, therefore, not correct to say (as many scholars have done) that the Buddha took for granted the belief in rebirth current in society at the time. As is evident from the Buddhist and the non-Buddhist literature, there was at the time a variety of views on the question of survival covering almost every possibility that one can think of.

Besides, the belief was not of very great antiquity. It is absent in the Vedas, it is merely hinted at in the Brāhmaṇas and the early Upaniṣads present a variety of views, some of which clearly reject rebirth. By the time of the Buddha, the Materialists had made such an impact on society that he classifies the prevalent theories of his time as those of the Eternalists and the Materialists. In addition, scepticism was so rampant that the elite (the viññū purisā) did not subscribe to any specific belief. They were no doubt interested in the problem and people like Pāyāsi even performed experiments to test the validity of the belief in survival. One of these was that of weighing the body immediately before and after death. Finally, it is hardly consistent with the spirit of the *Kālāma Sutta* where the Buddha asks people to adopt a critical attitude towards traditional beliefs.

The Buddhist theory of survival has its origin in the enlightenment of the Buddha and not in any traditional Indian belief. It is said that it was on the night of his enlightenment that he acquired the capacity to know his prior lives. It was when his mind was composed, clear, cleansed and without blemish, free from adventitious defilements, pliant and flexible, steadfast and unperturbed that he acquired this capacity to recall hundreds and thousands of prior lives and the prehistory of the universe, going back through the immensely long periods of the expansions and contractions of the oscillating universe. This is, in fact, called the first important item of knowledge, which broke through the veil of ignorance (ayaṃ paṭhamā vijjā).

As we have seen, the second important item of knowledge (dutiyā vijjā) was obtained by the exercise of the faculty of clairvoyance (dibba-cakkhu), with which the Buddha was able to see, among other things the survival of beings in various states of existence, the operations of karma, galactic systems, clusters of galactic systems and the vast cosmos.

## THE FIVE STATES OF EXISTENCE

In the *Mahāsīhanāda Sutta*, there is a reference to the five states of existence. They are as follows: (1) the lower worlds (duggati, vinipāta, niraya), (2) the animal kingdom (tiracchāna-yoni), (3) the spirit-sphere (petti-visaya), (4) human beings (manussā) and (5) devas or higher spirits.

While the 'lower worlds' (vinipāta) are also called niraya (hells), we must not forget that 'hells' (pātāla) in the popular sense are denied. It is said that the common man believes that there is a hell or nether world on the bottom of the ocean, but Buddha says that this belief is false and states that 'hell' is a term for painful sensations. Yet elsewhere there is a reference to worlds which the Buddha claims to see in which everything one senses is unpleasant and the thoughts that come to one's mind are disagreeable and foul. In contrast, it is said, that there are worlds in which everything one senses or experiences is pleasant. About the existence of devas, the Buddha says, when asked the question as to whether they exist, that he knows on good grounds that they do. When further questioned as to why he used the qualification 'on good grounds', he says that it is because it is commonly taken for granted that devas or higher spirits exist.

The five states of existence are graded according to the amount or degree of pain or pleasure experienced in them. According to this description, the human world is one in which one experiences 'more pleasant than unpleasant experiences' (sukhabahulā vedanā vediyamānaṃ) (M. 1. 75). In the spirit-sphere it is more unpleasant than pleasant. In the animal it is unpleasant, since animals are supposed to live in a state of constant fear with strong unsatisfied instinctive desires such as hunger and thirst. In the 'lower worlds' it is said to be very unpleasant. In the deva-worlds, on the other hand, it is extremely pleasant (ekanta-sukhā vedanā vediyamānaṃ).

The person who is pictured as faring on in these states of existence is conceived as one who is oppressed by the heat, exhausted, afraid and thirsty. The lower worlds are compared to a pit of coals into which one falls; animal existence is a pit full of excrement; existence in the spirit-sphere is like coming under a tree in a desert without much shade; human life is compared to coming under a large and shady tree, while the deva-world is compared to a well-furnished and beautiful palace. In contrast, Nirvanic existence is said to be analogous to the above person, who is oppressed with heat, exhausted and thirsty, reaching a lake where the waters are cool and clear, bathing in it, quenching his thirst and sitting or lying down in an adjoining glade, experiencing extreme happiness (ekanta-sukhā vedanā vediyamānaṃ).

From the descriptions given in the early texts, the usual tendency is for a person to survive as a departed spirit or a discarnate spirit in the spirit-sphere and come back to an earth-life, since the normal character of human beings is a mixture of good and evil and the stage of evolution of one's consciousness is attuned to existence in these worlds. But it is possible to regress to animal or subhuman forms of existence by neglecting the development of one's personality or character and becoming a slave to one's passions. It is also exceptionally possible to attain to existence in the deva-worlds. In the *Saṅkhāruppatti Sutta*, it is said that a person who is possessed of faith (saddhā), virtue (sīla), learning (suta), selflessness (cāga) and wisdom (paññā) can aspire to and attain to better states of existence among human beings or devas.

## INTELLIGIBILITY

The word used to describe the progression from existence to existence is 're-becoming' (punabbhava). Rebirth is only a special case of re-becoming when a person comes back to an earth-life. Rebirth in this sense takes place until a person attains a spiritual state of Non-returner (anāgām.) or Arahant. If there is any doubt about the interpretation of punabbhava as rebirth in these contexts, it may be dispelled by examining similar expressions such as 'he does not come back to lie in the womb' (na punar eti gabbhaseyyaṃ) (Sn. 29), used of an Arahant.

The question has been raised by some philosophers as to whether a conception of survival after death either in the form of rebirth or as a discarnate spirit is at all intelligible. If we preserve someone's heart or kidney in a living condition after his death, we would not say in respect of such an organ that so and so is now alive. It is therefore necessary for there to be some sense in which the reborn person or discarnate spirit should be able to claim identity with the dead person (when he was alive), even though all that can be established is continuity and not identity even in this life. To say that both have the same soul will not help because the existence of such a soul as an unchanging agent or recipient of actions is unverifiable.

The solution to this problem lies in the criteria that we employ to claim personal identity. In a single human life we normally use two criteria. One is the spatio-temporal continuity of the body. On the basis of this we can claim that so-and-so is a person who as a child went to such-and-such a school, although there may be nothing in common between the two bodies as far as shape and content is concerned. The other criterion is memory, on the basis of which someone may claim that he was such-and-such twenty years ago. When one life is concerned the two criteria normally support each other.

In the case of the reborn person or discarnate spirit, it is the memory criterion alone which can establish the identity. In this case, when the body criterion is employed, we have to say that 'he is not the same person' but when the memory criterion is employed we would have to say 'he is not another person'. So according to Buddhism 'he is neither the same nor another' (na ca so na ca añño) when we give a strictly accurate description, although in common parlance we may say that he is the same person.

# II

# The Buddhist Doctrine of Karma

I refer to this doctrine specifically as the Buddhist doctrine of karma in order to distinguish it from the other non-Buddhist doctrines of karma, which were taught by non-Buddhist thinkers prior to, during and even after the time of the Buddha. In this respect, it is important to note the significant differences between the Buddhist doctrine of karma and the doctrines of karma taught in Jainism, by certain Ājīvika thinkers as well as the Brahmins.

## MISCONCEPTIONS

This is particularly necessary since the Buddhist doctrine of karma is often confused with and assumed to be the same as the Brahmanical one. People tend to speak of or criticise the doctrine of karma as though there was only one such doctrine common to different religions such as Hinduism, Jainism and Ājīvikism, despite the fact that they profess different teachings about the nature, operations and attitude to the alleged phenomenon of karma.

Another misconception which is partly connected with the above misunderstanding is that the Buddhist doctrine of karma constitutes or implies a fatalist attitude to life and nature, a view put forward by some (not all) Western scholars and even subscribed to by some South Asian intellectuals both non-Buddhist and even Buddhist.

Yet another source of misunderstanding is the attempt on the part of certain scholars and other individuals to rationalise (quite unnecessarily) the doctrine of karma by interpreting it to mean the social or biological inheritance of man or both, ignoring altogether and distorting the authentic teachings of the Buddhist texts.

## MEANING

In the pre-Buddhist literature the word karma was used mainly in the sense of either religious rituals or the social functions and duties of man. In the latter sense the *Īṣa Upaniṣad* says: 'Let a man aspire to live a hundred years, performing his social duties' (kurvanneveḥa karmāṇi jijīviṣecchataṃ samāḥ) (2). This sense has survived in the Buddhist texts, where the word karma is used in the plural to denote the different professions or occupations of men. Thus, Buddhism recommends people to take up 'morally blameless occupations' (anavajjāni kammāni).

As a technical term, the word karma is used in the early Buddhist texts to denote 'volitional actions'. These actions may be 'morally good' (kusala), morally evil (akusala), or morally neutral (avyākata). They may be actions which find expression in bodily behaviour (kāya-kamma), verbal behaviour (vacī-kamma) and psychological behaviour (mano-kamma).

The morally good and evil actions are said to be liable to give rise to consequences, individual as well as social, pleasant and unpleasant on the whole, as the case may be. The individual consequences may be manifested in this life, the next life or the lives to come unless their potentialities are extinguished or they do not find an opportunity for fruition.

Conscious volition (cetanā) is a necessary condition of such a morally good, evil or mixed act, but does not constitute the whole of it except when it happens to be purely mental. Thus, we would not be guilty of the crime of murder merely because we had the intention of murdering somebody. As the *Atthasālinī* (p. 98) points out 'There are five constituent factors in an act of killing; (1) the existence of a living being, (2) the awareness of the existence of such a living being, (3) the intention of killing, (4) the effort or the means employed to kill and (5) the consequent death of the living being.'

The intention is necessary but not sufficient to constitute an act of killing. As the Vinaya rules point out, where the intention is absent but one's actions are instrumental in causing the death of a person, one may be guilty of an act of negligence but not of murder.

So the word karma is used to denote volitional acts which find expression in thought, speech or physical deeds, which are good, evil or a mixture of both and are liable to give rise to consequences, which partly determine the goodness or badness of these acts.

## BASIS FOR DOCTRINE

It is often assumed that the basis for the doctrine of karma in Buddhism is a rational argument implicit in the *Cūlakammavibhaṅga Sutta*. It is true that in this Sutta the Buddha seems to suggest purely rational grounds for believing in the doctrine of karma, but it would be mistaken to believe that the doctrine is accepted as true or as representing the nature of things as they are on these grounds.

In this Sutta, a brahmin youth meets the Buddha and asks him for an explanation as to why among human beings some are short-lived while others are long-lived, some are sickly while others are healthy, some are ugly to look at while others are handsome, some have little power or influence while others are influential, some are poor while others are rich, some are of a lower social status while others are of a higher social status.

The question is posed in the form: 'What is the reason and the cause for the inequality (hīnapaṇītatā) among human beings despite their being human?' The Buddha's reply was as follows: 'Beings inherit their karma and it is karma which divides beings in terms of their inequalities.'

We may argue that this embodies the following rational ethical argument, consisting of an empirical and ethical premise, viz. people are of unequal status, those of unequal status ought to be such only by virtue of their own actions – therefore, since this is not due to their actions in this life, it should be due to their actions in a prior life. This means that both karma and pre-existence are the case.

It is also true that this kind of rational ethical argument has appealed to many thinkers. Maurice Maeterlinck (1862–1949), poet, dramatist and essayist says: 'Let us return to reincarnation . . . for there was never a more beautiful, a juster, a purer, a more moral, fruitful and consoling, nor, to a certain point, a more probable creed than theirs. It alone, with its doctrine of successive expiations and purifications, accounts for all the physical and intellectual inequalities, all the social iniquities, all the hideous injustices of fate.' (See *Reincarnation, An East-West Anthology*, ed. Joseph Head and S. L. Cranston, New York, 1961, p. 200.) Professor Allan G. Widgery also speaks appreciatively of such an argument when he says: 'For it affirms that men are not born equal . . . and this affirmation appears to be more in accordance with the facts. . . . Men are regarded as different at birth: the differences being due to the manner in which in past lives they have built up their nature through the action of the law of karma' (ibid., p. 117).

But it would be mistaken to consider the passage in the above Sutta as presupposing a rational ethical argument with a concealed ethical premise. It is true as Ānanda has said of the Buddha that, 'so far as anything can be attained by reasoning (takka), thou has ascertained it' (yāvatakaṃ takkāya parrabbaṃ anuppattaṃ taya) (S. I. 56), but the doctrine of karma is not put forward in Buddhism as a product of mere speculative reasoning (takka), which is not adequate for the discovery of the facts of nature as the Buddha has elsewhere pointed out. The Buddha's statements even in this Sutta are based on clairvoyant observation and reasoning and not on mere rational speculation.

It is also mistaken to assume on the ground of the recognition of the fact of the known inequalities among mankind that Buddhism accepted the *status quo* of a static conception of society or denied the doctrine of what is known as 'the equality of mankind'.

For, as we shall see when we come to the social and political philosophy of Buddhism, Buddhism upholds the biological, social and spiritual equality of mankind and envisages a time in the future when with the economic, moral and spiritual regeneration of man there would come into being a social order in which people would be healthy and long-lived and the inequalities in power, wealth and social status would be greatly diminished.

In this context, we must not forget that one of the central teachings of Buddhism revolves round the conception of the destruction or elimination of the evil effects of kamma (kammakkhaya) by effecting a change in the basis of human motivation from that of greed (lobha), hate (dosa) and ignorance (moha) to selflessness (cāga), compassion (mettā) and understanding (paññā). Even the better social order of the future can be set up only by people who believe in moral and spiritual values and have to some extent cultivated the qualities of selfless service, kindness and wisdom.

## VERIFIABILITY

As we have said above, the statements about the operations of karma are made by the Buddha on the basis of inferences based on clairvoyant observation. The awareness of the nature of the operations of karma is said to be the second item of knowledge (dutiyā vijjā) obtained by the Buddha on the night of his enlightenment.

It is said: 'When his mind was thus composed, clear and

cleansed without blemish, free from adventitious defilements, pliant and flexible, steadfast and unperturbed, he turns and directs his mind towards an understanding of the death and rebirth (upapāta) of beings. Then with his pure, paranormal clairvoyant vision he sees beings – the high and the low, the beautiful and the ugly, the happy and the wretched – dying and being reborn according to their *character* (kamma).'

The three-fold knowledge (tisso vijjā) acquired by the Buddha, which is crucial for the attainment of enlightenment, consists of the knowledge of pre-existence, of the operations of karma and of the capacity to eliminate the inflowing impulses (āsava-kkhaya). It is the same knowledge had by the Arahants attaining emancipation of mind (ceto-vimutti) and in the *Thera-* and *Therī-gāthā*, the prayers of the brethren and the sisters; we constantly meet with the refrain: 'I have attained the three-fold knowledge, I have done the bidding of the Buddha' (tisso vijjā anuppattā kataṃ Buddhassa sāsanaṃ).

The operations of karma are, therefore, personally verified by the Buddha and his disciples. In the *Mahāsīhanada Sutta*, the Buddha refers to the way he tested the theory of karma as though he was testing a scientific hypothesis.

It is said:

'There are these five destinies, Sāriputta. What five? The lower worlds, the animal kingdom, the spirit-sphere (petti-visaya), human existence and the higher worlds. I know these lower worlds, the path which leads to them or the kind of conduct which takes you to that state of existence at death . . . Herein, Sariputta, I comprehend the mind of a certain individual with my mind as follows: "This individual is set on behaving in such a manner and follows such a mode of conduct that he is likely to be born in one of the lower worlds at death on the destruction of the body." I then observe him at a later time by means of clear, clairvoyant, paranormal perception – the same individual born in one of the *lower worlds* at death experiencing *great pain.* Just as if there were a pit of coals and a man were to come along, tired and exhausted, taking a path leading straight to it and a man possessed of sight were to observe him and say to himself: "This man is, surely, taking a path which will land him in a pit of coals," and later see him fallen in that pit experiencing great pain; even so . . . the *animal world* . . . experiencing *much unhappiness* . . . Just as if there were a cesspit and a man, tired and exhausted were to come along . . .; even so . . . the *spirit-sphere* . . . experiencing *more unpleasant than pleasant sensations* . . . Just as if there were a tree in a rugged place, with sparse foliage affording scanty shade and a man were to come along, tired and exhausted; even so . . . the *human world* . . . experiencing *more pleasant than unpleasant sensations* . . . Just as if there were a tree with dense foliage in a pleasant spot and a man were to come along, tired and exhausted . . .; even so . . . in a *higher world* . . . experiencing *extremely pleasant sensations* . . . Just as if there were a palace with all the comforts and luxuries and a man were to come along, tired and exhausted. . . .'

In the *Mahākammavibhaṅga Sutta*, the Buddha points out that certain yogins who have acquired the capacity for clairvoyant observation, nevertheless came to false conclusions and denied the fact of karma since they made invalid inferences from the observed data. This is what he says:

'Herein a certain yogin as a result of his efforts and application, attains a certain state of trance, in which he sees with his clear, clairvoyant paranormal vision a man who has misconducted himself born at death on the dissolution of his body in a happier and better world. He concludes as follows: "There are no evil actions (kamma) and no consequences of misconduct, for I have observed a man . . . Everyone whether he misconducts himself in this life or not, is born at death in a happier and better world." I do not agree [says the Buddha] with the claim of this yogin that there are no evil actions and no future consequences of misconduct. I am prepared to grant that this yogin has observed a man who has misconducted himself in this life, born at death in a happier and better world, but I do not agree with his conclusion that, therefore, all people, whether they misconduct themselves in this life or not, are born at death in a happier and better world. The knowledge of the Transcendent One (Tathāgata) with regard to operations of kamma are different . . . If a person who has misconducted himself in this life is born at death in a happier and better world, then he has either some time in his past done good deeds, which have resulted in these experiences, or at the time of his death has changed his ways and adopted the right view of life.'

The mistake that these yogins made, according to the Buddha, was to form generalisations on the basis of one or a few observations without observing a generality of cases and seeing that the apparent exceptions were explicable on other terms. The operations of kamma, it is said, are so complex that they are not fully comprehensible (acinteyya) (A. II. 80) except to the vision and understanding of a Buddha. Even with regard to the universe (loka-visaya), we noted that the Buddha could observe clusters of galaxies and the vast cosmos, while Anuruddha, the specialist in clairvoyance, could observe only a single galaxy.

### RELATION TO CAUSAL LAWS

The operation of these laws of karma was only a special instance of the working of causal laws in nature, in which there were physical laws (utu-niyāma), biological laws (bīja-niyāma), psychological laws (citta-niyāma), karmic laws (kamma-niyāma) pertaining to moral acts and their consequences and laws pertaining to spiritual phenomena (dhamma-niyāma). But the pattern of events in nature, according to Buddhism, are neither deterministic nor indeterministic. So causal laws are only probable and statistical and not deterministic.

Karmic laws, therefore, state tendencies rather than inevitable consequences. Several of these correlations are stated in the *Culakammavibhaṅga Sutta*. The general principle is that morally good acts tend to be followed in the long run by pleasant consequences and morally evil acts by unpleasant consequences to the individual. Since it is of the nature of good acts to promote the material and spiritual well-being of mankind, it follows from this general principle that one cannot gain one's own happiness at the expense of others.

Among the specific correlations are the following. Those who harm and hurt living beings tend to be sickly, while those who are compassionate towards them tend to be healthy. Those who are angry and irritable, scowl at and abuse people tend to be ugly, while the others who are not so tend to be beautiful. Those who are envious and jealous of the honour and respect bestowed on others tend to lose while the others tend to command, respect.

### MEDIEVAL ANALYSIS

In the medieval period we find kamma classified, first according to function (kicca) as what gives birth (janaka), what tends to support a tendency (upatthambhaka), what tends to obstruct a tendency (upapīlaka) and what destroys (upaghātaka). Secondly, according to the manner in which they come into function (pāka-dāna-pariyāya), they are classified as weighty (garuka), proximate (āsanna), habitual (āciṇṇa) and residual (kaṭattā). Thirdly according to the time of taking effect (pāka-kāla), there are four sorts – what is experiencable in this life (diṭṭhadhammavedaniya), in the next life (upapajjavedaniya), some time in the future (aparāparavedaniya), or never (ahosi). Fourthly, according to the place in which the effects occur, there is evil karma finding fruition in the worlds of sense-gratification, similar good karma and good karma which becomes effective in the subtle material worlds (rūpa-loka) and the immaterial ideational worlds (arūpa-loka).

## DISTINCTION

It is necessary to distinguish the Buddhist theory of karma from the other non-Buddhist theories. Firstly, it has to be distinguished from the Jain theory, according to which man could not develop morally and spiritually without undergoing all the consequences of his previous evil karma. The Jains hoped to achieve this by indulging in ascetic practices, which they believed helped to wear away the evil effects of past karma. The value of a moral act, likewise, depended on its physical expression rather than the intention, which is not so in Buddhism.

The Buddhist theory has also to be distinguished from an Ājīvika theory which asserted that all present actions and experiences are strictly determined by previous karma. Karma according to Buddhism, while being non-deterministic, was only one among many factors which conditioned the nature of the individual's experience of pleasure and pain. Among them was the physiological state of the body, which was partly a product of heredity or the biological laws (bījaniyāma) recognised in Buddhism. The other factors were changes in the physical environment (utuparināma), in social vicissitudes (visama-parihāra), the intentional activity of the individual (opakkamika) and lastly karma. Karma, it would appear, could operate separately in a psychosomatic manner or in co-operation with the other factors.

Since a number of factors operated in conditioning man's experience, it was wrong to say that pleasure and pain were due entirely to one's own actions (sayaṃ-katam sukhadukkhaṃ), nor were they due to the action of an external agent like God (paraṃ-kataṃ), nor to a combination of both (sayaṃ kataṃ ca paraṃ kataṃ ca), nor were they accidental (adhicca-samuppanna). Pleasure and pain were causally conditioned (paṭicca-samuppanna) and man by his knowledge of himself and nature could understand, control and master them.

## FATALISM, HEREDITY AND KARMA

Since karmic correlations were not deterministic, karma was only one of many factors conditioning the nature of experience, while past karma was extinguishable and modifiable in the context of one's present actions. Buddhism, it may be noted, was opposed to all forms of determinism: natural determinism (svabhāva-vāda), theistic determinism (issara-kārana-vāda) and karmic determinism (pubba-kamma-vāda) or any combination of them. According to one Brahmanical text, nature (prakṛti) compels man to act as he does, while nature itself is under the control or will of God.

As we have seen Buddhism states that man is conditioned by his heredity (bīja-niyāma), by his physical, social and ideological (salāyatana paccayā phasso, etc.), environment, by his psychological past (citta-niyāma) including his karmic heritage (kamma-niyāma), but he is not determined by any or all of them. He has an element of free-will (attakāra), or personal endeavour (purisa-kāra) by exercising which he can change his own nature as well as his environment (by understanding it) for the good of himself as well as others. In this sense man is master of his fate (atta hi attano natho).

The laws of heredity, likewise, are not to be confused with those of karma. Buddhism accepts both. As a result there may be situations in which the causal lines of karma and heredity coincide. A person may have a certain trait because he inherits it from one of his parents and also because he has a particular karmic reason or affinity for it.

Sometimes in the case of mental traits, the origin may be karmic rather than hereditary. As C. D. Broad stated in his examination of the philosophy of McTaggart, who urged a belief in rebirth and karma on philosophical grounds in his books *The Nature of Existence* and *Some Dogmas of Religion*: 'McTaggart points out that the assumption of selective affinity between certain kinds of mind and certain kinds of organism would explain likenesses in mental characteristics between parents and children which are often ascribed to the direct influence of heredity. Owing to heredity a man's organism will resemble those of his direct ancestors more closely than those of other people. Now similar organisms will be adapted to similar minds, and so zygotes which will develop into similar organisms are likely to attract similar minds and unite with them at conception.' Broad added: 'I think it must be admitted that this theory is ingenious and plausible' (*Examination of McTaggart's Philosophy*, Vol. II, Part II, Cambridge University Press, 1938, pp. 614–15). Besides, it can be seen how rebirth and karma can explain the (sometimes marked) temperamental differences in identical twins, who when they happen to be 'Siamese twins' have an identical and a common environment.

## CENTRAL TEACHING

It must, however, not be forgotten that the central teaching of Buddhism is not that of continuing to perform good karma for the sake of rewards in continued saṃsāric existence (which cannot be enjoyed without the subsequent suffering from the evil which finds fruition), but the elimination of the effects of karma (kammakkhaya).

The immediate ideal of the Buddhist should therefore be that of attaining the first stage of spiritual development (sotāpanna) by the elimination of attachment to notions of ego and ego-centred desires (sakyā-diṭṭhi); by the elimination of doubts regarding the Buddhist account of the nature and destiny of man in the universe (vicikicchā) through examination; inquiry into and partial verification of the truth of the Dhamma, and the realisation that religion is part and parcel of one's daily living and experience and not of obsessional attachment to rites and rituals (sīlabbata-parāmāsa). Such a person is 'not liable to fall below the status of human existence' (avinipatadhammo) and is destined to achieve the goal of enlightenment (niyato sambodhi-parāyano) before long. This is the path leading to the destruction of karmic effects (kammakkhaya) in which the good life is cultivated with the growth of selflessness, love and understanding for its own intrinsic worth and not for egoistic rewards.

# 12

# The Case for the Buddhist Theory of Karma and Survival

If we use the word 'rebirth' to denote the view that immediately or some time after death we return to an earth-life, then such rebirth is only a special case of re-becoming.

According to this Buddhist doctrine of re-becoming, there could be continuity of individuality in various planes of existence. We may survive as a discarnate spirit (Pali, gandhabba = Skr. gandharva) in the spirit-sphere (petti-visaya), as a denizen of the sub-human world or as an angelic spirit in the celestial planes of existence. Such survival, as the *Kathāvatthu* explains, is either in the gross material world (kāma-loka), the subtle material world (rūpa-loka) or the immaterial world (arūpa-loka). There is no intermediate existence (antarābhava) apart from existence in one of these three planes of becoming.

As we have seen, since human existence is a mixture of good and evil, the usual pattern as the texts make out, is to survive as a discarnate spirit and come back to a human existence. The practice of Buddhism by the cultivation of faith (saddhā), virtue (sīla), learning (suta), selflessness (cāga) and wisdom (paññā) makes it possible for a person to determine his future birth on the human or celestial planes. A person who has become a non-returner (anāgāmin) need not come back to human existence and an Arahant will not be born again in the spatio-temporally and causally conditioned cosmos.

NOVEL THEORY

Besides, the Buddhist theory of survival is a novel theory which is not to be found in the pre-Buddhistic literature. It was a doctrine of survival without the concept of a self-identical substance or soul. The physical form, perceptions, feeling, will or intellect were not the soul, nor did the soul own them, nor was a soul to be found within them, nor again were they to be located in a cosmic soul. There was no self apart from a complex of psycho-physical processes and man was defined as a bundle of dispositions (suddha-saṅkhāra-puñja). Though there was no self-identical (anaññaṃ) substance, there was a continuity (santati, santāna) of individuality, sometimes referred to as a stream of consciousness (viññāṇa-sota) or a stream of becoming (bhava-sota). Associated with a person's present body were the dispositions with potentialities for re-becoming (ponobhaviko bhava-saṅkhāro).

These planes of existence and the operations of karma were observed by the Buddha on the night of his enlightenment. His knowledge consisting of 'the recall of prior lives' (pubbe-nivāsa-anussati-ñāṇa) is described as follows:

'When his mind is thus composed, clear and cleansed without blemish free from adventitious defilements, pliant and flexible, steadfast and unperturbed, he turns and directs his mind to the recollection of his former lives, viz. one life, two lives . . . ten lives . . . a hundred lives . . . through evolving aeons, recalling in what place he was born, his name and title, his social status, his environment, experiences and term of life and dying there in what place he was next born and so on up to his present existence, he remembers the varied states of his former lives in all their aspects and details. Just as a man who has travelled from his village to another and from that to yet another, when to his former village by the same route, remembers how he came from that village, where he stayed and rested, what he said and what he did; even so, when the mind is composed . . .' (D. I. 81).

Since the Buddhist theory of survival is a composite theory, the case in support should include at least the arguments for survival as discarnate spirits as well as for rebirth.

Before we examine such arguments and the evidence, we have to meet the objection that the known facts of science concerning brain-mind phenomena suggest the impossibility of survival.

## TWO VIEWS

There are two classical views regarding the relationship between the mind and the body. One is the Identity Hypothesis which either denies the reality of mental experience or holds that such experiences are inseparable from aspects of neural or brain phenomena. The other is Dualism, which holds that mental and neural phenomena interact.

The extreme form of the Identity Hypothesis, called Central State Materialism, tries to do away with such causal factors as 'experience' or 'consciousness' and explain psychological behaviour as being solely the functioning of the central nervous system.

A less extreme view, which is still monistic, is the psychosomatic theory according to which psychological experience and brain phenomena are merely the two aspects of one reality. According to this theory the brain-mind combination does not function in a purely mechanical manner but, since brain and mind are two aspects of the same process, they both cease to function with the death of the person.

A modern form of the Dualist Theory would be the instrumental or the transmission theory according to which the brain would function as the instrument of the mind, being itself affected by it.

Buddhism, which discards the monistic and the dualistic hypotheses, would hold that there is some truth in each without subscribing to either. For Buddhism the human being in normal consciousness is a psycho-physical unit, in which the physical and psychical phenomena are in a state of mutual dependence (aññamañña-paccaya). Yet at the same time aspects of will can control, govern and produce mental activity. Also, when the body is brought within control and is in a state of perfect composure with its activities stilled (kāyasaṅkhārā niruddhā), it can exercise its extra-sensory powers of perception.

Buddhism, therefore, while rejecting the Identity Hypothesis that 'the mind and the body are the same' (tam jivaṃ tam sarīraṃ) and the Dualist Hypothesis that 'the mind and body are different' (aññaṃ jīvaṃ aññaṃ sarīraṃ) finds partial truth in each and thus puts forward a middle view.

## NEUROLOGY

The ideal scientist in the field of neurology is not expected to subscribe to any particular point of view. As Dr Wilder Penfield, Director of the Montreal Neurological Institute said in 1957; 'Any scientist who looks up from his work to declare, for example, that the truth is to be found in monism or dualism, or that there is a middle ground, ceases to be a scientist'. (Quoted from Professor Hornell Hart, *The Enigma of Survival*, Rider & Co., London, 1959, pp. 218–19.)

This does not, however, mean that the findings of scientists have no bearing on these theories. The advances made over the last fifty years are due to new electro-psysiological techniques which have made it possible to stimulate single nerve fibres and record responses from single nerve cells, the measurement of the electrical activity of the brain (EEGs), brain surgery and the study of the chemical basis of neural phenomena. They have shown that it is possible to alter somewhat the state of the personality or consciousness by physical or chemical means.

Consciousness, incidentally, cannot be argued or analysed away to the satisfaction of the extreme monists for it is a brute fact that certain physiological processes such as aspects of brain phenomena are accompanied by consciousness or self-consciousness, though it could have been otherwise.

## MEMORY

At the same time, this research has also shown that there is no one-to-one correspondence between phenomena and mental experience as the psychosomatic theory would like to maintain. Thus, memory is not uniquely located in particular points of the brain. Dr H. O. Hebb states in 1953 that 'it is very difficult to conceive of memory as a function of a localised region' (*Brain Mechanisms and Consciousness:* A Symposium, 1954).

Dr Penfield records that when a specific point in the brain of a woman patient was touched, she heard a mother calling her little boy. But eleven minutes later when the same point was touched with the electrode, the patient no longer heard the mother calling her little boy but instead heard the voices of people calling from building to building. In another case, the patient heard the same song vividly when each of four different points in the brain were stimulated. Lord Brain, F.R.S., the eminent neurologist states: 'Evidently in the brain, memory is not a unitary function nor is there any single part of the nervous system in which all memories are stored' (In 'Some Aspects of the Brain-Mind Relationship' in *Brain and Mind*, International Library of Philosophy and Scientific Method, London, 1965, p. 69.)

The lack of specific localisation is not confined to memory but is to be found in other functions as well. In 1912 Yerkes found that habits registered in one part of the nervous system of an earthworm might shift later on to another part, and a similar versatility was to be found in human brains relative to the effects of brain damage in children by Klebanoff, Singer and Wilensky in 1954. A senior lecturer in zoology working mainly on the brains of rats, reports as follows:

'Three of the preceding sections are headed respectively

"cortex", "limbic system" and "reticular system", but this anatomical arrangement does not correspond to the facts of function: the study of any of these systems soon becomes meaningless without reference to the others. During every few milliseconds, in the waking brain, information passes to and fro in a network of communication of which only the larger details are yet certainly known . . . In such a flux we cannot, with our present knowledge, properly speak of localisation of function, but only of the specific effects of injury or stimulation . . . A small injury can influence behaviour which certainly depends also on the functioning of the other parts; by contrast, some substantial injuries leave behaviour largely unaltered; and when behaviour is disturbed by lesions, there may be subsequent recovery due, evidently, to some compensatory process elsewhere. These facts at present defy explanation. All they do is to make accounts of neural function in terms of reflex arcs as absurd as interpretations of learning in terms of conditioned reflexes' (S. A. Barnett, *A Study in Behaviour*, Methuen & Co., London, 1963, p. 238).

Dr Grey Walter confessed a lack of knowledge about the nature of memory. He said: 'No sketch of the contemporary world of brain research would be complete without a hue of mystery because this is what catches the mind's eye. For me there are two great obscurities in our picture: memory and sleep' (*Frontiers of Knowledge*, Modern World Series, p. 99). Recently (April 1968), Dr Penfield referred to the limitations of present scientific research. He says: '. . . The more we learn about the mechanisms within the brain, the clearer it becomes that science has not thrown any real light on the nature of the mind . . . The only way the neuro-physiologist works is to study the action of the brain on one side and the changing stream of mental activity on the other. You can see the parallelism of the activity but you cannot understand the interrelationship' (News report from Toronto, *Times Weekender*, Friday, 12 April 1968).

INSTRUMENTAL THEORY

The brain functions or is made to function as a whole and there is no one-to-one psychosomatic correspondence between brain phenomena and the concomitant experiences. So despite the recent advances in biochemistry and microbiology, mental phenomena cannot be considered to be just one aspect of a single process in the brain.

Professor Sir John Eccles, who has been described by Sir Cyril Burt as 'the most eminent of living neurologists who has specialised in the study of the brain', has observed that 'the structure of the brain suggests that it is the sort of machine that a "ghost" might operate' where the word "ghost" is used 'to designate any kind of agent that defies detection by such apparatus as is used to detect physical agents' (*The Neurophysiological Basis of Mind*, London, Oxford University Press, 1953, pp. 278ff.).

This suggests that an instrumental theory of the brain cannot be excluded in the light of modern findings. We must not forget in this context that many physiological changes are initiated by the operation of aspects of will and that many diseases not only have a psychological origin (with or without a discoverable organic condition) but are curable by purely psychological means. We may note that physical pain with an organic basis can be relieved or removed by chemical means (i.e. drugs) or by the suggestions of hypnosis.

When in addition to all this, we have to take into account the realities of ESP (extra-sensory perception), the Identity Hypothesis becomes almost untenable.

John Beloff has written:

'This (i.e. parapsychological evidence), it seems to me, is the empirical reef on which the Identity Hypothesis is doomed to founder even if it can survive all other hazards. Most of its supporters do indeed recognise the danger but, like Feigl, pin their faith to the ability of science to explain the ESP phenomena eventually along more or less conventional lines (obscure brain functions, unsuspected sources of energy, etc.). Such faith though plausible enough twenty or thirty years ago is now increasingly unrealistic. The choice that confronts us today, I submit, is a very drastic one: either we must blankly refuse to credit the evidence or we must be prepared to accept a radical revision to the whole contemporary scientific world-picture on which materialism has taken its stand' (*Brain and Mind*, pp. 50–1).

That the parapsychological phenomena constituting ESP have come to stay and are presently accepted as valid by leading scientists, psychologists and philosophers is evident from a recent publication (1967) of a book called *Science and ESP* in the *International Library of Philosophy and Scientific Method.*

The brain may be compared to a computer and electronic machines can be constructed to perform certain operations of abstract thinking (such as logical and mathematical calculations) with a greater speed, precision and accuracy than the human mind is capable of. But however much such computers may stimulate human behaviour, they cannot have psychological experiences, express personal behaviour as opposed to mere imitation, and have the degree of creativity and spontaneity that a human mind is capable of exhibiting.

Summing up recent scientific findings on the body-mind problem, Professor Hornell Hart states: "To look at the body-mind problem without bias, it is essential that we recognise two pivotal facts: (1) that damage to brain structure may block or distort what the 'I'-thinker wants to transmit; and (2) that the chemical condition of the brain has marked effects on the moods and attitudes of the 'I'-thinker himself.... Whatever it is that thinks 'I' in any one of us is not a constant, unchanging reality. Nor is it something which progresses smoothly and consistently along a regular trend" (*The Enigma of Survival*, p. 219).

### BUDDHIST VIEW

All this seems to support the Buddhist theory of the mind, which holds that 'conscious mental and cognitive phenomena function in dependence on their physical basis' (yam rūpaṃ nissāya manodhātu ca manoviññānadhātu ca vattati, *Paṭṭhāna*), that certain aspects of will can direct, govern and produce mental activity as well as verbal and bodily behaviour and that, when the body and the brain are stilled with the attainment of the Fourth Jhāna (and sometimes even otherwise), the mind can exercise its powers of extra-sensory perception which are potentially present.

So none of the modern findings with regard to the mind and its relation to the brain, nor the assertions of modern brain physiologists in any way preclude the empirical possibility of survival after death. This does not mean that survival after death is a fact but that it is an open possibility to be proved or disproved or made probable or improbable in the light of relevant evidence.

### OTHER OBJECTIONS

There are other objections that are raised specifically against the concept of rebirth. They fall into three categories: (1) that rebirth is a self-contradictory concept, (2) that it cannot account for the increase in the human population, which is a fact, and (3) that biogenesis or reproduction by fission at the lowest levels of life is inexplicable on the basis of the rebirth theory.

The first objection is that the concept of rebirth involves the identity of two or more persons one of whom lives now. It is held that the identification of two or more persons regarding them as one and the same person is either meaningless or self-contradictory. This is based on the belief that the identity of the person consists in the identity of the body, which is certainly the case in the law courts. But as the philosopher

John Locke pointed out, with specific reference to the case of rebirth, we also apply a mental criterion in our identification of persons.

If someone suffers from an attack of total amnesia, which involves a complete black-out of his past memories, resulting in a complete change of life, we would be inclined to say he is now a new person, that he is not the same person as before. For example, Dr Jekyll and Mr Hyde who have the same body are regarded as two different persons. This means that, as regards the identity of persons, we normally employ two criteria, that of the continuity of the body and that of the continuity of memory and mental dispositions. In the rebirth case all that is claimed is that in a significant sense there is a continuity (santati) of the mind of the individual from one earth-life to another.

This makes it meaningful to say that two persons, historically removed from each other in time, are one and the same individual because they have a continuous mental history. The modern positivist philosopher, Professor A. J. Ayer of Oxford, granting the meaningfulness and the logical possibility of rebirth, says: 'I think that it would be open to us to admit the logical possibility of reincarnation merely by laying down the rule that, if a person who is physically identified as living at a later time does have the ostensible memories and character of a person who is physically identified as living at an earlier time, they are to be counted as one person and not two' (*The Concept of a Person*, Macmillan, London, 1963, p. 127). The logical objection is, therefore, untenable.

The second objection is that it cannot account for the increase in human population. This objection would be valid if the theory requires that any human birth at present presupposes the death of a prior human being on this earth. Such a theory would also make it impossible for human beings to evolve out of anthropoid apes since the first human beings to evolve would not have had human ancestors (unless their samsaric ancestors were from other planes of existence). But according to the early Buddhist view of the cosmos, there are hundreds and thousands of galaxies spread out in space, containing 'thousands of suns, moons, earths and other inhabited spheres'. It is also the case according to the Buddhist theory of rebirth that the prior life of a human being may be animal. It is, therefore, possible according to this theory to account for the increasing number of present human births in terms of the deaths of human beings, animals or non-human beings in this as well as on other planets in the universe.

As regards the third objection from biogenesis, it can hardly affect the Buddhist theory. Although according to some Brahmanical theories, rebirth is possible even at the level of plants, it appears to be the case according to Buddhism that rebirth takes place at a higher level of evolution, when a 're-becoming mind' has been formed with the persistence of memory. After his enlightenment, the Buddha refers to some of his Jain practices as an aspirant to Buddhahood in the following words: 'I used to walk up and down conscientiously extending my compassion even to a drop of water, praying that the dangerous bacteria in it (khuddake pane visamagate) may not come to harm' (M.I. 78). The context seems to suggest that this was a waste of time. Further objections arise in relation to the mind-body.

## BODY-MIND PROBLEM

The case against the possibility of survival in the light of what we know about the mind is fully stated in a book by Dr C. Lamont called *The Illusion of Immortality* (Philosophical Library, New York, 1950). A sound criticism of its contents is to be found in Chapter 13 of a book by Dr C. J. Ducasse, Emeritus Professor of Philosophy, Brown University, called *A Critical Examination of the Belief in a Life after Death* (Illinois, 1961).

The Buddhist theory of the relationship between body and mind can account for the basic facts stated in Lamont's book as well as the criticisms of Ducasse. Lamont's case is based on the following facts:

1. that 'the power and versatility of living things increase concomitantly with the development and complexity of their bodies in general and their nervous systems in particular'.
2. that 'the genes or other factors from the germ cells of the parents determine the individual's inherent physical characteristics and inherent mental capacities'.
3. that, during the course of life 'the mind and the personality grow and change, always in conjunction with environmental influences, as the body grows and changes'.
4. that 'specific alterations in the physical structure and condition of the body, especially in the brain and cerebral cortex, bring about specific alterations in the mental and emotional life of a man'.
5. that 'conversely, specific alterations in his mental and emotional life result in specific alterations in his bodily condition'. (See Ducasse, op. cit., p. 114).

Ducasse shows that (5) contradicts Lamont's contentions against Dualism. He further cites the case of psychosomatic disease to show that primarily mental states cause physical changes in the body. Psychosomatic medicine, for example, today recognises the fact that mental states such as anxiety, tension and worry sometimes cause painful stomach ulcers.

Now what is the Buddhist theory? Buddhism clearly holds that conscious mental and cognitive experiences function in dependence on a physical basis. A statement in the *Paṭṭhāna* reads as follows: 'That physical basis in dependence on which the category of mental experience (mano-dhātu) and the category of cognitive experience (mano-viññāṇa-dhātu) function, this physical basis is to the category of mental experience and the category of cognitive experience and to phenomena associated with it, a condition by way of dependence' (nissaya-paccaya).

Because of this dependence it is not surprising that (1) is true and (4) occurs, namely the alterations in the physical basis resulting in alterations in consciousness.

Yet the dependence is not one-sided. As the Buddhist texts elsewhere state, 'the mind follows in the wake of the body' (kāyaṃvayaṃ cittaṃ) and 'the body follows in the wake of the mind' (cittaṃvayo kāyo). The relation between the psyche (viññāṇa) and its hereditary psycho-physical basis (nāmarūpa) is one of 'mutual dependence' (aññamañña paccaya). The will and other psychological factors can initiate some of the mental and physical changes that take place as suggested in (5).

Again, since according to Buddhism, the psycho-physical basis of our bodies is partly due to what is derived from mother and father and 'biological laws' (bīja-niyāma) operate, it is not surprising that (2) is *partly* true, namely that genetic factors condition our physical and some of our mental characteristics.

When the Buddha told Sāti that it was wrong to hold that consciousness fares on from life to life without change of identity (aññaññaṃ), he illustrated this by showing that consciousness was causally conditioned. It is conditioned by the state of our body, which is partly a product of hereditary factors. It is also conditioned by the external environment. On account of the eye and visual phenomena, there arises in us visual consciousness. Similarly in respect of the other senses, there arise forms of consciousness associated with their respective sense-objects.

Likewise, it is said that on account of the impact on the conscious mind (mano) of ideas (dhammā), there arise various forms of conceptual consciousness. When these ideas do not come to us through language from our social and external ideological environment, they impinge on the conscious mind from our own unconscious. As a result of this our consciousness changes and grows and this in turn affects our subsequent behaviour. This is how the Buddha explains to Sāti that the psyche (viññāṇa) is not an unchanging entity but is in a state of dynamic growth and becoming in close association with the conditioning of the body.

In the case of visual stimuli, etc. they physically affect the senses in giving rise to their respective impressions (paṭigha-samphassa) but in the case of ideas that arise in the mind in remembering, imagining, thinking, etc. the contact with the conscious mind is said to be only nominal (adhivacana-samphassa).

It is these impressions and ideas and their by-products that accumulate in our memory and form part of our mind. So what is stated in (3), namely that 'the mind and personality grow and change always in conjunction with environmental influences as the body grows and changes' is partly true. As we have seen above, it is stated in the Buddhist text themselves.

So while Buddhism holds that the person is a psycho-physical unit (nāmarūpa), it does not subscribe to the Identity Hypothesis that the mind and the body are one and the same entity or to the Dualistic Hypothesis that the mind and the body are entirely different.

Besides, Buddhism holds that if awareness (sati) can be retained while the impressions and ideas that impinge on the conscious mind are inhibited, the activity of the body is gradually stilled and the emotions of sensuous love (kāma-chanda) and hate (vyāpāda) subside, then the mind being intrinsically resplendent (pabhassara) gradually acquires certain extra-sensory powers of perception (abhiññā).

What we outlined earlier was the relationship of the conscious mind (manodhātu, manoviññāṇadhātu) to its physical basis, but we must not forget that according to the Buddhist theory the 'stream of consciousness' has two components without a sharp division between them (ubhayato abbocchinnaṃ), the conscious mind and the unconscious, in which accumulate the emotionally charged experiences that we have had going back through childhood and birth into previous lives. Besides, with the expansion and development of consciousness (vibhūta saññī), it attains a paranormal state.

How much of our memories in the unconscious are associated with the brain? Do they include the memories of prior lives as well? What is the nature of the association between the potentially paranormal mind and the brain? Does the paranormal mind function at its best when the activity of the brain and the body is quiescent (kāyasaṅkhārā niruddhā) under its control? The total psyche (viññāṇa) of a person comprising the conscious mind, the memories and dispositions in the unconscious and the potentially paranormal mind is said to be 'associated with and linked to the body' (ettha sitaṃ ettha paṭibaddhaṃ). But it is not clear how close or how loose the association of its several aspects are.

The Buddhist texts speak of two forms of telepathy, direct and indirect. Indirect telepathy, it is said, is had 'by attuning oneself with the thought-vibrations of a person as he thinks' (vitakkayato vitakka-vipphāra-saddaṃ sutvā). Direct telepathy does not require this mediating process. Is the activity of the brain required for indirect telepathy while it is unnecessary for direct telepathy?

Previously we tried to show that the modern findings in regard to the mind and its relation to the brain do not preclude the possibility of survival after death. While reiterating this point we tried to give here a more detailed account of the Buddhist solution to the body–mind problem.

The arguments of the critics from the nature of the mind and its relation to the brain, if valid, would hold against any theory of survival after death, including the Buddhist. The other objections which we dealt with in our previous talk could only be levelled against a rebirth theory. They were, that rebirth was a self-contradictory concept in that it claimed that many persons were one and the same person, that it could not account for the increase in the human population and that biogenesis or a-sexual reproduction at the lowest levels of life was inexplicable on the basis of a rebirth theory.

### ANOTHER OBJECTION

If any of the above arguments were valid, they would have shown that a rebirth theory was not merely improbable but impossible. But we saw that the arguments were based on false premises and did not affect the Buddhist theory of rebirth. Where there was continuity of mind in the form of actual or potential memory and mental dispositions, then, in popular parlance, we can speak of the many lives of one person. The increase of population would not present a difficulty where pre-existence could be in the form of animal lives or those of non-human beings in this as well as other planets in the universe. Biogenesis ceases to be a problem if rebirth takes place only at a higher level of biological evolution.

One of the commonest objections against a theory of rebirth, which implies pre-existence, is that we do not remember our past lives. The objection may take three different forms. First, that we do not have any memory of prior lives and that, therefore, there is no evidence of our having lived in the past prior to our present birth. Secondly, that memory is indispensable to the identity of a person. Thirdly, that unless we have memory, rebirth is to no purpose, since no moral or other lesson is learnt in the process.

We may first dispose of the third form of this argument. We are concerned only with the question as to whether re-becoming or rebirth is a fact and not whether it is a good thing to be reborn. We cannot argue from what ought to be or what is best to what actually is the case. It is generally admitted that such an argument has no basis in fact, since, if it is true, the world would be very much different from what it is. Besides, there is a variety of rebirth theories and the question as to which one is true cannot be made on the basis of the ethical consideration as to which one is the best to believe in. For, quite apart from differences of opinion as to what is best (whether, for example, it would be better to remember or not to remember), there is no justification, as we have shown, in arguing that what is best is in fact the case.

The second form of the objection is that memory is indispensable to the identity of a person. If by this is meant that, unless a person has authentic memories of a past life, we cannot be at all certain that he is the same as one who lived before, there is some substance to this objection. But it would not be necessary to prove that this was so in the case of all people.

If a sufficient number and variety of people can be shown to have such authentic memories then, although we may not be able to identify the prior lives of other human beings, it would be a reasonable presumption that they too had prior lives and are potentially capable of remembering this at some time or another.

To come back to the first form of the objection that we have no memory of having lived before, then, if rebirth is a fact, it is certainly not true of all human beings that they do not recollect their prior lives. For there are at least a few who do while many others could be assisted to recall their previous lives.

It is possible, of course, to argue that the lack of memory regarding prior lives is no proof that we have not lived before, any more than lack of memory regarding the first year of our lives on the part of all or most human beings is no proof that we did not live in the first year of our life. It is true that mere absence of memory of a certain event or phase of life is no proof that such an event did not take place or that we did not live through such a phase of life.

Yet this is an argument from silence. In the case of our present life, we have another criterion to go on, namely the criterion of bodily continuity, and other people can testify to the fact that we existed in the first year of our lives and lived through certain experiences. But in the case of rebirth we have no evidence at all if we do not have actual or potential memories. Memory is, therefore, very relevant to the problem of rebirth.

However, it is necessary to point out that the word 'memory' is used in two senses. In a secondary sense, 'having memory' is a matter of retaining a skill or capacity that we acquired. If someone learnt how to swim when he was a child and can now swim very well without having to re-learn it and without even being able to recall that he learnt to swim as a child, we still say that he remembered how to swim though he has forgotten that he had learnt it as a child.

If rebirth be the case, is it not likely that some of the capacities or skills we have or acquire without much difficulty in this life may be due to our having learnt them in a prior life, especially where they cannot be fully accounted for in terms of heredity or learning in this life?

The explanation not only of capacities and skills but of differences of temperament or 'weaknesses', which also fall into this category, would have to be the same. Now identical twins (as opposed to fraternal twins) are said to have the same heredity and when they happen to grow up as 'Siamese twins conjoined to each other, they have more or less a common environment. Now if individual differences and variations are due entirely to the factors of heredity and environment alone, there should be identity of temperament and character on the part of these twins. At least there should not be marked differences in their dispositions and temperaments. But the facts are otherwise.

Thus H. H. Newman, who made a specialist study of twinning, says with regard to the original 'Siamese twins', Chang and Eng: 'The author of a study made when the twins were in London was impressed with the lack of any strong resemblance between Chang and Eng. Much emphasis was placed on their different dispositions and temperaments. Change was inclined to drunkenness, while Eng was a tee-totaller' (*Multiple Human Births*, New York, 1940, pp. 64–5).

With regard to these identical twins, in general, his observations are as follows:

'In describing several pairs of these strange twins, writers have commented upon their lack of close similarity. Such twins have been regarded as the only kind of twins that are beyond question derived from a single egg and therefore surely identical in their hereditary make-up. One would expect such twins, since they have not only a common heredity but a common environment (for they must be in the same environment all the time), to be even more strikingly similar than pairs of separate twins that are not so intimately associated. The fact is, however, that Siamese twins are almost without exception more different in various ways than any but a few pairs of separate one-egg twins. One of the most difficult problems faced by the twinning specialist is that of accounting for this unexpected dissimilarity of the compenents of Siamese twin pairs (Ibid., pp. 67–8).

Could this difference not be due to a third factor other than heredity and environment, namely the psychological past of the two individuals? If so, is it not likely that even in other individuals as well there could be capacities, skills, temperaments, weaknesses, etc., which are due to 'memories' (in the secondary sense defined above) of prior lives rather than to the factors of heredity and environment. Geniuses or child prodigies, whose extraordinary accomplishments cannot be accounted for in terms of heredity or environment, would only be special cases of such a carry-over of skills from one life to another.

Apart from the use of the word 'memories' in the above secondary sense, we use the word in its primary sense to denote the 'recall of authentic experiences of one's past'. In this sense there are quite a few who have claimed to have remembered experiences of their alleged prior lives. Some of them are spontaneous cases of recall while others are due to the intervention of hypnotists, who have carried out age-regression experiments. How authentic are these memories and what reason have we to believe that they are potentially present in many if not all human beings? These are questions that we shall seek to answer.

### UNSATISFACTORY ARGUMENTS

We need in due course to examine the evidence for recall of experiences from prior lives. Yet, before we proceed to do so, it is necessary to dispose of some unsatisfactory arguments that are sometimes adduced in support of the doctrine of rebirth. They may take many forms.

There is a tendency to urge that some belief is true because almost everybody holds it. Yet the universality of a belief does not entail its truth. Nor at the same time does it entail its falsity. It is sometimes maintained that many primitive peoples of the ancient world believed in survival or the doctrine of rebirth. But this does not imply that the belief is either true or false. Its truth or falsity has to be established independently.

The relevance of the universality of the belief as evidence of its truth becomes more interesting when it is realised that people in a state of deep hypnosis give an account of experiences in alleged prior lives, lived on earth, whatever their conscious beliefs may be. There is evidence that Materialists and Theists holding a variety of views on the subject of survival after death without subscribing to the doctrine of rebirth or pre-existence, give alleged accounts of prior lives, recounting details of their experiences.

Does this imply the truth of the belief? Not necessarily, for it is possible that all their beliefs could be illusory, though the universality of such an illusion has to be accounted for. But the experiences they recount certainly constitute evidence for the truth or falsity of the belief in rebirth. We shall carefully examine this evidence later on.

Another form in which an argument for survival is presented, is that a human need or want implies the existence of what is needed or wanted. We need or want food. Therefore, it is suggested, there must be food. Many people feel the need for immortality or at least survival after death. Therefore, it is suggested, there must be such immortality or survival.

However, this is an argument that cuts both ways. For others may argue that we believe in rebirth or survival because we need to believe or desire to entertain such a belief. But what we like to believe is not necessarily true, and, therefore, this is no evidence of the truth of the belief.

Freud in his work called *The Future of an Illusion* tries to show that people entertain certain religious beliefs, like the belief in the existence of God, for instance, because there is a deep-seated craving in us for security amidst the insecurity of life and the uncertainty of the beyond. According to him people believe in God dogmatically because of such a deep-seated craving. It is an object of wish-fulfilment and, in this specialised sense, an 'illusion'.

This does not, however, necessarily mean that the belief is false. As Freud himself pointed out, a girl may believe in the existence of a Prince Charming who may one day come and propose to her because she likes to believe this, but this does not necessarily mean that such a person does not exist. So the desire to believe in rebirth or survival does not necessarily show that the belief is false just as much as the desire to disbelieve in rebirth does not imply that the contrary belief is false.

The Buddhist view on this matter is both relevant and interesting. Our desires influence or condition our beliefs, to which we tenaciously cling (taṃhā paccayā diṭṭhupādānaṃ) but this does not necessarily mean that these beliefs are always false, for when they happen to be 'right beliefs' (sammā diṭṭhi), they are in fact true.

So although desires affect our beliefs, this fact has no relevance to the truth or falsity of the beliefs. We have, however, because of our emotional involvement with these beliefs, to weigh the evidence for or against their truth or falsity without prejudice. As Buddhists we have to examine the truth even of the belief in rebirth objectively, without being prejudiced for (chandā) or against (dosā) or being affected by fear (bhayā), even if it be the fear of the beyond, or being guided by our erroneous beliefs (mohā). So the desire to believe does not affect the truth or falsity of the belief, but we have to guard against the prejudice resulting from these desires in our quest for truth.

## AUTHORITY AND REVELATION

Another set of arguments for survival is based on authority. It may be stated that many poets and mystics as well as rational thinkers, brought up in a tradition which condemned the belief, nevertheless professed it.

The classic case is that of Giordano Bruno, who is said to have stated in his profession of faith before the Inquisition: 'I have held and hold souls to be immortal. . . . Speaking as a Catholic, they do not pass from body to body, but go to Paradise, Purgatory or Hell. But I have reasoned deeply, and, speaking as a philosopher, since the soul is not found without body and yet is not body, it may be in one body or in another, and pass from body to body. This, if it be not [proved] true, seems, at least, likely. . . .'

All that this seems to suggest is that the belief is worth examining and it does not in any way imply the truth of the belief.

The argument from revelation is also unacceptable to science and Buddhism. It is true that certain texts in the Vedic tradition, particularly the middle and late Upaniṣads, profess a belief in rebirth, but there is a variety of views on the subject of survival in the Vedic tradition itself. In one of the early Upaniṣads rebirth is denied. It is said: '. . . there are these three worlds, the world of men, the world of departed spirits and the world of the gods. The world of men is obtained through a son only, not by any other means' (*Bṛhadāraṇyaka Upaniṣad*, 1.5.15).

While there are these contradictions within revelational

traditions, the different theistic revelations also contradict each other on the problem of survival. So the doctrine of rebirth cannot be established by an argument from authority or revelation, since authority and revelation are not acceptable means of knowledge.

### METAPHYSICAL AND ETHICAL ARGUMENTS

The metaphysical arguments are no better. Apart from the fact that they make use of unverifiable concepts like 'soul', the arguments are of doubtful value and are generally discredited today. One of the traditional arguments for survival has been that the 'soul is a substance', substances are indestructible, therefore the soul is indestructible, i.e. 'immortal'. But apart from the difficulty of the concept of a 'soul', the notion of an indestructible substance is discredited today.

With regard to rebirth, we have already met with a sample of such a metaphysical argument in that of Giodano Bruno. Such arguments, based on pure reasoning, intended to prove the truth of rebirth, are to be met with, for example, in the work of John McTaggart. But they have little appeal today since it is recognised that matters of fact cannot be proved by pure reasoning (takka), as the Buddha himself pointed out (mā takka-hetu).

The ethical argument has a greater appeal but this is so only for those who accept its presuppositions.

### AGE-REGRESSION

The above arguments are, therefore, for one reason or another, unsatisfactory and have little force in proving the truth of rebirth or survival. The truth or falsity of rebirth, therefore, rests on the relevant empirical evidence. We may classify the main evidence into two sorts, (1) experimental and (2) spontaneous. The other evidence may be considered separately.

The experimental evidence is based on age-regression.

Under hypnosis a subject can recall or relive his past experiences. With regard to this life when regressed to age six, for instance, the subject would behave, write and talk as he or she did at that time and recall the past experiences which it may not be possible to recall by normal means. The handwriting and the memories could be independently checked. Such experiments have convinced psychologists and psychiatrists today that the authentic buried memories of one's childhood experiences, which cannot be called to mind in normal consciousness, can be unearthed by hypnosis.

It may be asked whether the subject is not just responding to the suggestion of the hypnotist and is merely play-acting or shamming. That this is not so has been proved experimentally.

H. J. Eysenck reports, 'In one case it was found that when a twenty-year-old girl was regressed to various ages she changed the chalk to her left hand at the six-year level; she had started writing with the left hand, but had been forced to change over at the age of six' (*Sense and Nonsense in Psychology*, Penguin Books, Reprint 1961, p. 48).

In another case a thirty-year-old was hypnotised and regressed to a level of about one year of age on a chair arranged in such a way that with the release of a latch it would fall back into a horizontal position. When the latch was released the behaviour elicited was not that of an adult but of a child. An adult, it is said, would quite involuntarily extend both arms and legs in an effort to maintain balance. Since the subject made no movement of the limbs but screamed in fright and fell backward with the chair, urinating in the process, Eysenck comments: 'It is unlikely that such behaviour is simply due to play-acting' (ibid., p. 49).

Intelligence and achievement tests have been used to assess the nature of the behaviour of regressed subjects and it has been found that 'people tend to behave on tests of this type in a manner roughly appropriate to the given age'. Eysenck's observations with regard to the possibility of faking such behaviour, are as follows: 'Such reactions, of course, could easily be faked, but it has been shown that when, for instance, the eye movements of subjects are photographed, a considerable lack of ocular co-ordination and stability is found when regression to a relatively young age occurs. Such physiological phenomena are characteristic of young children and are difficult, if not impossible, to produce voluntarily' (ibid., p. 49).

A remarkable fact is that the psychological experiences had, when the physiological condition of the body was different, been re-enacted. To quote Eysenck again: 'Even more impressive is another case of a subject who had had a colloid cyst removed from the floor of the third ventricle. Prior to this removal, the subject had been suffering from blindness in the left half of the right eye. After the operation, vision had become normal, but when the subject was regressed to a time shortly before the operation the visual defect again re-appeared during the regression' (ibid.) The expected physiological reaction is not only appropriate to the age but reflects the physiological condition of the body at the time.

In the light of the experimental evidence Eysenck concludes: 'Experiments such as those described in some detail above leave little doubt that there is a substantial amount of truth in the hypothesis that age regression does, in fact, take place, and that memories can be recovered which most people would think had been completely lost' (ibid., p. 51). This is the consensus of opinion among orthodox psychologists today.

So genuine memories not accessible to normal recall are generally evoked or the experiences relived at the suggestion of the hypnotist in age-regression. So at least as far as this life is concerned, to say that memories recalled under age-regression are hallucinatory or delusive is not correct.

## PRIOR LIVES

The majority of orthodox psychologists and psychiatrists, however, are reluctant to concede that accounts given of and the experiences lived through alleged prior lives are genuine. In such cases they tend to dismiss these accounts and experiences of prior lives as fantasy or a product of dramatization and role-playing based on material derived from the experiences of this life. They are prepared to grant that the subject's behaviour 'will give the appearance of reincarnation' (F. L. Marcuse, *Hypnosis Fact and Fiction*, Penguin Books, Reprint 1961, p. 184) but deny that the reincarnationist interpretation is valid.

So the position is that many psychologists and psychiatrists are prepared to concede the fact that under age-regression a hypnotised subject will give detailed descriptions of an alleged prior life but would not agree with the validity of a reincarnationist interpretation of the data.

The main reason for this seems to be the logical and methodological difficulties involved in accepting an explanation in terms of the hypothesis of rebirth rather than a careful attempt on the part of these psychologists and psychiatrists to understand or explain the data itself.

We have tried to show that neither the logical nor methodological difficulties are valid. We pointed out that the concept of rebirth does not lead to contradictions. Even a positivist philosopher such as Professor A. J. Ayer has stated that the concept of rebirth is meaningful. Besides, as we have argued, there is a growing realisation that the phenomenon of consciousness cannot be explained away purely in terms of physico-chemical phenomena, while the validity of extra-sensory perception precludes that psychological explanations be contained (where the data require this) within the narrow and limiting framework of mechanistic materialist assumptions. The data therefore require to be examined with an open mind.

## THE EVIDENCE

All important is the nature of the evidence and its authenticity and the legitimate conclusions that we can come to in explaining this evidence with the help of the various hypotheses that may be adduced to explain it. When hypotheses cannot be accepted or rejected outright, they may be held with varying degrees of probability according to relevant criteria.

One of the earliest recorded experiments of psychologists was that of Theodore Flournoy, Professor of Psychology in the University of Geneva, who experimented with one of his subjects at the end of the last century and recorded the data and findings in a book published in 1899 (*Des Indes à la Planète Mars*, Geneva, 1899).

One of the prior lives of his Swiss subject was as an Arab chief's daughter, who married a Hindu prince about four centuries before. The subject spoke and wrote in the languages (Arabic and Prakrit), which she knew in the regressed state but not in her normal life, and gave details of experiences in this life, re-enacting and reliving some of the scenes. The facsimiles of the writing are reproduced in pages 289 and 313 of the book.

Before we examine this case, we may turn our attention to a more popular work published in 1942. This would enable us to see the issues involved in the interpretation of the data more clearly. Since Buddhists are or ought to be interested only in objective facts or in 'things as they are' (yathābhūtaṃ), it is important that we approach the subject with a critical mind without an initial bias for or against the theory of rebirth.

## 'RESEARCHES IN REINCARNATION AND BEYOND'

The work is by Rev. A. R. Martin, an ordained teacher of the Coptic Church and is entitled *Researches in Reincarnation and Beyond* (1st edn., Pennsylvania, 1942). It is dedicated to 'all seekers for truth or not it be in accordance with their former teachings or preconceived ideas' (p. 11). The book records the alleged experiences of people hypnotised by him or trained to recall their prior lives.

His comments with regard to the evidence and the records are as follows: 'The questions and their answers thereto were carefully recorded, usually in shorthand, exactly as given. Great care was taken to ask no "leading questions", thereby eliminating the possibility of implanting ideas in the mind of the reviewer, thus making certain to bring out only that which was recorded in the reviewer's subconscious mind. These correlations of important persons and events often occurring hundreds of years ago, were carefully checked in reference books, histories, encyclopaedias, etc., and were found correct as given by the reviewers. This information was known to come solely from the knowledge already in the reviewer's subconscious mind, for it was known that such knowledge was not contained in his intellectual mind of this present life' (ibid., pp. 7–8).

He claims that these explorations into the subconscious minds of various people 'worked out through powers of mind, absolutely without the use of any kind of drug' was attempted after a group of about twelve persons of various ages had for years examined various conflicting teachings of speculative philosophy on the subject of an after-life and were dissatisfied with them.

The author lists a number of beliefs about the nature of an after-life held by people in the West. The first was that 'death ends all . . .' (ibid., p. 4), the second that 'the consciousness – soul – dies and is buried with the body and remains there until a time called the resurrection when all persons who have ever lived from the beginning of creation to the time of the resurrection will come forth, from the land or the sea or wherever they may be, to be judged and sent either to an eternal heaven or an eternal hell of fire and brimstone from which there is no escape' (ibid., p. 4), the third was the view that there is 'an intermediate place of punishment or remorse from which the dead can be released through prayer and liberated into an eternal heaven . . .' (ibid., pp. 4–5). Several other such views are listed. The author says that he 'has lived all of his present life (to this time) in the United States' (ibid., p. 3), and was himself 'raised to manhood under the instruction of the second belief' (ibid., p. 6), and that none of those who thus met regularly to investigate these matters 'even "leaned toward" reincarnation' (ibid., p. 6).

If this is so, then considering particularly the fact that no 'leading questions' were asked, it is all the more remarkable that they were able to recall prior lives lived on earth. It is a curious fact, which calls for an explanation by itself, that those who in their normal conscious experience are materialists or theists, who do not believe in pre-existence or rebirth, give alleged accounts of prior lives under deep hypnosis. Where the subject is asked to concoct an account of an alleged 'prior life', this may be attributed to the suggestion of the hypnotist but where such prior lives are described without any express instructions on the part of the hypnotist to do so, this fact in itself calls for an explanation.

In an article appearing in the magazine *Two Worlds*, 'Can Reincarnation be proved by Hypnotism?', May 1964, pp. 247–9, H. C. Miranda states:

'Sometimes the subject during what is called "wakeful state" is not a reincarnationist, or even has never heard about such an idea, or else belongs to a creed that denies it emphatically.

'One very intelligent man, a Protestant, asked the hypnotist in a deep, booming, slow voice, "Why do you ask such a question?" The question was repeated, "Were you or were you not born for the first time?"

'He still hesitated, as if to conquer a strong inner opposition, and then began to describe his life a couple of centuries ago in a monastery somewhere in Spain.

'When he awoke, slowly and by reversing the age-regression process, the tape was played back to him. He was amazed because he did not know about reincarnation and never thought it possible.

'A bright, beautiful, mature woman talked freely about reincarnation and other related subjects. When she listened to the playback she said, "I must be crazy to say such things". She is a diehard Roman Catholic.'

### ORIGIN OF PHOBIAS

Granted that the experiences related in the above-mentioned book are authentic and factual, many of our problems in this life can be understood in terms of their causal origins in a prior life.

This is very much like the manner in which the submerged traumatic experiences of this life (as explained in Freudian psychology) are the causal factors which account for various symptoms.

Dr Eysenck records the case of a Mrs Smith, who suffered from recurrent asthmatic attacks; her work necessitated her going into various hospitals but in doing so she experienced a very strong fear reaction. The sight of a pair of hairy arms or knives also produced such a reaction. Under hypnotic age-regression, she was able to recall and relive the incidents which were responsible for this condition. It was the shock caused by an operation for mastoidectomy performed on her at the age of sixteen months, which she had forgotten. Dr Eysenck describes the situation as follows:

'During a self-induced trance one day, she was regressed to an early age, when she experienced a previously completely forgotten incident with unusual clarity. She seemed to be lying on a table under brilliant lights. A man was standing beside her holding a small knife. A vague, threatening object was descending from above her head, and settled down over her face. She was terror-stricken and tried to rise, but two hairy arms grabbed her and roughly forced her back. She continued to struggle, but was violently shaken and slapped repeatedly by someone. Finally, the object came down over her face and smothered her. On inquiry, it was found that at the age of sixteen months a mastoidectomy had been performed on her and that she had been very sick afterwards with complications caused by severe shock' (Eysenck, op. cit., pp. 51–2).

The origin of this phobia was traced to a childhood incident in this life. But it is interesting to compare in this connection one of the experiences recorded in the above-mentioned book. which locates the origin of a phobia in an incident of an alleged prior life. It is described as follows:

'A middle aged woman . . . when riding in a car driven twenty miles an hour or more, the motion produced such a fear within her that she would become very nervous and ready to jump out of the car. As a result she could ride only in cars driven around fifteen miles an hour. This fear of speed made it almost impossible for her to travel by train, bus, etc. Upon entering a past life review, she found herself to be a young girl travelling on a train with her parents, brothers and sisters. As the train passed over a trestle bridge it was wrecked, killing all the members of the family but herself, along with many others who were on the train. Her injuries were so severe that she was badly crippled and rendered an invalid for the remainder of that life. The speed had been such a dominant factor in this accident and its impression was so deep that the subconscious fixation outmanifested in this life as intense fear whenever any degree of motion was felt by her' (Eysenck, ibid., p. 44).

### KARMA?

If the experiences recounted in the Rev. Martin's book are authentic and factual, they also appear to throw some light on the operations of *karma*.

In one case, five previous lives of a person are recorded. In the fifth life previous to the present, the person's first recollection was that of 'awakening as a white baby in a log cabin' (Martin, op. cit., p. 90). The cabin was attacked by Red Indians, one of whom took her along and brought her up as a

Red Indian maiden. Eventually, she was taken away by a British trader with whom she lived in a small hut until he decided to leave her and cross the mountains in search of gold. He offered to take her back to the Indian tribe, but conscious of her white parentage and coming motherhood she refused. Instead, faced with the prospect of being alone in the hut, it is said that she committed suicide by shooting herself on 'the right side of her face.'

In the very next birth, she is stated to have been born as a crippled child named Sammy, whose entire right side was paralysed. The subsequent birth is supposed to have been as a US soldier of the South during the Revolution, when he was accosted by a British subject who stabbed him in the right side of the abdomen causing his death.

In the following birth, she was born as a girl named Nancy, whose mother worked for a wealthy family. A son of this family, it is said, fell in love with this girl and wanted to marry her, but his parents objected and had her married to a farm-hand. She subsequently journeyed West in a covered waggon and settled in Illinois, where two children were born. Nancy died at the age of thirty as a result of abdominal disorders. Her next life was as a person who became well-known as an operatic singer called 'Miss Nellie', a daughter of a wealthy family near Baltimore, Maryland. She was happily married but before long her husband was shot dead and it is said that she 'died of a broken heart'. The author describes and comments on part of her present life as follows: 'When she was fifteen years old, the first of these negative conditions resulted in a paralysis of the right side of the face and neck. At this age she knew nothing of reincarnation nor of the influence of past lives upon the present. The overcoming of the paralysis, slight traces of which are still apparent, was accomplished in a period of six to seven years through rest and quiet' (ibid., p. 94).

If the facts are right, are we to attribute her birth as a child paralysed on the right side in her fourth previous life and her paralysis of the right side of the face and neck in this life as well as, perhaps, her deaths from abdominal injuries or disorders as karmic consequences of her suicide while being with child in her fifth previous life?

Taken literally, if the experiences recounted here are authentic and true records of prior lives, they exemplify the truths of both rebirth and karma. But what justification have we for accepting these experiences at their face value?

## NORMAL HYPOTHESES

A person with a sceptical frame of mind may very well indulge in doubt and claim that one of several hypotheses other than rebirth could adequately account for the alleged facts. Some may even doubt whether the book I refer to exists and whether all this is not a concoction of mine! This would be the extreme hypothesis of fraud. The reply to this is that the book is to be found in some libraries, for instance the library of the University of Ceylon. A less extreme position that one could take would be to doubt whether the author of the book was not merely trying to bring out a sensationalist publication from which he might financially benefit and that he made it all up. One way of verifying this would be to contact the author and through him the people concerned as the author himself wants those interested to do (see ibid., p. 17). But this is unnecessary since this kind of evidence can be made available with the help of a suitable hypnotist and hypnotisable subjects.

Once it is established that the book contains an account of authentic experiences accurately recorded, we may still doubt the assumption that they are genuine memories of past lives. We may try to explain them as being due to the role-playing of the subject, who has proceeded to give dramatised accounts of alleged prior lives on the basis of material drawn from this life. We would then resort to the hypothesis of *Fantasy* or *Self-deception*, unless the author can prove to us, as he says he could, that 'it was known that such knowledge was not contained in his intellectual mind of this present life' (ibid., p. 8). This hypothesis would be difficult to exclude in the present circumstances unless it can be shown that specific items of knowledge later verified from encyclopedias etc. were not known to the subject (as the author claims to be the case). However, the fact that some of these alleged experiences solved some of the present psychological problems of some of these subjects is a factor to be taken into consideration in judging the genuineness of these experiences, though this test is by no means conclusive.

Another 'normal' explanation would be to assume that such 'experiences' can be derived genetically from one's ancestors. Apart from the fact that there is no independent evidence of such hereditary derivation of specific 'memory experiences' (leaving out capacities and aptitudes), the hypothesis requires an ancestral link between the two personalities. This is very unlikely at least in those cases, in which the prior life is located in such countries as Persia or Egypt.

## PARANORMAL HYPOTHESES

If the normal hypotheses fail to account for the facts, we have to resort to paranormal hypotheses to explain the evidence.

Granted that the 'memories' correspond with historical facts and knowledge of them is not derived from any experiences in this life, it is possible to suggest that they are the product of a telepathic, clairvoyant or retrocognitive faculty operating along with dramatisation and role-playing. On such a hypothesis, these persons did not actually live in the past but acquired information about past events by paranormal or extrasensory means and dramatised such a past life. Such a hypothesis appears to be more extravagant than a simple one of 'rebirth'. For, apart from not explaining all the data (e.g. the claim to identity, the serial nature of the recall in age-regression, etc.), there is little evidence of such wide and penetrative powers of telepathic, clairvoyant or retrocognitive perception except, perhaps, in a few extraordinary individuals.

For similar reasons, the hypothesis of *Spirit-possession* appears to be less plausible in accounting for the data. For, in spirit-possession, the alleged spirit communicating through the medium claims to be a different person from the personality associated with the body. In the case where a claim to rebirth is made, this is not so.

If a paranormal explanation is to be preferred, 'rebirth', therefore, appears to be more plausible than the others, the data being what they are. But the data presented in Rev. Martin's book do not clearly rule out the possibility of explanation in terms of fantasy or self-deception, as defined above, unless it can be shown and not merely stated that specific items of knowledge regarding the past were not available to the subject in the course of his present life (for which in this book we have merely to take the author'; word). This can be shown to be so in some of the better documented case-studies, which we shall take up now.

As we said earlier, the evidence for rebirth (which is only a special case of re-becoming) falls into three categories: (1) the experimental evidence, (2) the spontaneous evidence and (3) the other evidence.

## THE EXPERIMENTAL EVIDENCE

We have already given samples of the experimental evidence. However, one may criticise these experiments as not being conducted under strictly controlled conditions, although the author mentions several precautions he had taken to eliminate subjective bias.

Let us now take examples where the experimental controls appear to have been more satisfactory. In the case investigated by Professor Theodore Flournoy, the account given reads as follows:

'It appeared the Helene Smith had twice lived upon the earth before her present incarnation. Once five hundred years ago as an Arab chief's daughter, (Simandini by name) she became the favourite wife of a Hindu prince. This prince, Sivrouka, reigned over the kingdom of Kanara, and constructed, in 1401, the fortress of Tchandragiri. This romance was developed with a wealth of detail; and the astonishing features of it were first, that research in old and little-known books on Indian history confirmed some of the details, such as the names of places and persons described; secondly, that Simandini uttered (in the trance automatisms) many Hindu words and phrases, sometimes appropriately used, sometimes mingled with other words which the experts failed to identify, and wrote also similar phrases in Arabic script. Further, the entranced medium would act the role of Simandini, putting other members of the circle into the vacant places of the drama.' (See William McDougall, *An Outline of Abnormal Psychology*, Reprint, 1952, p. 511.)

In the professor's own words: 'All this various mimicry and this exotic speech have so strongly the marks of originality, of ease, of naturalness, that one asks with stupefaction whence comes to this daughter of Lake Leman, without artistic training and without special knowledge of the Orient, a perfection of art which the best of actresses might attain only at the cost of prolonged studies or by residence on the banks of the Ganges' (ibid., pp. 511–12).

The professor confesses that he has not been able to resolve the mystery especially the Hindu language and the historical statements about the kingdom of Kanara, which were verified in an old and rare book to which the subject had had no access. Yet he concludes that the 'Hindu drama was a subconsciously elaborated fantasy, incorporating very skilfully fragments of knowledge picked up in haphazard fashion' (ibid., p. 512).

His explanation is the standard one resorted to by most

orthodox psychologists when confronted with evidence of this sort, namely that here we get only dramatisation and role-playing based on elements of information picked up in this life. Professor Flournoy is, however, constrained to 'admit that some knowledge was displayed, the acquisition of which by normal means would seem to have been well-nigh impossible' (ibid., p. 515).

Yet, this does not seem to explain the ease, the spontaneity and accuracy with which she sang Hindi (Prakritic) songs and wrote in a Prakritic script. Nor does it explain the factual information she gave, the claim she made that she was in fact the wife of a Hindu prince in her previous life and the serial account of the life and the incidents she gave.

Let us take another case, the case of Mrs Anne Baker, reported by Dr Jonathan Rodney (*Explorations of a Hypnotist*, Elek Books, London, 1955). Mrs Baker, a Lancashire housewife who has never studied French or been to France and whose education was very ordinary, spoke perfect French under hypnosis, referred to the death of Marie Antoniette as if it had just happened, gave her name as Marielle Pacasse and spoke of a street named Rue de St Pierre near Notre-Dame Cathedral.

Subsequent investigations revealed that the name Marielle is rare now but was much in vogue about 1794 and although there was no such street at present, there was in fact a street of that name in the vicinity 170 years back (see pp. 165–6). Here again a normal explanation would not do. Apart from the knowledge of French, one would have to say that the knowledge about the streets of Paris about two centuries back was either acquired clairvoyantly or telepathically from the dead.

An explanation in terms of spirit-possession is also possible though highly improbable. One could say that the discarnate spirit of the dead Marielle Pacasse now inhabits the body of Mrs Baker. Normally, in the case of spirit-possession, the discarnate spirit claims to be a separate personality and possession is not continuous, whereas in this case, whenever Mrs Baker was hypnotised, she claimed to be Marielle Pacasse in her previous life. So to account for all the facts, 'rebirth' is the simpler paranormal hypothesis.

Another case which cannot pass unnoticed is the famous 'Bridey Murphy' case. When Mrs Virginia Tighe was hypnotised on six occasions between November 1952 and August 1953, she recalled a life as Bridey Murphy in Ireland. It created a wide interest in 'rebirth'. It will be interesting to see Professor C. J. Ducasse's assessment of the case when it first came into the limelight and later after careful reflection in the light of the verified facts.

In an opinion published in *Tomorrow* (Vol. 4, No. 4, pp. 31–3) in 1956, soon after the case became known, Professor Ducasse suggests three hypotheses to account for it:

'That the former is a reincarnation of the latter is *one* hypothesis that would account for the veridicality of those details. A *second* hypothesis that would also account for their veridicality is that of illusion of memory; that is, the hypothesis that Mrs Tighe, in childhood or later, heard or read of the life of an Irish Bridey Murphy and then forgot this; and that, under hypnosis, the ideas so acquired were recalled by Mrs Tighe, but not the manner in which she had acquired them: and hence that they were indistinguishable by her from memories of events of a life of her own. A *third* hypothesis, which would also explain the veridicality of the verified details is that while in deep hypnosis, Mrs Tighe exercises powers of paranormal retro-cognition latent at other times, and vastly more far-reaching than those whose reality has been experimentally proved by Rhine, Soal, and others.'

Going on the assumption that Mrs Tighe's knowledge of Ireland was erroneous (as was thought at the time), Ducasse favoured the *second* hypothesis.

Later, when further investigations vindicated the truth of

Mrs Tighe's statements and the attempts at 'debunking' the 'rebirth' theory were seen to be mainly inspired by religious prejudice and based on false assertions, Professor Ducasse changed his views and favoured the *first* hypothesis (i.e. rebirth) without ruling out the possibility of the third. He does so in his book, *A Critical Examination of the Belief in a Life after Death*, Springfield, Illinois, 1961.

Here he refers to the items mentioned by Bridey, which could not be easily explained away. One of the most significant was that in her previous life she bought foodstuffs from Farrs and John Carrigan. Extensive research on the part of Mr John Bebbington, Belfast Chief Librarian, disclosed the fact that these two grocers were found listed in a Belfast city directory for 1865–6. Besides, they were 'the only individuals of those names engaged in the "foodstuffs" business' there at the time.

Bridey also referred to a rope company and a tobacco house, which were in operation in Belfast at the time, and this too was found to be correct. Another remarkable fact was that Bridey's statements, which according to experts on Ireland were irreconcilable with known facts, were shown after further investigation not to be so. Ten such facts are listed To take one example, one was to the effect that her husband taught law at the Queen's University in Belfast sometime after 1847. *Life Magazine*, on the basis of so-called expert opinion, attacked this on the ground that there was no law school there at the time, no Queen's *College* until 1846, and no Queen's *University* until 1908. However, further investigation showed that this was incorrect. There was documentary evidence to show that on 19 December 1845, Queen Victoria ordained that 'there shall and may be erected . . . one College for students in Arts, Law, Physic . . . which shall be called Queen's College, Belfast' (op. cit., p. 286). 'The Queen's University in Ireland' was founded by her on 15 August 1850 (ibid.).

Such accuracy may be due to either extraordinary clairvoyant powers on the part of the subject or to the simple fact that these were genuine memories of her past life. Since she did not display any such clairvoyant powers in other respects during hypnosis, the latter appears to be the more plausible explanation.

## SPONTANEOUS EVIDENCE

The spontaneous evidence consists of accounts given by individuals, mostly children, of their alleged prior lives, which when subsequently checked prove to be historical and accurate and could not have been derived from any normal source in this life.

There are several such cases from all over the world and reports of them are to be found in newspapers and magazines. But in coming to valid conclusions on their basis one has to rely on the trustworthy verified accounts of scientists. The evidence should be first recorded without bias and one should then see what theory best accounts for the data.

In this respect, one of the best studies so far is that of Dr Ian Stevenson. He makes a detailed study and evaluation of twenty cases in one of his books (*Twenty Cases Suggestive of Reincarnation*, New York, 1966, pp. x and 362).

Let us briefly review the case of Imad Elawar, as studied and reported in this book. Imad was born on 21 December 1958 at Kornayel and talked of a previous life when he was between a year and a half and two years old. He mentioned a considerable number of names of people and some events in this prior life as well as about certain items of property he claimed to have owned. He said he lived in the village of Khriby and had the name Bouhamzy. He had a woman (mistress) called Jamille, who was beautiful and a 'brother' called Amin, who lived at Tripoli, etc.

The father, however, discredited the story and scolded Imad for talking about an imaginary past life. Once, it is said, he even recognised a resident (Salim el Aschkar) of Khriby in the presence of his paternal grandmother. The parents attached more importance to Imad's statements after this. But no systematic attempt to verify the authenticity of Imad's statements were made until Dr Ian Stevenson undertook to investigate the case.

Khriby was situated about twenty-five miles away from Imad's home. The road from Kornayel was an extremely winding mountain road. The items were carefully recorded prior to the investigations at Khriby. It was ultimately revealed that of the fifty-seven items mentioned, fifty-one were correct. In Dr Stevenson's own words: 'Of the fifty-seven items in the first tabulation, Imad made ten of the statements in the car on the way to Khriby before we reached that village. But of these ten, three were incorrect. Of the remaining forty-seven items, Imad was wrong on only three items. It seems quite possible that under the excitement of the journey, and perhaps sensing some expectation of hearing more statements on our part, he mixed up images of the "previous life" and memories of his "present life". In any case, his "score" for this group of statements definitely fell below that for the forty-seven made before we left Khriby' (ibid., pp. 257–71).

Some of the items were very specific, as when he said that they were building a new garden at the time of his death and that there were cherry and apple trees in it, that he had a small yellow automobile, a bus, etc.

Besides the verification of these items of information, there were significant recognitions of persons and places, sixteen of which are listed. For example, we may note the recognition of the place where Ibrahim Bouhamzy (the previous personality) kept his dog and his gun. He also recognised the sister of Ibrahim, namely Huda, and the portrait of Ibrahim's brother Fuad. He was also able, it is said, to recall his last words before death, which his sister, Mrs Huda Bouhamzy, remembered and which were, 'Huda, call Fuad.'

When we consider the above as well as the similarity in the character traits between the previous and the present personalities, chance-coincidence has to be virtually ruled out. Since neither fraud, self-deception or racial memory could account for the evidence, a paranormal explanation is called for. And of all the different paranormal explanations, such as telepathy-cum-clairvoyance plus personation, spirit-possessions, etc., rebirth appears to be the most plausible. This was, in fact, Dr Stevenson's own general conclusion after studying several cases of this type.

In the spontaneous case there is no hypnotist to put any suggestion into the mind of the child. We may say, however, that the child's beliefs about a prior life are a product of his fantasy. But such an explanation ceases to be feasible in the above instances, when the so-called 'fantasies' turn out to be historically true and they were not derived from any source in this life.

## OTHER EVIDENCE

We have already referred to other evidence for rebirth when we tried to suggest that temperamental differences in identical twins, which cannot be due to heredity and environment, may be accounted for in terms of the impact of the psychological past of the person, which goes back into prior lives. We have also seen how some phobias prevalent in this life have not only been traced to traumatic experience in prior lives but have been cured by re-living the experience and discovering the origin of it.

Although it is possible to give other explanations of the so-called *déja-vu* experiences, the experience of feeling 'I have been here before', some of them, at least, seem to point to or call for an explanation in terms of pre-existence. There is a recorded case of an American couple, who found that some parts of Bombay were extremely familiar to them, despite the fact that they were visiting the place for the first time. To test their knowledge, it is said, they went to a certain spot, where they expected to see a house and a banyan tree in the garden. They, however, did not find them but were told by a policemen in the vicinity that he recalled having heard from his father that they had been there and that the house belonged to a family named Bhan. Curiously, this couple had called their son Bhan, because they liked the name. (W. C. White, 'Cruise Memory', *Beyond the Five Senses*, ed. E. J. Garrett, J. B. Lipincott, New York, 1957; cited by Dr Stevenson). Such stories are, however, anecdotal and one cannot attach much importance to them. They are of value only when one is certain of their authenticity.

Dr Raynor C. Johnson suggests that certain recurrent dreams may be memories of experiences had in prior lives (see *A Religious Outlook for Modern Man*, Hodder & Stoughton, London, 1963, pp. 184ff.). A brief excerpt from an account of one such dream reads as follows:

'The dream was of being a prisoner in a place that I knew to be the Tower of London. I had not seen it in real life, but I had no doubt where I was. It was very cold weather (in waking life, a hot summer). I was aware that I had been condemned to death . . . This, I used to dream over and over again, and after being in the dream a vigorous man, to wake up and be a little girl felt rather strange. At last the dream changed, and I was standing on a scafford which must have been newly erected as it smelt of sawdust. Everything was decorous and decent. The executioner knelt and apologised for what he was about to do. I took the axe from his hand and felt it, and handed it back, bidding him do his duty . . . When I woke up I made a drawing of the axe, which was of a peculiar shape. Some time after this I asked to be taken to the Tower of London, and I explained to a friendly gunsmith that I wanted to write history but could not understand the battles perfectly until I understood the weapons. "You are right, Missy," he said, and demonstrated to me the various uses of pike, lance, crossbow, etc. I then asked had he an axe that beheaded people? He said, "Yes, this certainly beheaded the

Jacobite Lords, but it is supposed to be very much older." Somehow, I was not surprised that it proved to be the exact shape of the axe in my dream . . .'

Here again we can suggest that this is not the only explanation possible but when we read about several such dreams one begins to wonder whether they are not a hang-over from one's past-life experiences.

We have further evidence for rebirth from clairvoyants. The best attested case in the twentieth century is that of Mr Edgar Cayce. A general account of his life and doings is to be found in a book by Dr Gina Cerminara (*Many Mansions*, William Sloane Associates, New York, 1950, Twelfth Printing 1964, p. 304).

There is good evidence that Cayce had remarkable clairvoyant powers, with which he successfully diagnosed illnesses even without actually seeing the patient. But what is more remarkable is that he went on to give accounts of the prior lives of some of these individuals (some of which were historically verified). He also gave the alleged karmic causes of their present illnesses.

We have already seen how suicide had certain karmic effects in subsequent lives. Cayce in his readings (which are still preserved and are available for study at the Association for Research and Enlightenment, Virginia Beach, U.S.A.) records the different kinds of karmic effects following in the wake of the different kinds of actions done in the past. In one case, it is said, a person was born blind in this life because in his third life previous to this, *circa* 1000 B C, he was born in Persia as 'a member of a barbaric tribe whose custom was to blind its enemies with red-hot irons, and it had been his office to do the blinding' (ibid., pp. 50–1).

13

# The Conditioned Genesis of the Individual

The term paṭicca-samuppāda denotes, in general, the Buddhist theory of causality. Here we are concerned with the special sense of this term, which came to denote the conditioned genesis of the individual. In this special sense, the term is used to denote the factors which condition and result in the process called 'the individual' in the course of his saṃsāric existence.

There are four related senses in which the term is used.

First, it is used to denote what are known as the two principles of causal determination. Stated in an abstract and logical form, it reads as follows: 'this being so, that is so' (asmiṃ sati idaṃ hoti) and 'this not being so, that is not so' (asmiṃ asati idaṃ na hoti), i.e. whenever A, then B, and whenever not A, then not B. This may be called the Abstract Formula of Causal Determination.

Secondly, it is used to denote the two principles of causal determination stated in a dynamic form as having application to the world of concrete reality: 'this arising, that arises' (imass'upp dā idaṃ uppajjati) and 'this not arising, that does not arise'. This may be called the Concrete Formula of Causal Determination.

Thirdly, it is used to denote the causal laws which operate in nature, whether they be physical laws (utu-niyāma), biological laws (bīja-niyāma), psychological laws (citta-niyāma), etc.

Finally, the word is used in a special sense to denote the causal laws which operate in bringing about the continued genesis of the individual. Here we are concerned primarily with this last sense of the term.

However, we must not forget that we cannot understand the full significance of this special use of the term to denote the conditioned genesis of the individual without calling to mind its general meaning.

We may recall here that Buddhism steers clear of the two extremes of strict Determinism as well as of total Indeterminism. At the time of the rise of Buddhism, there were thinkers who held the view that changes took place in nature without any pattern at all. According to them, all changes were haphazard, fortuitous, accidental and were due entirely to chance. These were the Indeterminists.

On the other hand, there were thinkers who were utterly opposed to this point of view. They not only held that there was a definite pattern in the nature of the changes that took place, but argued that this pattern was rigidly determined. Among these rigid Determinists were Theists who argued that, since the world was created by an omniscient and omnipotent God, all events (including the actions of human beings) are due to the will of God. Besides theistic determinism, there was the Natural Determinism of the Naturalists (svabhāva-vāda), according to whom everything that happened in nature was strictly determined by natural forces. In addition, there was karmic determinism, according to which everything that happened to a person was due entirely to his past karma (pubba-kamma-vāda).

The Buddhist theory of causality was opposed to both these extreme points of view: to Indeterminism, which denied any pattern altogether, as well as to the theistic and naturalistic forms of Strict Determinism, according to which there was a rigid pattern over which man had no control.

Buddhism is, therefore, opposed to the view that there is only the play of chance in the manifestation of phenomena, as also to the views that everything is due to the will of God or to the operations of rigid deterministic laws of nature.

These ideas are important when we come to study the doctrine of the conditioned genesis of the individual. What happens to the individual and the changes wrought in him are not arbitrary and due to chance, nor are they due to the will of God nor, again, to the operation of rigid physical, bio-chemical and economic laws of nature over which he has no control at all. In keeping with the Buddhist theory of causality, man is *conditioned* by various factors, hereditary, psychological and environmental, but he is not *determined* by them.

Buddhism also avoided explanations in terms of agents, whether human or extra-human. Thus to say that pleasure and pain were caused by the agency of one's own soul or by an external agency such as God, or by one's own soul or self as well as by God, are all erroneous. On the other hand, to say that pleasure and pain were uncaused is equally erroneous. So all the following four alternatives are discarded as unsatisfactory, viz.

1. Pleasure and pain were caused by one's own self (sayaṃ-kataṃ sukha-dukkhaṃ)
2. Pleasure and pain were caused by an external agency paraṃ-kataṃ sukha-dukkhaṃ)
3. Pleasure and pain were caused both by the self as well as by an external agency (sayaṃ-kataṃ ca paraṃ-kataṃ ca sukha-dukkhaṃ).
4. Pleasure and pain were not due to the self or an external agency but were *fortuitous* (adhicca-samuppanna), i.e. uncaused.

According to the Buddhist theory, pleasure and pain were causally conditioned (paṭicca-samuppanna). They may be causally conditioned by the physical environment, by the physiological condition of the body, by the social environment, by one's own present actions or by karma (or by any combination of them). So explanations are given in terms of causally conditioned factors without recourse to metaphysical concepts such as a soul or some sort of agency.

This idea is brought out in the *Śālistamba Sūtra*. Here it is said that although 'the element of heat' (tejo-dhatuḥ) is a causal factor in making a seed grow, it does not do this out of its own will: 'It does not occur to the element of heat "I shall bring this seed to maturity"' (*Ārya Śālistamba Sūtra*). Although the *Śālistamba Sūtra* is a Mahāyāna Sūtra, the same idea is to be found in the *Aṅguttara Nikāya* with regard to psychological causation. Here it is said that 'a person who lacks remorse need not make an act of will (to the effect) "let joy arise in me". For, it is of the nature of things that joy arises to one who lacks remorse' (A. V. 2). So, even in psychological causation, a conscious act of will was not always considered necessary in bringing about a subsequent psychological state.

In one place the Buddha points out that to say that 'the experience and the one who experiences are one and the same' (sā vedanā so vediyatīti . . ., S. II. 23), and therefore that the experience of pleasure and pain are one's own creation, is one extreme point of view. To say that 'the experience and the one who experiences are different' (aññā vedanā añño vediyatīti . . .), and therefore that the experience of pleasure and pain are due to an external agency, is the other extreme point of view. The Buddha, it is said in this context, avoids these extreme points of view which do not correctly represent the facts, and teaches the doctrine in the middle by means of conditioned genesis.

So the doctrine of conditioned genesis attempts to explain phenomena, as in science, in terms of causal correlations without recourse to explanations in terms of first causes or metaphysical substances such as a soul or agent.

In some of the pre-Buddhistic Upaniṣads, which taught the doctrine of rebirth and karma (though not exactly in the

Buddhist sense), an attempt is made to explain rebirth and karma by having recourse to the doctrine of the soul, which was the common factor (as the unchanging agent) in the different lives of the individual. It was the agent of all actions as well as the recipient of reactions. So it was the same unchanging agent, which caused the actions and experienced their reactions.

These Eternalists who posited the persistence of an unchanging agent or ātman were opposed by the Materialists who denied the continuity of individuality altogether by saying that one who undergoes experiences in this life was different altogether from any previous person. The Buddha avoids these two extremes by means of the doctrine of conditioned genesis. The *Saṃyutta Nikāya* states: 'In the belief that a person who acts is the same as the person who experiences . . . he posits Eternalism. In the belief that the person who acts is different from a person who experiences . . . he posits Materialism. Avoiding both these extremes, the Transcendent One preaches the doctrine in the middle: "Ignorance conditions volitional acts . . ." ' (S. I. 20, 21).

So we see that the doctrine of conditioned genesis tries to explain phenomena in terms of causal correlations without assuming the existence of metaphysical entities like a 'soul'.

It is, at the same time, an explanation of the origin and cessation of suffering or the unsatisfactory nature of conditioned existence. After stating the whole series of inter-related phenomena such as 'ignorance conditions volitional acts, etc.', it is concluded: 'In this manner there arises this mass of suffering . . . and in this manner there ceases this mass of suffering' (S. II. 21).

We find in other religions and philosophies that many explanations of the present condition of the individual are in terms of metaphysical first causes or final causes. The theists try to explain the condition of the individual by asserting that the individual is a creation of God considered as a first cause. The materialists try to account for the individual in terms of purely material factors considered as a first cause in the evolution of the world. The dualists, as in Saṅhkya philosophy, assume two primordial first causes such as Matter (Prakṛti) and Spirit (Puruṣa).

Yet, in the doctrine of conditioned genesis, ignorance (avijjā) is not a first cause in this sense. In this way, too, the doctrine is an attempt to explain phenomena 'in the middle' without recourse to first causes or final causes. Explanations in terms of a first cause posit a cause such as God or Matter in the beginning of time, and explanations in terms of final causes try to explain things in terms of ultimate ends such as a goal or purpose, which things serve. But, in the doctrine of conditioned genesis, there are no first or final causes.

Ignorance is not a first cause, although it is selected as a convenient starting point to explain a series of inter-connected phenomena.

'Ignorance' is to be found here and now in the present. It constitutes the sum-total of our erroneous beliefs, as well as true beliefs not amounting to knowledge, about the nature and destiny of man in the universe. We cannot know the first beginnings of such ignorance on the part of beings in an oscillating universe which expands and contracts without beginning or end. But we can know that our present ignorance is causally conditioned and that, by acquiring full knowledge and realisation of our nature and destiny, we can put an end to our ignorance even in the present. As stated in the texts: 'The first beginning of ignorance is not known (such that we may say) that before this there was no ignorance and at this point ignorance arose . . . but that ignorance is causally conditioned (idappaccayā avijjā) can be known' (A. V. 113).

Ignorance is, therefore, not conceived as a first cause except in the purely relative sense that we may start with ignorance, which is itself (as we shall see) conditioned by other factors. It is said that anyone who understands the causal process in the genesis and development of the individual would not seek for explanations in terms of first causes or uses. After enumerating the doctrine of conditioned , the Buddha asks the monks on one occasion the ng rhetorical question: 'Would you, O monks, knowing and seeing thus, probe [literally, run behind] the prior end of things . . . or pursue [literally, run after] the final end of things?'

Buddhism starts with the present and explains specific phenomena in terms of general laws. This is also what the scientists try to do in their investigations into the nature of phenomena in their respective branches of study. In doing so, it does not try to give explanations in terms of first causes or other such univerifiable metaphysical entities. This is the distinctive contribution of Buddhism in its investigation of phenomena concerned with man's nature and destiny.

This is why the doctrine of causal genesis is considered to be the central teaching of Buddhism. It contains the truth about the nature of the individual and his destiny as discovered by the Buddha in the final stage of his enlightenment. In a stanza which was widely known, it is said that 'the Transcendent One speaks of the causes of conditioned events which arise from causes'. In one place the Buddha says: 'He who sees the doctrine of conditioned genesis, sees the Dhamma, and he who sees the Dhamma, sees conditioned genesis' (M. I. 191).

It unfolds the predicament of man as he is found in the present, conditioned (but not determined) by his past experiences going back into prior lives, by heredity and the physiological condition of the body, the impact of the environment, physical and ideological, and the different kinds of desires which rage within him.

The explanation of specific events in the history of specific individuals is in terms of general causal laws or correlations. As we shall see when we examine this in detail, the statement, 'ignorance conditions our volitional activities' (avijjā paccayā saṅkhārā) shows how our erroneous beliefs as well as our true beliefs (not amounting to knowledge) about the nature and destiny of the individual along with other factors condition our good and evil volitional actions of body, speech and mind. It is a statement whose truth can be at least partially verified by us when the different kinds of relations which hold between our 'beliefs' and 'good and evil volitional acts' are clarified.

Such relations between 'beliefs' and 'volitional acts' hold whether we observe or discover them, and whether we approve or disapprove of them. Such correlations are objective, for 'causation has the characteristics of objectivity (tathatā), empirical necessity (avitathatā), invariability (anaññathatā) and conditionality (idappaccayatā)' (S. II. 26). Hot things tend to get cold and cold things hot in a closed system, whether scientists observe or discover this and approve or disapprove of it. Those who observe such phenomena tend to deduce from them general causal laws.

In a similar fashion the Buddha states: 'Whether Transcendent Ones arise or not, this order exists namely the fixed nature of phenomena, the regular pattern of phenomena or conditionality. This the Transcendent One discovers and comprehends; having discovered and comprehended it, he points it out, teaches it, lays it down, establishes, reveals, analyses, clarifies it and says, "look!" ' (S. II. 25).

This unique and central teaching of Buddhism was described by the Buddha as a doctrine which was 'not only profound (gambhīro) but appears profound' (D. II. 55). It is the failure to penetrate and realise this doctrine that has prevented beings enmeshed in saṃsaric existence from transcending the limitations of conditioned existence, which necessarily involves birth in lower realms of beings.

It is not surprising, therefore, that the majority of scholars who approached the study of this doctrine with the preconceptions of other religions and metaphysical systems failed altogether to understand it.

The mistake that many of them (e.g. Jacobi, Pischel, Schayer) made was to think of Ignorance as the first cause in an evolutionary series accounting for the beginning and the development of cosmic phenomena emerging from the chaos of ignorance. Others thought of ignorance as the childhood condition of man and the series as representing stages in the growth of man beginning with birth and culminating with his death. Yet others (Kern) considered ignorance as the state of sleep and the rest as what happens when we gradually awaken from sleep.

A sympathetic scholar of Buddhism, Dr Paul Dahlke, who had some remarkable insights into aspects of Buddhist philosophy, thought that 'the whole chain of the conditions of origination represents one single karmical moment of personal experience'. This, no doubt, leads to contradictions, as the Ven. Nyanatiloka pointed out (see *Guide Through the Abhidhamma Piṭaka*, Colombo, 1957, p. 158). For if we say this, we find, for instance, that birth (jāti) as well as decay and death (jarāmaraṇa) must take place at one and the same moment! Dalhke seems to have been aware of these contradictions and the difficulties involved in his interpretation, for he speaks of 'the apparent lack of logic, nay, the apparent contradictions' within the series. A local Buddhist scholar quotes this statement and adds, 'To this statement of Dahlke the writer is ever so grateful', since he himself could not comprehend the traditional explanation.

The reason for his failure to comprehend the traditional explanation is interesting, since it is a common source of error. He says: 'Unless I can comprehend the paṭicca-samuppāda as applicable in all its links to that reality which only is accessible to me – my present living – and, thereby, prove to myself its validity, I am afraid it is something that I will have to take upon faith.'

The traditional explanation breaks up the twelve links into three lives, the first two being in the past, the next eight in the present and the last two in the future. Yet, to imply that the past and the future are not accessible to me in the present, is not correct since the present life, from the point of view of the past, is the future, and from the point of view of the future life, is the past. So we do not have to take the first two links or the last two on faith since they can be experienced in this life itself. We can be aware of our ignorance here and now, although ignorance was also present in our past life. What has to be taken on faith is the linkage between the past and the present as well as the past and the future.

Such faith is Buddhistic since it is a 'rational faith' (ākāravatī saddhā) which can be replaced with knowledge or realisation, when one can develop the capacity to see one's past lives. If all that is taught in Buddhism must be accessible to our present experience, then there would be no necessity to develop 'higher knowledge' (abhiññā) or extra-sensory forms of experience.

All this does not mean that there are no scholars who have given a correct explanation of the doctrine of conditioned genesis. The one given by the Ven. Nyanatiloka is the best and the most authentic that I have seen so far.

This doctrine of causal conditioning should not seem so strange in a world dominated by science, which tries to explain specific phenomena as being causally conditioned in the light of general laws without recourse to metaphysical substances or agents or primordial first causes. However, as we have pointed out, we must not lose sight of the fact that 'causal conditioning' as taught in Buddhism is not deterministic. So, despite the fact that we are conditioned by our psychological past, by heredity (bīja-niyāma) and by the environmental present, both physical and ideological, we have an element of initiative or freedom (ārabbha-dhatū) by the exercise of which we can change the course of the future.

Yet, at the same time, we must not forget that no other doctrine has been so misunderstood and misinterpreted by scholars, some of whom were sympathetic towards Buddhism. If we take the first sentence of the formulae describing the nature of the conditioning of the individual, viz. 'Ignorance conditions our volitional activities' (avijjā paccayā saṅkhārā) we find that most scholars took 'Ignorance' as a primordial first cause, despite the fact that this is explicitly denied in the Buddhist texts. For them, 'Ignorance' was the original state of unconscious existence in the beginning prior to evolution. With the process of evolution, there was blind groping on the part of all things or beings, but still no conscious awareness or purpose in their actions. So 'avijjā paccayā saṅkhārā' was interpreted to mean that a 'state of original ignorance was followed by that of blind groping' in the history of evolution.

Another such 'explanation' is that by 'ignorance' is meant a 'state of deep sleep', while 'activities' refer to our semi-conscious activity, which follows our awakening from sleep. Still another 'explanation', which is favoured by some Ceylonese scholars, is that 'ignorance', 'activities', as well as all the factors referred to in the formulae, such as 'birth' and 'death', co-exist in every single moment of our existence!

However interesting all these 'explanations' may be, they are all contradicted by, and are not consonant with, what is found in the early Buddhist texts and the interpretations of Buddhist tradition. It would, therefore, be wiser on our part to examine the explanations actually given in the Buddhist texts.

## THE TEXTUAL EXPLANATION

What does avijjā paccayā saṅkhārā actually mean? To understand this sentence it is necessary that one should, at least, understand what these words mean.

What is meant by avijjā? Or, as the question is posed in the texts themselves, katamā ca avijjā? The answer given is that 'by ignorance is meant lack of knowledge with regard to the unsatisfactoriness of things (dukkhe aññāṇaṃ), lack of knowledge with regard to the cause of the unsatisfactoriness of thinks, lack of knowledge with regard to the cessation of this sense of unsatisfactoriness and lack of knowledge with regard to the path leading to this cessation' (S. II. 4).

The word saṅkhārā, on the other hand, means 'volitional acts'. Although scholars have given all sorts of arbitrary translations of this term, its meaning has been clearly defined in the *Vibhaṅga* (P.T.S. Text, p. 135). Here it is said that saṅkhārā), constitute, (1) meritorious volitional actions (puññabhisaṅkhārā), (2) demeritorious volitional actions (apuññabhisaṅkhārā) and (3) imperturbable volitional actions (āneñjābhisaṅkhārā). These are subdivided into those which find expression through the body (kāya-saṅkhārā), speech (vacīsaṅkhārā) and the mind (mano-saṅkhārā).

Let us leave aside the imperturbable volitional actions, which are defined as 'good volitional acts which occur in the states of impersonal mystical consciousness or arūpa-jhāna' (kusalā cetanā arūpāvacarā).

We then have meritorious volitional actions of body, speech and mind as well as demeritorious volitional actions of body, speech and mind. The meritorious volitional acts are defined in the *Vibhaṅga as* 'acts of good intention (kusalā cetanā) pertaining to the sensuous material world and the subtle material world, consisting of acts of charity (dāna), restraint (sīla) and mental culture (bhāvanā)'. The demeritorious volitional acts are defined as 'acts of evil intention (akusalā cetanā) pertaining to the sensuous material world (kāmāvacarā)'.

If we help someone in distress, do a charitable deed, say what we believe to be true, especially when this is helpful to others and not so helpful for ourselves, act with benevolence, even towards our enemies, then we are doing morally good actions or meritorious volitional acts. If, on the other hand, we cause harm to others out of malice, appropriate other people's property by fraudulent means, indulge in slander and hate people who may criticise us, then we are doing morally evil acts or demeritorious volitional actions.

Now what the above statement says is that our lack of knowledge concerning the four noble truths conditions our good and evil volitional acts. Lack of knowledge concerning the four noble truths is lack of knowledge concerning the nature and possible destiny of man in the universe. We lack knowledge concerning the nature and possible destiny of man in the universe when we entertain erroneous beliefs about man and his destiny in the universe and also when we have true beliefs about man and his destiny in the universe merely on the grounds of faith, whether rational or blind. The erroneous beliefs cannot be reckoned as knowledge because they are erroneous, and the true beliefs because they are mere beliefs not amounting to knowledge.

It is a fact that our beliefs condition our volitional acts. Many people, especially in the modern world, in the firm belief that this is the only life, do not believe that we are in any way responsible or accountable for our actions. Opportunism, expediency, the continued indulgence in the pleasures of sense and sex in the quest for pleasure as well as the multiplication and gratification of desires for the same end constitute their pattern of life. It is true that this kind of living, for from giving happiness, results in boredom, anxiety, conflict and tension. Yet, for them, the beliefs of all religions are superstitions of a by-gone age. Moral values do not exist. Their beliefs about the nature of man and the amoral ethic which accompanies these beliefs make them commit what is reckoned to be evil with impunity.

On the other hand, there are those who believe that good actions have their reward in an after-life and do good in the hope of attaining a better life in the next existence or in a heaven. So both good and evil actions are conditioned by our beliefs which may be true or false.

## CAUSAL CORRELATION

According to Buddhism, those who act in the belief that there is no after-life or that there is an after-life are guided by ignorance. Those who deny an after-life are ignorant of the fact that there is one. On the other hand, those who merely believe in an after-life do not have knowledge of the fact. Both lack knowledge about the nature and destiny of man and are impelled by ignorance. Though impelled by ignorance, their actions are not strictly determined by ignorance since man has within himself the capacity to get rid of his ignorance.

So we see a causal correlation between 'ignorance' and 'volitional activities' such that 'whenever there is ignorance there is a tendency for volitional acts to come into being as a result of ignorance' (avijjāya kho sati saṅkhārā hoti, avijjā-paccayā saṅkhārā, S. II. 7), and that 'whenever there is no ignorance there are no volitional activities and with the cessation of ignorance there is a cessation of volitional activities' (ibid.). The Arahant or the perfect person does not experience the tensions of choice and decision which are involved in 'volitional actions'; his actions are purely spontaneous (kiriya-matta) and are good by nature without involving a tendency to fruition in subsequent lives.

It may appear paradoxical to some as to how good actions may be caused by ignorance. There is no doubt that the early texts quite explicitly state that good as well as evil volitional actions can be performed under the influence of ignorance. It is said: 'When a person under the influence of ignorance performs a meritorious volitional act, his consciousness tends to become meritorious; if he performs a demeritorious act, his consciousness tends to become demeritorious' (avijjāgato yam purisa-puggalo puññaṃ ce saṅkhāraṃ abhisaṅkharoti, puññūpagaṃ hoti viññāṇaṃ . . .) (S. II. 82).

The question is posed rhetorically by Buddhaghosa in his *Visuddhimagga* (P.T.S. Text, p. 543), viz. 'How can ignorance which has a decidedly undesirable effect and is blameworthy be the cause for meritorious action . . . ? How can sugar-cane issue from a nimb-seed?' Buddhaghoṣa's answer is that there need not be a similarity between cause and effect, and therefore 'this ignorance though it may have a decidedly undesirable result and is blameworthy in its intrinsic nature should be considered as a cause, so far as possible, of all meritorious actions . . .'. Earlier, Buddhaghoṣa illustrates how this happens in the case of ignorance: 'Craving for becoming is the specific condition of action which leads to a happy fate. Wherefore? Because the average man, overcome by the craving for becoming, strives to do the various kinds of deeds leading to a happy fate such as abstinence from taking life . . .' (ibid., p. 525).

In a pictorial representation of the 'wheel of becoming' (bhava-cakra) in an Ajanta painting (seventh-century), 'ignorance' is depicted as a 'blind man with a stick'. This is a very apt portrayal of the role of ignorance. Some stanzas from the ancient teachers (porāṇā) of the Buddhist tradition throw light on this illustration. They are quoted by Buddhaghoṣa in the *Visuddhimagga* and along with his preamble, the passage reads as follows:

'Blinded by ignorance, he is like a blind man who wanders about the earth, encountering now right and now wrong paths, now heights and now hollows, now even and now uneven ground and so he performs acts now of merit, now of demerit and now imperturbable. Hence it is said:

As one born blind who gropes along
Without assistance from a guide,
Chooses a road that may be right
At one time, at another wrong,
So while the ignorant man pursues
The round of births without a guide,
Now to do merit he may choose
And now demerit in such plight.
But when the Dhamma he comes to know
And penetrates the Truths beside,
Then Ignorance is put to flight
At last, and in peace would he abide' (ibid., p. 544).

We may note that the blind man with the stick sometimes goes on wrong paths and sometimes on the right path, though he may not know that it is the right path. 'Volitional activities' are here depicted as 'a potter with wheel and pots'. This, again, is an apt illustration. These activities of ours are motivated partly by physiological and psychological causes, of which we are not fully aware. All we do in turning them into 'volitional activities' is to give them a push or restrain their momentum as the potter does with his wheel.

ELABORATIONS

The different types of volitional activities, both good and evil, that we indulge in are well illustrated in a passage of the Saṃyutta Nikāya. According to the text, as a result of ignorance (avijjā-paccayā) we perform volitional acts of the body (kāya-saṅkhārā), of speech (vacī-) or of the mind (mano-), either of our own accord (sāmaṃ) or at the instigation of others (pare), with full awareness of what we are doing (sampajāna) or without full awareness of what we are doing (asampajāna) (S. II. 40).

While the earliest texts of the Pali Canon defines 'ignorance' as 'ignorance of the four noble truths' as stated above, we find further elaborations in the *Abhidhamma Piṭaka* and the Chinese Āgamas. In the *Dhamma-saṅgaṇi*, for instance, ignorance is defined not merely as ignorance of the four noble truths but as 'ignorance regarding the past (pubbante aññaṇa), ignorance regarding the future (aparante aññaṇa), ignorance regarding the past and the future, ignorance regarding the conditioned nature (idappaccayatā) of causally conditioned events (paṭicca-samuppannesu dhammesu)' (1,061). In the Chinese *Saṃyukta Āgama*, corresponding to the *Vibhaṅga Sutta* of the *Saṃyutta Nikāya* (S. II. 2–4) of the Pali Canon, there is mentioned in addition to the above 'ignorance of the interior, the exterior, both interior and exterior, action, consequence, both action and consequence, the Buddha, the Dhamma, the Saṅgha, etc.'. The Sanskrit version of this Sūtra was found in two brick inscriptions at Nālandā (see *Epigrapiha Indica*, XXI, pp. 179– 99).

These further elaborations are only extensions of the original concept. A person who lacks knowledge regarding the four noble truths may entertain a wide variety of false beliefs, or some if not all true beliefs about the nature and destiny of man in the universe. He may entertain or cling to any one of a variety of materialistic sceptical or eternalist beliefs about the nature and destiny of man. He may believe in a variety of causes for man's predicament. He may or may not believe in an ultimate goal of existence. Even if he does believe in a goal, he may not do so by treading the eight-fold path. He may believe that some goal is assured him by the grace of God or the necessity of evolution. He may not believe in causal conditioning, but instead hold to the view that the process of events in nature is entirely haphazard or one strictly determined by purely material causes. All these beliefs would have some impact on his values and volitional activities. This is what the statement, 'Ignorance conditions volitional activities' (avijjā paccayā saṅkhārā) implies.

Since only one view would be true, and an immense variety of views would be false, and we do not have knowledge of this one true view if it is a mere set of beliefs accepted on faith, we can imagine the extent of man's ignorance about his own condition, nature and destiny in the universe.

## ERRORS

There are certain errors one must guard against in the interpretation of the causal formulae, of which 'ignorance conditions volitional activities' is the first. It is not implied, as the texts quite clearly point out, that ignorance alone conditions our volitional acts. In Buddhist causal theory any causal situation is complex. What we pick out as a cause is only a predominant factor which operates along with other factors in bringing about an effect.

So is 'ignorance'. Ignorance is one of the 'impelling' or 'motivating' causes (hetu) of actions. The term 'hetu' is used in the *Abhidhamma* in this specialised sense of 'motivating cause'. The word is formed from the hu- 'to impel' with the suffix -tu and means 'impeller'. Among the factors that motivate man's actions – good, evil, mixed and neutral – are, on the one hand, greed, hatred and ignorance, and, on the other, their opposites, namely selflessness, compassion and understanding. So, alongside ignorance, motivating man's actions are the desires.

The desires and beliefs together condition man's actions. When we desire a cool drink and quench our thirst by taking one, we are impelled by both desires and beliefs. There is, on the one hand, the desire to drink or the thirst, which makes us restless and seek a drink. On the other hand, there are the beliefs (which may be true or false) that a drink may be had from the refrigerator, etc. So it is these two factors, namely desires and beliefs, which result in the activity, which constitutes the quest for a drink.

Likewise, just as much as 'ignorance conditions our volitional actions', it is said that 'volitional actions too reinforce our ignorance' (Saṅkhāra-paccayā pi avijjā, *Vibhaṅga Sutta*, 141). Supposing we do an evil act under the influence of our desires and false beliefs. The evil act in turn reinforces our false belief and makes it harder to dislodge. We try to justify our evil act, and the belief impelling it (hetu-paccaya), associated with it (sampayutta-paccaya) and supporting it (nissaya-paccaya) becomes a 'rationalisation' we cling to in the face of the evil act that we have done. If, for example, we scold someone in anger, we tend to hold and cling to the belief which led to the scolding, due to the tendency on our part to justify the scolding. So there is the relationship of 'mutual dependence' (aññamañña-paccaya) as well between 'ignorance' and 'volitional actions'. So the causal correlation between 'ignorance' and volitional actions' involves several 'relationships' (paccaya) between the two.

So the first statement of the causal formulae means that 'ignorance conditions our volitional actions' as explained above. A careful study of and reflection on our volitional actions will reveal the desires and beliefs (erroneous or otherwise) lurking behind them, and the truth of the above statement can thereby be verified.

## PARTIAL CONDITIONED EXPERIENCE

According to the Buddha, all this variety of opinion on this subject is due to the partial, relative and conditioned character of the thought of the thinkers who put forward these points of view. This is, in fact, what is said in the *Brahmajāla Suta*, where the Buddha has classified the main views that thinkers put forward with regard to the nature and destiny of man in the universe.

The Buddha says that the religious teachers and philosophers, who were Eternalists (Sassata-vādā), Semi-Eternalists (Ekacca-Sassatikā), such as the Theists (Īssara-nimmāna-vādā), who asserted that God was eternal while his creation was not, Cosmologists (Antānantikā), who asserted various theories about the extent of the universe, Sceptics (Amarā-vikkepikā), Indeterminists (Adhiccasamuppannikā) Primordialists (Pubbanta-kappikā), who speculated about pre-existence and first-causes, Eschatologists (Uddhamāghātanikā), who speculated about survival and final causes, Materialists (Ucchedavādā), who believed in the annihilation of the personality at death, and various Existentialist Moral Philosophers (Diṭṭhadhammanibbāna-vādā), who posited their various philosophies, did so 'on the basis of conditioned and limited personal experience' (chahi phassāyatanehi phussa phussa paṭisaṃvedenti) (D. I. 45).

As a result, the Buddha argues, their experiences have aroused their desires (vedanā paccayā taṇhā), and these, in turn, have resulted in entanglements (taṇhā paccayā upādānaṃ) which result in further becoming (bhava) and rebirth (jāti). It is only, says the Buddha, 'when a person can understand the origin and limits of conditioned personal experience (phassāyatana), its values, its defects and how one transcends it that he can comprehend something higher than this (. . .ayaṃ imehi sabbeh'eva uttaritaraṃ pajānāti' (D. I. 45).

It is, therefore, not sufficient to have a merely intellectual appreciation of the four noble truths or the central truths of Buddhism. Even such a person who entertains 'the right view of life' (sammā-diṭṭhi), still has only a mere 'view' (diṭṭhi). He may have true beliefs about the nature and destiny of man in the universe, but they are still mere beliefs not amounting to knowledge. So, while starting with 'right beliefs' (sammā-diṭṭhi) as the guide of life, one should try to attain 'right understanding' (samma-ñāṇa).

Unless and until 'right understanding' is attained, all people, whether they be Buddhists or non-Buddhists, entertain either erroneous beliefs or true beliefs (not amounting to knowledge) about the nature and destiny of man in the universe. As a result, they have diverse opinions about the reality of moral actions and the nature of good and evil. So their volitional actions, whether they believe in the value or moral efficacy of such actions or not, are conditioned by the various opinions they hold, which may be characterised as 'ignorance'.

It is possible that they may not consciously or clearly hold such opinions, which would be the case if they do know what they believe about these matters, or are not very articulate in their beliefs; but even in such a case they are guided by ignorance in their volitional actions.

So this is the seemingly simple though truly profound truth expressed in the sentence 'ignorance conditions volitional acts' (avijjā paccayā saṇkhārā). As we have shown earlier, these volitional acts may be done of our own accord (sāmaṃ) or at the instigation of others (pare), with full awareness of what we are doing (sampajāna) or without full awareness of what we are doing (assampajāna) (S. II. 40).

At the same time, we must not forget what we have already stated, namely that 'ignorance' is only one of the main factors with and conditioning our volitional activities. It o means the only factor, since another important conditioning our volitional actions are the different of desires in us. In fact, it is the beliefs and desires together which largely motivate our behaviour and thereby condition our volitional activities.

VOLITIONAL ACTS AND CONSCIOUSNESS

The next statement of the formulae of causal conditioning reads, 'volitional acts condition consciousness' (saṅkhārā paccayā viññāṇaṃ). The later explanation of this statement is to be found in the Commentaries, and the Visudhimagga is somewhat sophisticated, but one of the earliest explanations, which has been neglected, is simple and straightforward. It says: 'If a person under the influence of ignorance performs meritorious actions, his consciousness acquires a meritorious bent (puññūpagaṃ hoti viññāṇaṃ), if he performs demeritorious actions, his consciousness acquires a demeritorious bent, and if he performs "imperturbable" actions, his consciousness acquires an "imperturbable" bent' (S. II. 82). If we take this explanation as valid, what it means is that the tone or moral tone of one's consciousness is affected by the nature of the volitional actions performed by us.

The first verse of the *Dhammapada* underlines the importance attached to the factor of 'will': 'Psychological states are led by will, governed by will and are a product of will' (manopubbangamā dhammā mano-seṭṭhā manomayā). It is such willed actions which change our psychological nature and eventually cause our happiness or unhappiness in so far as happiness is karmically caused.

The *Nidāna Saṃyutta*, which deals extensively with causal formulae, has three sections devoted to the subject of 'will' or 'intention' (cetana). What is stated in the first passage reads as follows: 'What one wills (ceteti), decides (pakappeti) and registers in one's unconscious (anuseti) becomes an object for the persistence of consciousness (ārammanaṃ hoti viññānassa thitiyā). When such an object is present, consciousness finds a footing in it (ārammane sati patiṭṭhā viññāṇassa hoti), and when consciousness is established therein and comes to maturity, there results a renewed birth in the future (tasmiṃ patiṭṭhite viññāṇe virūlhe āyatiṃ punabbhāvabhinibbatti hoti)' (S. II. 65). We have translated the word 'anuseti' as 'registers in the unconsciousness'. The meaning of the word as given in the Pali Text Society Dictionary is as follows: '1. to dwell on, harp on (an idea); 2. (of an idea) to obsess, to fill the mind persistently, to lie dormant and be continually cropping up' (s.v. anuseti). The word is formed from the prefix anu-, meaning 'on or under', and the √sī, meaning to lie down. Here what is meant is that these psychological states lie beneath the state of the conscious mind but continue to affect it.

What the above passage states is that when we perform willed actions, involving choice and decision, the form and tone of our consciousness is thereby changed and this tends to determine the nature of our next life. So there is a causal connection between will (cetanā), consciousness (viññāṇa) and the next life (āyatiṃ punabbhavābhinibbatti).

In the *Saṅkhāruppatti Sutta* of the Majjhima Nikāya, which deals with the question of 'birth according to one's will' (saṅkkharuppatti), it is said that a person who is possessed of faith (saddhā), virtue (sīla), learning (suta), selflessness (cāga) and understanding (paññā) can acquire almost any kind of birth at will in his next life either among humans or in higher worlds among the galactic systems of the universe. When such a person wishes for some form of future existence, it is said, 'he fixes his mind on such thoughts (taṃ cittaṃ dhati), concentrates on such thoughts and develops such thoughts so that those acts of will (saṅkhārā) and that life of his (vihāra) when developed and often dwelt upon (bhavitā bahulīkatā) tends to bring about such an existence (tatr'uppatiyā saṃvattanti)' (M. III. 99, 100). Here, again, the sequence is that of acts of will causing a growth in one's personality as reflected in his faith, virtue, learning, selflessness and wisdom resulting in the light of his wishes in a renewed form of existence which is to his liking.

Of the three passages we referred to in the *Nidana Saṃyutta*, the second reads as follows: 'What one wills, decides and registers in one's unconsciousness becomes an object for the persistence of consciousness. Such an object being present, consciousness finds footing in it, and when consciousness is established therein and comes to maturity, there is eventually an entrance into a new personality' (. . . tasmiṃ patoṭṭhite viññāne virūḷhe *sāmsarūpassa avakkanti* hoti, S. II. 66).

The third passage proceeds as above, and then states: '. . . when consciousness is established therein and comes to maturity it acquires a certain bent or tone (nati). This determines its activity (āgatigati, literally coming and going) and this in turn its decease and rebirth (cutūpapata)' (S. II. 67).

The sequence in all these passages is the same. The acts of will (cetanā, saṅkhārā) condition the nature and tone of our consciousness (viññāṇa, citta) and this, in turn, conditions the next life and the new personality (āyatiṃ punabbhavābhinibbatti, cutūpapāta nāmarūpassa avakkanti). So while 'ignorance conditions our volitional activities' (avijjā paccayā saṅkhārā), as explained above, these volitional activities are the predominant factor in conditioning the nature and tone of our consciousness.

As we know, according to the Buddhist theory consciousness is not an unchanging entity, or soul, as explained in dealing with the heresy of Sāti in the *Mahātaṇhālsaṅkhaya Sutta*. It is constantly changing under the impact of the external world and our own past experiences. But the nature of our consciousness is not strictly determined by these factors which condition it, since predominant among the factors which determine the nature and direction in which our consciousness develops and matures are our will (cetanā) or acts of will (saṅkhārā). It is our own will or these acts of will which can or do make a tremendous difference to our future development. They can transform the nature of the human individual for good or for evil. Environment, heredity and our own psychological heritage from the past are, no doubt, factors which condition the nature of our consciousness, but the fundamental factor which governs our future is our will as expressed in our acts of will, which transform our nature or state of our personality or consciousness (viññāṇa).

Properly utilised, it is the most effective instrument that we possess in changing our future from what, out of neglect, it may otherwise be. So while the first statement of the causal formulae taught that 'our beliefs or ignorance regarding the nature and destiny of man condition our volitional acts' so that we tend to act in all sorts of ways and justify them, the second statement of the causal formulae asserts the equally profound truth that 'our acts of will or volitional activities condition the nature, form and tone of our consciousness' (saṅkhārā paccayā viññāṇam).

The meaning of the third statement of the causal formulae, namely that 'the nature of our consciousness conditions the nature of the new individuality in the next life' (viññāṇa paccayā nāmarūpaṃ) should also be somewhat clear from the passages we have cited above, but before we examine this third statement, it would be worthwhile to consider another traditional explanation, which has been given to the statement 'volitional activities condition consciousness'.

## ANOTHER INTERPRETATION

This is to be found in the *Visuddhimagga* of Buddhaghoṣa and the Commentaries, although it quotes in support certain statements of the *Dhammasaṅgaṇi*, which is a book of the *Abhidhamma Piṭaka*.

The explanation is as follows. Sankhārā or acts of will are here treated as previous karma. By 'consciousness' is to be understood the five forms of consciousness associated with the senses such as visual consciousness, auditory consciousness, etc., as well as the consciousness which is a product of mental activity (mano-viññāṇa-dhātu) such as memory, reflection, imagination, reasoning, etc. Now, it is argued that acts of will constituting our previous karma condition the nature of our consciousness in a subsequent life.

It is in this manner that Buddhaghoṣa explains the statement. He says: 'In the statement "volitional activities condition consciousness", consciousness is of six kinds beginning with visual consciousness . . .' (*Vism.*, 545). He quotes in support certain passages from the Dhammasaṅgaṇi. These passages are not directly relevant to the explanation of the formulae of causal conditioning. For instance, one of them quoted from the *Dhammasaṅgaṇi* when taken in its context reads as follows: 'What psychological states are morally neutral? When *as a result of* (vipākaṃ) good karma done and accumulated in the realm of sensuous existence there arises *visual consciousness* accompanied by a neutral tone and associated with visual objects . . .' (ibid., 431).

Here visual consciousness among other forms of consciousness is represented as a product of previous good karma. There is no doubt that karma conditions the forms of consciousness that we have in subsequent lives. If we intentionally blind other people, then there is a tendency to be born blind. So our lack of visual consciousness would be due to a demeritorious act of will done in a past life. So there is, no doubt, a karmic connection between forms of consciousness and acts of will done in previous lives. It is in this sense that the Ven. Nyanatiloka following Buddhaghoṣa explains the statement 'volitional activities condition consciousness': 'Here by "consciousness" (viññāṇa) are meant only those classes of consciousness which are the results (vipāka) of wholesome or unwholesome karma-formations done in former existence . . .' (see *Guide Through the Abhidhamma Piṭaka*, Colombo, 2nd edn, 1957, p. 165).

While not denying these facts of conditioning, and the

possibility of explaining this statement in the aforesaid manner as well, it is important not to lose sight of the explanation given in the earliest authentic texts of the *Sutta Piṭaka*, which stress the fact that our volitional acts proximately change the nature and bent of our consciousness in this life itself quite apart from their remote consequences in subsequent lives, which are also not be denied. Besides, acts of will considered as karmic factors should condition not only the state of our consciousness in subsequent lives but other factors in our lives as well.

Considering the citations that we have given, it would appear that the interpretation we gave earlier would be the more natural explanation though the latter explanation does not contradict it. It merely supplements it. Another reason why this explanation appears to be more authentic would become clear when we examine the explanations given in the *Sutta Piṭaka* of the next statement of the formulae, namely that 'consciousness conditions the (new) individuality' (viññāṇa paccayā nāmarūpaṃ).

From what we have cited already, it is clear that our acts of will condition the character of our consciousness, it is the nature and tone of our consciousness, which conditions the nature of our successive personality: 'What one wills (ceteti), decides and registers in our subsconscious (anuseti) becomes an object for the persistence of consciousness. When such an object is present, consciousness finds a footing in it and when consciousness is established therein and comes to maturity, there results a renewed birth (punabbhavābhinibbatti) in the future' (S. II. 65). In another passage (already quoted), it was said: '. . . when consciousness is established therein and comes to maturity, there is eventually an entrance into a new personality (nāmarūppassa avakkanti hoti)' (S. II. 66). Or again: '. . . when consciousness is established therein and comes to maturity, it acquires a certain bent or tone (nati), this determines its activity and this in turn its decease and rebirth (cutūpapatā)' (S. II. 67).

All these passages confirm the fact that it is the nature of our consciousness, which refers to a phase and the state of the dynamic stream of consciousness (viññāṇa-sota), which conditions the nature and form of the new personality we inherit in our successive life. This subsequent life may be in various planes of existence, but since most people survive as a discarnate spirit (gandhabba, Skr. gandharva) and are reborn in an earth-life, the new personality is here depicted as rebirth in a human condition.

As we have already pointed out, three factors are necessary for a human birth, the presence of the ovum, its fertilisation by the sperm of the father as well as the interaction and integration of the zygote (i.e. sperm and ovum together) with the dynamic stream of consciousness (viññāṇa-sota), which is also called 'the discarnate spirit' (gandhabbo ca paccupaṭṭhito hoti). So the new personality after integration (avakkanti) is a product of the two parents and the dynamic stream of consciousness, which in the later texts is called 'the re-linking consciousness' (paṭisandhi-viññāṇa).

Modern biological science would not admit the existence of such a dynamic stream of consciousness charging and interacting with the zygote. It therefore assumes that the child conceived in the mother's womb is a purely hereditary product of the parental stock. At conception, a normal human being receives twenty-three chromosomes from the father's sperm and twenty-three from the mother's ovum. Each chromosome is composed of many individual determiners of heredity called genes. Modern biologists and psychologists consider the human person as being a product entirely of heredity and environment. It is, therefore, one of their basic assumptions that what cannot be due to heredity must necessarily be due to the environment.

It is now more or less established that physical characteristics at birth are due almost entirely to heredity, but it is assumed that the personality characteristics, such as temperament, are due to the interaction of the environment. In a study of identical twins (who have the same heredity because they are a product of the bifurcation of a zygote composed of one sperm and one ovum, a fact which is itself unexplained), it is said that 'the authors came to the conclusion that the physical characteristics are least modified by the environment, intellectual characteristics somewhat more and personality characteristics most of all' (quoted from Ernest R. Hilgard, *Introduction to Psychology*, Harcourt, Brace & World Inc., 1962, p. 436).

Buddhism, while granting that 'the laws of heredity' (bīja-niyāma) condition, on the whole, the physical and physiological characteristics of the person, holds that the temperamental and such personality characteristics, including aptitudes and skills, are on the whole conditioned by the psychological past of the individual. This is a theory that should be carefully examined by biologists and psychologists in the light of all the known facts since there is some significant evidence from science even at present in favour of the Buddhist theory. We have already cited some of this evidence.

We are presently trying to explain the statement that 'consciousness conditions the (new) psycho-physical individuality' (viññāṇa paccayā nāmarūpam). According to the texts, there is mutual interaction and integration of the two in the formation of the new personality. It is said: 'Just as much as two bundles of reeds are to stand erect supporting each other, even so conditioned by the (hereditary) psycho-physical factors is the consciousness, and conditioned by the consciousness are the psycho-physical factors' (S. II. 114).

In the *Mahānidāna Sutta* of the *Dīgha Nikāya*, there occurs the following dialogue between the Buddha and Ananda, which throws light on the relationship of the two:

It has been stated that 'conditioned by consciousness is the psycho-physical individuality'. This assertion, Ananda, is to be understood in the following manner: 'If consciousness did not come into the mother's womb, would the psycho-physical individuality spring up in the mother's womb?'

It would not, O Lord.

If consciousness, Ananda, comes into the mother's womb and departs, would the psycho-physical individuality be born into this world?

It would not, O Lord.

Therefore, this is the cause, the source, the origin and the condition [for the birth of the] psycho-physical individuality, namely, the consciousness.

Now, it is also stated that 'conditioned by the psycho-physical individuality is the consciousness'. This assertion is to be understood in the following manner: 'If, Ananda, consciousness did not find a foothold in a psycho-physical individuality, would the arising again of birth, decay, death and suffering be manifested?'

It would not, O Lord.

Therefore, Ananda, this is a cause, a source, an origin and a condition [for the manifestation of] consciousness, namely the psycho-physical individuality.

To this extent can one speak of one being born, decaying, dying, passing away and being reborn . . . to this extent can one speak of a cycle of births in this world, namely owing to the mutual interaction of the psychophysical individuality with the consciousness (nāmarūpaṃ saha viññāṇena). (D. II. 62–64)

The next statement of the causal formula asserts that 'conditioned by the nature of our personality is our external world' (nāmarūpa paccayā salāyatanaṃ). What we translate as the 'external world' here is the term 'salāyatana', which is used to refer to both the five sense organs (such as the eyes, ears, nose, tongue and body-sensitivity) and the mechanism of the mind (manāyatana) as well as their objects, viz. visible forms, sounds, smells, tastes, tangibles as well as ideas, concepts, opinions and theories. This 'external world' of ours is very much conditioned by our psycho-physical personality. For example, if we were born blind for psychological or physical reasons, then the world of colours and shapes would not exist for us. Likewise the world that we perceive through our sight is very much conditioned by our psychological natures. While what we actually see depends partly on the texture of the visual organs and the state of our brain, we may be conditioned to notice and pay greater attention to certain aspects of our visual environment owing to our past psychological conditioning and habits.

Likewise the ideas and concepts that we have depend partly on the condition of the 'basis of our mind' (manāyatana), the ideas, opinions and theories we are exposed to in our social and ideological environment as well as the receptivity of our own mind as a result of which we may show a special interest in some sorts of ideas as against others.

A statement in the *Paṭṭhāna* also throws light on the nature of mental phenomena and their relation to the body and the external world. It is said: 'The field of visual forms, sounds, smells, tastes and tangibles are, to perceptual activity and phenomena connected with it, a condition by way of pre-nascence (purejāta-paccaya). The physical base (rūpa) in dependence, on which there arises perceptual activity (mano-dhātu) as well as conceptual activity (manoviññāṇa-dhātu), is a condition by way of pre-nascence for perceptual activity and phenomena connected with it; but for conceptual activity and phenomena connected with it, it is sometimes (kiñcikale, v. 1. kañcikāle) a condition by way of pre-nascence (purejāta-paccaya) and sometimes not a condition by way of pre-nascence' (*Paccaya Niddesa*, 10).

What this means is that physical objects, sounds, smells, etc., exist prior to and independent of their being perceived and become a condition for perceptual activity and associated mental phenomena (such as feelings) to manifest themselves. Likewise, the physical basis of the mind exists prior to, and becomes a condition for the arising of perceptual activity and associated phenomena (such as feelings). But the physical basis of the mind is not always prior to the conceptual activity of the mind (manoviññāṇadhātu) such as memory, reasoning, imagination, etc. since their residues are present in the dynamic unconscious, which is prior to the formation of the physical basis of the mind although their subsequent arousal and recall is dependent on the physcial basis (rūpa) of the mind. It seems to follow from this that all conscious mental activity has a physical (i.e. physiological) basis, while all that is present in the dynamic unconscious of the stream of consciousness need not be located in this physical basis, although this consciousness is associated and connected with one's body (ettha sitaṃ ettha paṭibaddhaṃ).

The meaning of the next statement, which is to the effect that 'conditioned by the external world are the impressions' (salāyatana paccayā phasso), is fairly clear. The external objects impinge on our sense in the form of stimuli, and when the mind is attentive to them produce sense-impressions. As the texts say, 'on account of the organ of sight and visual objects there arise eye-consciousness and the meeting of the three constitutes a visual impression' (cakkhuṃ ca paṭicca rūpaṃ ca paṭicca uppajjati cakkhu-viññāṇaṃ) tiṇṇaṃ saṅgati phasso) (S. II. 72). The sense-impressions caused by the five senses are called 'actual contacts' (paṭigha-samphassa), while the impressions caused by the manifestation of ideas or concepts in the mind are called 'nominal contacts' (adhivacana-samphassa). On the basis of our conceptual activity and also as a result of our social and ideological environment, numerous ideas, concepts, opinions and theories pass through our minds. So we see that on account of the external world and the activity of our minds, there arise various impressions.

These 'impressions give rise to or condition our feelings or sensations' (phassa paccayā vedanā), which may be pleasant, unpleasant or neutral. 'The feelings condition our desires' (vedanā paccayā taṇhā), the impressions (sensuous or mental) associated with pleasant feelings condition or arouse the desires for sensuous or sexual gratification (kāmā-taṇhā) and the desires for egoistic pursuits (bhava-taṇhā) such as the desire for possessions, for power, for fame, for personal immortality, etc. On the other hand, the unpleasant feelings condition or arouse our desire for elimination or destruction (vibhava-taṇhā).

Then, these 'desires condition our entanglements' (taṇhā paccayā upādānaṃ). These 'entanglements' may be with objects, places or persons (kāmupādāna), philosophical, religious or political ideas or theories (diṭṭhupādāna), habits, customs, rites or rituals (sīlabbatupādāna) as well as our beliefs in soul or substance (attavādupādāna). For example, if our ego instincts (bhava-taṇhā) are strong, we hold on to or cling to some belief in a soul because this gratifies our desires for security and personal immortality in an insecure and uncertain world where we fear that death may be the end of everything. Likewise we cling to objects or persons when they afford us pleasure and gratify our various desires. So we cling to all the things, persons, habits and ideas which afford us pleasure by providing satisfaction for our desires, and form sentiments of attachment around them in the vain hope that they would continue to be sources of pleasure since man acts on the principle of seeking pleasure and avoiding pain (sukhakāmā hi manussā dukkhapaṭikkūlā)

On the other hand, we are repelled by the things that cause displeasure. They become the objects of aggression or repulsion (paṭigha) and we direct our hatred (dosa) against them since they arouse our desire for elimination or destruction (vibhava-taṇhā). We form sentiments of hate around these things, persons, habits or theories, and so they too become our 'entanglements'. The satisfaction of this desire for elimina-ation and destruction also affords us sadistic pleasures.

Our entanglements may be of a higher order if we treat as secure states of personality, or as a 'soul', the higher stages of jhanic experience. So it is 'these kinds of things, persons, habits, theories or states of experience around which we formed entanglements, which condition our future becoming' (upādāna paccayā bhavo) in different planes of existence. 'This becoming conditions our birth' (bhava paccayājāti) and 'birth in these conditions results in decay and death' (jāti paccayā jarāmaraṇaṃ).

This is the 'wheel of becoming' (bhava-cakra) that we are caught up in, but the emergence from this condition is also pictured as a process of conditioning: 'Suffering is instrumental in arousing faith in moral and spiritual values, such faith results in gladness and composure of mind, giving rise to insight regarding reality and eventual salvation' (dukkhūpanisā saddhā . . .) (S. II. 31). However, in the last resort, it is the understanding of the nature of our conditioning which liberates us and makes it possible for us to attain the Unconditioned (asaṅkhata).

As we can see, the doctrine of conditioned genesis shows how we are conditioned by the environment, by our heredity (bija-niyāma) owing to the fact that our personality is made up of the fusion of the dynamic consciousness coming down from a previous life with what is derived from our parental stock, our psychological past going back to prior lives and the desires and beliefs which motivate our behaviour. Yet, although we are *conditioned*, we are *not determined* by these factors since we have an element of initiative (ārabbha-dhātu) or freedom from constraint which makes it possible for us within limits to control and direct our future course of saṃsāric evolution and make the future different from what it may otherwise be.

14

# The Buddhist Ethical Ideal of the Ultimate Good

Moral philosophers use the term 'good' in two important senses. There is the sense in which we speak of what is 'good as an end' or what is 'intrinsically good'. There is also the sense in which we speak of what is 'good as a means' or what is 'instrumentally good'. The two senses are inter-related. For what is instrumentally good, or good as a means, is necessary to bring about what is intrinsically good, or good as an end.

When the *Dhammapada* says that 'health is the greatest gain' (ārogyā paramā lābhā), it is, in a sense, treating the state of health as being what is good as an end. For whatever our gains may be, most people are prepared to lose them or use them in order to recover their health if they fall ill. Besides, it is only if we are healthy that we can adopt the means to gain material or even spiritual riches. If health is a desirable end to achieve or is good as an end, then what is instrumental in achieving this state of health is good as a means. Since medicines, even when they are bitter, are often useful as a means to the cure of illnesses, they are deemed to be good as a means, or instrumentally good.

Although some people would regard a state of physical health in the above sense as being good as an end, others may say that good health is only a relative end since the ultimate end or goal that we should seek is happiness, and good health is only a necessary condition for happiness. So while no one would say that bitter medicine is good as an end, many people would regard a state of health as being good as an end only in a relative sense, as contributing to one's well-being and happiness. One's well-being and happiness would, therefore, be for them an ultimate end in a sense in which even physical health is not. Besides, in the world in which we live, we can enjoy a state of physical health only in a relative sense since we may fall ill from time to time and even healthy men eventually die.

In this chapter we shall be concerned only with what is ultimately good from the Buddhist point of view. Buddhism presents a clear conception of what is ultimately good, and what is instrumentally good in order to achieve it. What is instrumentally good to achieve this end is regarded as good as a means. This consists mainly of right actions and the other factors that help in bringing about what is ultimately good.

These right actions may often be called good as opposed to evil actions. But we shall avoid the phrase 'good actions' and consistently use the phrase 'right actions' (as opposed to 'wrong actions) in speaking about what is primarily necessary in order to achieve what is good as an end.

In the Buddhist texts, the terms that are most often used to denote 'right actions' are kusala or puñña. Kusala means 'skilful' and denotes the fact that the performance of right actions requires both theoretical understanding as well as practice. The person who has attained the ideal or the highest good is referred to as a person of 'accomplished skill or the highest skill' (sampanna-kusalaṃ paramakusalaṃ). Akusala, its opposite, means the 'unskilful'. Puñña, as used of right actions, means what is 'meritorious', as opposed to pāpa, which means 'demeritorious'. It is not a term that is employed to denote the highest good. In fact, the person who has attained the highest good is said to have 'cast aside both meritorious and demeritorious actions (puñña-pāpa pahīna).

As we shall see in examining the nature of right actions, this does not imply that meritorious actions (as opposed to demeritorious) ones are not necessary for the attainment of the highest good, nor that those who have attained are amoral. The path to salvation or the path leading to the highest good in Buddhism is a gradual path, and although we may start with our egoistic or self-centred desires as a motive for self-advancement, they have progressively to be cast aside until eventually the goodness of the actions alone remains without the personal motivation for doing good.

If we acquaint ourselves with the nature of the ethical ideal or the conception of what is intrinsically good or good as an end, we would be in a better position to understand the Buddhist conception of right and wrong.

Moral philosophers have conceived of the ethical ideal in various ways. Some have thought of it as pleasure and others as happiness. Yet others considered the notion of duty or obligation as central to ethics, while others again think of the goal as perfection.

What is the Buddhist conception of the ideal? Buddhism conceives of the ethical ideal as one of Happiness, Perfection, Realisation and Freedom. These ethical goals, in fact, coincide, and the highest good is at the same time one of ultimate Happiness, moral Perfection, final Realisation and perfect Freedom. This is the goal to be attained in the cosmic or personal dimension of existence.

This is a goal for one and all to attain, each in his own interest as well as that of others. Besides, there is a social ideal which it is also desirable to bring into existence. This is broadly conceived of as 'the well-being or happiness of the multitude or mankind' (bahujanahitāya bahujanasukhāya). Here 'well-being and happiness' is conceived of both materially as well as spiritually. The ideal society in which this well-being and happiness will prevail in an optimum form is conceived of as both socialistic, being founded on the principle of equality, and democratic, as affording the best opportunities for the exercise of human freedom. Such a society is also just, as it is based on principles of righteousness.

We shall explore the nature of these conceptions in greater detail in examining the social philosophy of Buddhism. We shall also examine in Chapter 15 the relationship that exists between the social ideal and the personal ideal. Although from an individualistic point of view 'the path to the acquisition of wealth is one, while the path to Nirvana is another'(aññā hi lābhupanisā aññā nibbāna-gāmini) even the social ideal can be attained, it is said, only by people, who are motivated to act in accordance with the Ten Virtues (dasa kusala-kamma) in a society built on firm economic, political and moral foundations.

What is the role of pleasure and the performance of one's duties in relation to the Buddhist ethical ideal? Let us first take the role of pleasure. Buddhism recognises the importance of the hedonistic principle that man is predominantly motivated to act out of 'his desire for happiness and his repulsion for unhappiness' (sukka-kāmā hi manussā dukkha-paṭikkūlā). In fact, the central truths of Buddhism, 'the four truths concerning unhappiness' (dukkha-sacca), are formulated in the manner set forth so as to appeal to man's intrinsic desire for happiness and the desire to escape from or transcend his unhappiness.

Pleasure is classified in the Buddhist texts according to its different grades, and it is stated that 'the most refined and sublimest form of pleasure' (utaritaraṃ paṇītataraṃ) is the bliss of Nirvana. This 'experience of the bliss of freedom' (vimutti-sukha-paṭisaṃvedī) is so different from the conditioned pleasure and happiness of worldly existence that there is a reluctance on the part of the texts to use the word *vedanā* (feeling) of it since *vedanā* as represented in the formula of conditioning is always conditioned.

The attitude to pleasure in the Buddhist texts is a realistic one. It does not deny the fact or value of pleasure. The limited good (assāda) a well as the evil consequences (ādīnava) of even the gross forms of pleasure are recognised. The Buddha did not advocate a form of asceticism whereby we should shun all pleasures by closing our eyes and ears (and becoming like the blind and the deaf) to objects which arouse sensuous pleasure. Instead the Buddha wanted those who were addicted to such pleasures to realise their limitations.

One form of pleasure that we experience is by the gratification of our desires. We get satisfaction from time to time by gratifying our desire for sensuous pleasures and sex (kāma-taṇhā). We get such temporary satisfaction, again, by gratifying our egoistic instincts (bhava-taṇhā), such as the desire for self-preservation (jīvita-kāma), for security, for possessions, for power, for fame, for personal immortality, etc. We also get satisfaction by gratifying our desire for destruction (vibhava-taṇhā) or aggression (paṭigha) or the elimination of what we dislike. The enjoyment of these pleasures is often accompanied by rationalisations or erroneous beliefs, such as, for instance, that we have been created for a life of enjoyment of this sort or that we should eat, drink and be merry today for tomorrow we die.

What is important is not to shun pleasure or torment the body, but to realise for oneself the limitations of pleasures and the diminishing returns they afford, so that eventually we can transcend them by a life of temperance and restraint and enjoy the immaterial or spiritual forms of pleasure (nirāmisa-sukha) which accompany selfless and compassionate activity based on understanding. One must give up the gross forms of pleasure for the more refined and superior kinds of happiness. As the *Dhammapada* states, 'If by renouncing a little pleasure we can find a great deal of happiness, then the prudent man should relinquish such trifling pleasures on discovering an abundant happiness' (mattā sukha-pariccāgā passe ce vipulaṃ sukhaṃ, caje mattā sukhaṃ dhīro samphassaṃ vipulaṃ sukhaṃ) (Dh. 290).

This is only an extension of the hedonistic principle that man has a tendency to seek pleasure and to recoil from pain, and therefore that he ought to do what is both rational and possible by giving up the gross forms of pleasure for the more sublime forms until he eventually attains the supreme bliss of Nirvana.

These more sublime forms of pleasure are correlated with forms of activity which are spiritually elevating and socially desirable. It is not always necessary that one should literally renounce the worldly life in order to cultivate them. Both laymen and monks can attain the first stage of spiritual progress (sotāpanna) as well as some of the later stages. A person who can perform the duties associated with his livelihood, provided it is a right mode of living (sammā ājīva), with a sense of selfless service to his fellow men out of concern, compassion and understanding, can act without a narrowly selfish motivation and derive happiness from his work. The Buddha compared the spiritual gains to be had from the lay life and the life of the monk to agriculture and trade. Agriculture gives slow but steady returns, while trade gives quicker returns though it is more risky. According to the Buddha, nothing could be worse than the outward renunciation of the lay life in order to live a life of corruption and hypocrisy as a recluse. Such a person, apart from the disservice he would be doing to the community, would be digging his own grave.

However, the ignorance that clouds the judgment of man is such that a man who enjoys the grosser forms of pleasure cannot experience anything more refined or more sublime, since he is addicted to them. So what often happens is that he experiences less and less of both pleasure and happiness because of his reluctance to go against the current (paṭisotagāmi) until eventually he becomes a slave to his passions, losing both his freedom and happiness as well as every other quality which can bring him closer to the ethical ideal.

While Buddhist ethics recognises and appeals to the hedonistic, it does not fall into the error of hedonism by asserting that pleasure alone, abstracted from everything else, is what is worth achieving. The hedonistic ideal of supreme happiness, for example, is also identical with the therapeutic goal of perfect mental health.

So the path to happiness is also the path to mental stability, serenity, awareness, integration and purity of mind. The

Buddha classified diseases as bodily (kāyika) and mental (cetasika) and it is said that while we have bodily diseases from time to time, mental illness is almost continual until arahantship is attained, so that only the saint or a person with a Nirvanic mind can be said to have a perfectly healthy mind.

While the four noble truths, as we have pointed out, on the one hand indicate the path from unhappiness to perfect happiness, it is also in the form of a medical diagnosis. From this point of view, the truths give an account of (1) the nature of the illness, its history and prognosis, (2) the causes of the illness, (3) the nature of the state of health that we ought to achieve and (4) the remedial measures to be taken in order to achieve it.

This diseased state of the mind is due to the unsatisfied desires and the conflicts caused by the desires that rage within our minds both at the conscious and unconscious levels. Thus the desire for sense pleasures and selfish pursuits is found as a subliminal or latent tendency as well (rāgānusaya; cp. kāma-rāga, bhava-rāga). It is the same with our hatred or aggression (paṭighānusaya). Mental serenity, stability and sanity can be achieved neither by free indulgence in our desires (kāma-sukhallikānuyoga) nor by ascetic repression and self-torment (attakilamathānuyoga). When we become more aware of the way these desires operate in us by the exercise or practice of awareness (satipaṭṭhāna), we gradually attain a level of consciousness in which there is a greater degree of serenity and stability. The culmination of this development, when the mind is purged of all its defilements, is the perfect state of mental health, which coincides with the experience of the highest bliss.

Buddhism points to the sources of unhappiness, or the causes of suffering, not to make us unhappy or brood over our lot, but in order that we may emerge from our condition with stronger, happier and healthier minds. Such people could say in the words of the *Dhammapada*:

'So happily we live, free from anger among those who are angry'
(susukhaṃ vata jīvāma verinesu averino) (Dh. 197).
'So happily we live in good health amongst the ailing'
(susukhaṃ vata jīvāma āturesu anāturā) (Dh. 198).
'So happily we live relaxed among those who are tense'
(susukhaṃ vata jīvāma ussukesu anussukā) (Dh. 199).

The person who has attained the ideal is said to have fulfilled all his obligations (kata-karaṇiya) since the greatest obligation of everyone, whatever else he may do, is the attainment of the goal of Nirvana. But, till he does this, man has all his social duties to perform towards the various classes of people in society. The duties and obligations of parents and children, employers, husbands and wives, religious men and their followers, etc., are given in the *Sigālovāda Sutta*, while the duties and rights of a king or taste and its citizens are recorded in the *Aggañña* and *Cakkavatti-sīhanāda Suttas*. Even such duties and obligations are to be performed in a spirit of selfless service, love and understanding, so that we are treading the path to Nirvana in the exercise of these obligations.

So while the ultimate end is one of perfect happiness and mental health, it is not one in which one is obliged to perform one's duties for duty's sake. Likewise, when the Arahant serves society as the several enlightened monks and nuns mentioned in the *Thera-* and *Therīgathā* did, they did so out of a spontaneous spirit of selflessness, compassion and understanding.

It is, therefore, a mistaken notion to hold, as some scholars have held, that the Arahant is amoral and could even do evil with impunity. It is true that an Arahant 'casts aside both meritorious and demeritorious actions' (puñña-pāpa-pahīna). By this is meant only that he does not do any acts, whether they be good or evil, with the expectation of reward, nor do these acts have any efficacy for bringing about karmic consequences in the future. They are mere acts (kiriya-mattā) of goodness, which flow spontaneously from a transcendent mind, which shines with its natural lustre with the elimination of craving, hatred and delusion and is wholly filled with selflessness (cāga), loving-kindness (mettā) and wisdom (paññā).

The following passage illustrates the process and nature of this attainment:

'In whatever monk who was covetous, covetousness is got rid of . . . wrath, grudging, hypocrisy, spite, jealousy, stinginess, treachery, craftiness, . . . who was of evil desires, evil desire is got rid of, who was of wrong view, wrong view is got rid of. . . . He beholds himself purified of all these unskilled states and sees himself freed (vimuttaṃ attānaṃ samanupassati) . . . When he beholds himself freed, delight is born; rapture is born from delight; when he is in rapture, the body is impassible; when the body is impassible, he experiences joy; being joyful the mind is concentrated. He dwells, suffusing one direction with a mind of loving-kindness (mettāsahagatena cetasā), likewise the second, third and fourth; just so, above, below, across; he dwells having suffused the whole world everywhere, in every way with a mind of friendliness that is far-reaching, widespread, immeasurable, without enmity, without malevolence. He abides with a mind full of pity (karupā) . . . sympathetic joy (muditā) . . . equanimity (upekkhā) . . . without enmity, without malevolence. It is as if there were a lovely lotus pond with clear water, sweet water, cool water, limpid, with beautiful banks; and a man were to come along from the east, west, north, or south, overcome and overpowerd by the heat, exhausted, parched and thirsty. On coming to that lotus pond he might quench his thirst with water and quench his feverish heat. Even so . . . one who has come into this Dhamma and discipline taught by the Buddha, having thus developed loving-kindness, pity, sympathetic joy and equanimity, attains inward calm' (M. I. 283).

We find it expressly stated of the saint that he is a 'person of accomplished skill (sampanna-kusala), of the highest skill (parama-kusala), who has attained the highest attainment, an invincible recluse', who is endowed with 'right aspirations (sammā-saṅkappa) such as compassion (avihiṃsā vitakka), which do not require to be further disciplined (asekha)'. The Arahant's state is, therefore, one of moral perfection, though it is not one of 'conditioned morality but natural or spontaneous morality'; he is said to be 'naturally virtuous and not virtuous through conditioning' (sīlavā hoti no ca sīlamayo).

This state of bliss or ultimate happiness, perfect mental health and moral perfection, is also described as a state of supreme freedom (vimutta) and realiation (sambodhi, paññā). The mind is master of itself (vasī) and one has supreme control over it. The inflowing impulses (āsavā) do not disturb it.

The criticism has been made that the quest for Nirvana is a form of escapism. But this criticism is without basis since the person who attains Nirvana does so with full understanding of the nature of the world as well as of himself. If he ceases to be henceforth attracted by the pleasures of the world, it is because he can assess their worth and their limitations. The real escapists are the people who cannot, in fact, face reality as a whole and try to drown their fears, anxieties and sorrows by indulging in their passions. They are easily upset by their circumstances and find consolation in some form of neurosis. But the person who has a Nirvanic mind, or is anywhere near it, is 'unruffled by the ups and downs of the world, is happy, unstained and secure' (phuṭṭhassa lokadhammehi cittaṃ yassa na kampati, asokaṃ virajaṃ khemaṃ).

In such a state one has 'no fear or anxiety' (abhaya) at all. The highest good or the ethical ideal for each person is, there fore, conceived of as a state of bliss, mental health, perfection, freedom and realisation. It is a state that is stable (dhuva) and ineffable (amosadhamma) as well.

# 15

# Buddhist Ethics

Ethics has to do with human conduct and is concerned with questions regarding what is good and evil, what is right and wrong, what is justice and what are our duties, obligations and rights.

Modern ethical philosophers belonging to the Analytic school of philosophy consider it their task merely to analyse and clarify the nature of ethical concepts or theories. For them, ethics constitutes a purely theoretical study of moral phenomena. They do not consider it their province to lay down codes of conduct, which they deem to be the function of a moral teacher, a religious leader or a prophet.

However, there are some philosophers, even in the modern world, as, for example, some of the Existentialists, who consider it the duty of the philosopher to recommend ways of life or modes of conduct which they consider desirable for the purpose of achieving some end which they regard as valuable. Kierkegaard, for instance, considers that there are three stages of life, namely, the aesthetical or sensualist, the ethical and the religious. He indirectly recommends in his philosophy that we pass from one state to another. The aesthetical or sensualist way of life, according to him, leads to boredom, melancholy and despair, so it needs to be transfigured in the ethical stage, and so on.

In the philosophy of the Buddha, we have an analytical study of ethical concepts and theories as well as positive recommendations to lead a way of life regarded as 'the only way' (ekāyana magga; eso 'va maggo natth' añño dassanassa visuddhiyā) (Dh. 274) for the attainment of the *summum bonum* or the Highest Good, which is one of supreme bliss, moral perfection as well as of ultimate knowledge or realisation. This way of life is considered both possible and desirable because man and the universe are just what they are. It is, therefore, justified in the light of a realistic account of the nature of the universe and of man's place in it.

While this way of life in its personal or cosmic dimension, as it were, helps us to attain the highest Good, if not in this very life, at least in some subsequent life, it also has a social dimension in so far as it helps the achievement of 'the well-being or happiness of the multitude or of mankind as a whole' (bahujana-hita-bahujana-sukha). The well-being and happiness of mankind is another end considered to be of supreme, though relative, value in the Buddhist texts and this well-being and happiness is conceived of as both material and spiritual welfare.

Buddhist ethics, therefore, has a close connection with a social philosophy as well. This social philosophy is also fully developed. We have in the Buddhist texts an account of the nature and origin of society and the causes of social change. There is also an account of the nature and functions of government, the form of the ideal social order and how it is likely to be brought about.

In dealing with the ethics and social philosophy of Buddhism, we are trying to answer the question, 'What should we do?' In previous essays, we tried to give answers to the questions, 'How do we know?' and 'What do we know?' The question, 'What should we do?' has a personal as well as a social dimension. In a Buddhist frame of reference, the question, 'What should we do?' concerns, on the one hand, what the goal of life should be or is and what we have to do for self-improvement, self-realisation and the attainment of the highest Good. On the other hand, thc question has a social dimension and concerns what we have to do for the good of society or 'for the welfare and happiness of mankind'. The questions, 'What should we do for our own good?' and 'What should we do for thc good of others or society?' are mutually related, and what the relationship is, according to Buddhism, we shall examine later on.

Now, when we ask the question, 'What should we do?' the answers we give presuppose a certain account of reality. Let us illustrate this. In one stanza in the *Dhammapada* the sum and substance of Buddhist ethics is summed up as follows: 'Not to do any evil, to cultivate the good and to purify one's mind – this is the teaching of the Buddha' (183). Now someone may raise the question as to how we can be without doing what is called 'evil' and cultivate what is called the 'good' unless human beings have the freedom to do so.

If all our present actions, choices aad decisions were strictly determined by our psycho-physical constitution, which is partly hereditary, by our environmental influences, by our psychological past, or by all together, how is it possible for us to refrain from evil or do good? The very possibility of our refraining from evil and doing good therefore depends on the fact that our choices and decisions are not strictly and wholly determined by such factors and are in this sense 'free'. So ethical statements become significant only if there is human freedom in this sense. But the question as to whether there is human freedom in this sense is a question pertaining to the nature of reality. Is man so constituted that he has the capacity for 'free' action in the above sense without his actions being strictly determined by external and internal causes?

If not, these ethical statements cease to be significant. It does not make sense to ask a human being to refrain from evil if, considering his nature, he is incapable of doing so. If, however, man is 'free' in the above sense, it would be significant to ask him to exercise his choice in a certain way, which is what we do when we ask him to refrain from evil and do good. But whether he is 'free' or not in the above sense is not a question concerning ethics but a factual question concerning human nature. The answer belongs to the theory of reality and not ethics. This is an instance as to how ethics is related to the theory of reality. Or, in other words, how the answer to the question, 'What should we do?' is related to the answer to the question, 'What do we know about man and the universe?'

This question as to whether freedom in the above sense or free will is a fact is not the only one. There could be further questions. Even though one could, to some degree, refrain from evil aad cultivate the good, despite all the influences external and internal to which one is subject, one may still ask what use it is for oneself to refrain from evil and do good.

One may maintain that if sporadic acts of evil or good do not change one's nature for the better, or make one's lot happier, and if death is the end of life, what purpose does it serve to refrain from evil, to do good and to cleanse the mind? Here, again, one of the answers would be that if this activity does not change our nature for the better or make our condition happier, and death is, in fact, the end of life, there would not be much purpose in refraining from evil, doing good and cleansing the mind, even if we had the freedom or capacity to do so. So all this would be to some purpose only if such activity changed one's nature for the better and made one's condition happier in the long run, and if death was not, in fact, the end of individuality.

But the question as to whether this was so is a factual question. Does refraining from evil and doing morally good acts tend to change one's nature for the better and make one's condition happier in the long run in a world in which physical death is not the end of individuality? It is only if the answer to this question, too, is in the affirmative that it would seem worthwhile or desirable in a moral sense (as opposed to a merely social sense) of refraining from evil, doing what is good and purifying the mind.

Although it would appear to be worthwhile to do this if the answer is in the affirmative and there is human survival after death, and the refraining from evil, thc cultivation of the good and the purification of the mind results in a happier state for the individual, it may still be asked whether there is an end to such a process. Is there a highest Good, or must the process of refraining from evil and cultivating the good go on for ever, with progression and regression? Here, again, the question as to whether there is an end which is one of supreme bliss, perfection and realisation of an unconditioned state of ultimate reality is a purely factual question. It is only if there is such a state that an end to conditioned existence would be possible.

So an ethical statement which recommends the attainment of a highest Good, and lays down a way of life for such attainment, would be significant only if there is such a state which can be considered the highest Good for each and all to attain, and if the way of life does, in fact, lead to it. The question as to whether there is such a highest Good, and whether the way of life recommended leads to it, is, however, a factual question which has to be established independently of the ethical recommendations.

It would, therefore, be the case that the ethics of Buddhism would be significant only if certain facts are true, viz. (1) there is freedom or free will in the sense enunciated, (2) there is human survival or the continuity of individuals, (3) this continuing is such that the avoidance of evil and the cultivation of the good along with the purification of mind tends to make our nature better and our condition happier, while the opposite course of action has the reverse effect, and (4) there is a state when the mind is pure and cleansed of all defilements – a state of bliss, perfection, realisation and ultimate freedom.

In examining the Buddhist account of reality, we have already shown the truth of (2), (3) and (4). We have shown that there is pre-existence and survival after death, constituting a 'continued becoming' (punabbhava). We have shown that karma (in the Buddhist sense) is operative and that morally good, evil and mixed acts make a difference to one's nature and are followed by pleasant, unpleasant and mixed consequences, as the case may be. We have shown that there is 'that realm' (atthi . . . tad āyatanaṃ, Ud. 80) of Nirvana beyond space-time and causation which is the ultimate Good that all should attain and without which it would not be possible to transcend conditioned existence.

It remains for us to examine more fully than we have done, whether or not the Buddha asserts the reality of freedom or free will in the sense explained. By 'free will' in a Buddhist context, it is not meant that there is a will, choice or decision which is unaffected by causal factors that affect it, but that our volitional acts or will, choice or decision, while being *conditioned* by such factors, is not wholly shaped or *strictly determined* by them, since there is in man 'an element of initiative' (ārabbha-dhātu) or 'personal action' (purisa-kāra) or 'individual action' (atta-kāra), which can, within limits, resist the factors that affect it. But for this factor of human personality, 'moral responsibility' would be a farce and the forces that impel us to act would be responsible for our actions.

This is, in fact, what the Buddha says. On the one hand he distinguishes the Buddhist theory of the 'causal genesis' (paṭicca-samuppāda) of events from all forms of Strict Determinism, whether theistic or natural. According to the theistic version of Strict Determinism, every outcome in the universe is foreknown and predetermined by an omniscient and omnipotent Personal God. In such a situation, all our experiences would be 'due to the creation by God' (Issara-nimmāna-hetu). If so, argues the Buddha, God is ultimately responsible for the (good and) evil that human beings do.

Such theistic Determinists lived during the time of the Buddha. We must not forget that they are also found today. Dr Hastings Rashdall, Fellow of New College, Oxford, whose two volumes on *The Theory of Good and Evil* (Oxford University Press, 1907) are widely recommended and read by students of ethics even today, was such a theistic Determinist. He says in one place in his book: 'And after all a doctrine of Free-will which involves a denial of God's Omniscience cannot claim any superiority over such a theistic Determinism as I have defended on the score of avoiding a limitation of the divine Omnipotence' (vol. II, pp. 343, 344). He is led to believe in Determinism because of his total distrust of Indeterminism at the time when scientists believed in deterministic causation, prior to the discoveries of quantum physics. Dr Rashdall, however, gives this scientific doctrine of his times an idealistic twist and says: 'When the theory of Determinism is held in connexion with a philosophy which finds the ultimate ground and source of all being in a rational will, it is impossible to escape the inference that the Will of God ultimately causes everything in the Universe which has a beginning – including therefore souls and their acts, good and bad alike' (ibid., p. 339).

Having taken up this position, he finds the consequences not too palatable and difficult to explain away, for he says: 'Yet from the metaphysical or theological point of view we must admit also that the soul is made or caused by God: and one cannot help asking oneself the question why God should make bad souls, and so cause bad acts to be done' (ibid., p. 340). He also admits the central difficulty of his position, which he tries to explain away unsatisfactorily, viz., 'We have seen then that the only point at which a difficulty is created either for Morality or for Religion by the acceptance of Determinism lies in its tendency to make God in a sense the "author of evil" . . .' (ibid., p. 345). So we see that the logic of theistic Determinism is no different from the Buddha's time to the present.

The Buddha also rejects different forms of natural Determinism. One such theory was that our experiences or (the good or) evil we do is 'due to our (hereditary) physiological constitution' (abhijāti-hetu). Another theory upheld psychic determinism (cf. Freud) and held that 'all our present acts and experiences are entirely due to our past actions' (pubbekatahetu). In addition, there were at the time of the Buddha 'natural Determinists' (svabhāvavādins), who held that all events were strictly determined by natural forces. Pūraṇa Kassapa was a 'Determinist' (niyativādi), who held such a theory. As a result of his natural Determinism, he was like the nineteenth-century rationalists of Europe, an Amoralist, who denied that there was good or evil as such, since man was not responsible for his so-called 'good' or 'evil' acts.

It is important to remember that the Buddhist theory of causation was opposed to all such Deterministic theories, both theistic and natural, as also to the theory of total Indeterminism (adhicca-samuppana) or Tychism, which denied causal correlations in nature altogether. As such, the Buddhist theory of causation seems to accept an element of indeterminacy in nature, which in the case of human actions manifests itself as the free-will of the individual, which is *conditioned* but not totally determined by the factors that affect it.

While the Buddha distinguished his causal theory from Determinism, he also faced the question of free-will and asserted its reality in no uncertain terms. On one occasion, it is said, a certain brahmin (aññataro brāhmaṇo) approached the Buddha and told him that he was of the opinion that there was no free-will on the part of himself (atta-kāra) or others (para-kāra). The Buddha admonished him and asked him how he could say such a thing when he himself of his own accord (sayaṃ) could walk up to the Buddha and walk away from him.

On this occasion, the Buddha says that there is such a thing as 'an element of initiative' (ārabbha-dhātu), and as a result one can observe beings acting with initiative and this says the Buddha is what is called 'the free-will of people' (sattānaṃ atta-kāro). He also goes on to say that there is 'an element of origination' (nikkama-dhātu), an 'element of endeavour' (parakkama-dhātu), an 'element of strength' (thāma-dhātu) and an 'element of perseverance' (ṭhiti-dhātu) and an 'element of volitional effort' (upakkama-dhātu), which makes beings of their own accord act in various ways, and that this showed that there was such a thing as free-will (A. III. 337, 338).

All this goes to prove that the Buddha faced the problem of free-will at the time and reiterated the view that asserted the reality of human freedom or free will without denying at the same time that this free-will was conditioned but not wholly shaped or determined by factors which affected it. There are certain things beyond our powers but there are at the same time certain powers which one can exercise within limits. For example, I cannot, even if I tried my utmost, speak a thousand words a minute, but I can certainly vary my speed of utterance within limits merely to show that I have the power to do this. It is this power that we all have within limits for refraining from evil and doing good. The more we exercise this power the more freedom and spontaneity we acquire.

Many scholars have failed to see that Buddhism upheld a theory of non-deterministic causal conditioning along with the doctrine of free-will. As a result Buddhism has been represented by some Western scholars as a form of fatalism because of their misunderstanding of the doctrine of karma as well as the doctrine of causation.

This misunderstanding, however, is not limited to Western scholars. A Sinhala Buddhist scholar, a layman, has represented the Buddhist teaching on this matter as follows in a paper read before a Philosophers' Conference: 'What does Buddhism have to say regarding free-will? The question does not seem ever to have been asked of the Buddha, but, if he had been asked, he would probably have answered that the question does not arise or that it is inaccurately put. There can be no such thing as a free will outside the causal sequence which constitutes the world process' (G. P. Malalaskera, 'The Status of the Individual in Theravāda Buddhist Philosophy', in *The Status of the Individual in East and West*, Ed. Charles A. Moore, University of Hawaii Press, Honolulu,

1966, p. 73). Another Buddhist scholar, a monk, says the following: 'The question of Free Will has occupied an important place in Western thought and philosophy. But according to Conditioned Genesis, this question does not and cannot arise in Buddhist philosophy . . . Not only is the so-called free-will not free, but even the very idea of Free Will is not free from conditions' (Walpola Rahula, *What the Buddha Taught*, Gordon Fraser, Bedford, 1959, pp. 54–5).

These three doctrines, namely upholding the reality of free-will (kiriyavāda) as opposed to the denial of free-will (akiriyavāda) in the sense specified, upholding the reality of survival after death (atthi paro loko) as opposed to the denial of survival (natthi paro loko), and upholding the reality of moral causation (hetu-vāda) as opposed to the denial of moral causation (ahetu-vāda), form the basis of Buddhist ethics. They are upheld because they are considered to be verifiably true.

It is these doctrines which make individual moral responsibility meaningful. Without them there is no sense in which we can be said to be morally responsible for our actions, although we may be so socially. In the *Apaṇṇaka Sutta*, where the Buddha addresses rational sceptics, he states that even if one is sceptical about free-will, survival and moral causation, it would be pragmatic and rational to act on the basis that they are true rather than their opposites, for in such a case, whatever happens, we do not stand to lose. If we act on the basis that free-will, survival and moral causation are true, then if they turn out to be so, we would be happy in the next life, and if not true, praised by the wise in this life, whereas if we do not act on this basis, then, if they are true, we would be unhappy in the next life, and if they are not true, we would be condemned by the wise in this life for acting without a sense of moral responsibility.

While the ethics of good and evil (in a moral sense as opposed to what is merely socially good and evil) require the above three postulates, which, according to the Buddhist account of reality, are facts, the ethics of salvation from conditioned existence require the postulate of an Unconditioned Reality, which, according to Buddhism, is also a fact.

Man and the universe being what they are, thc ethical and spiritual life (which in a sense is part of it) is both possible and the most desirable in our interests as well as of others.

# 16

# The Buddhist Conception of Evil

We have shown that Buddhism considered the attainment of Nirvana to be intrinsically good. It was the highest state of well-being, characterised by bliss, perfection, realisation and freedom. It was a condition in which our finitude comes to an end, for 'there was no criterion with which to measure the person who has attained the goal' (atthaṃgatassa na pamānaṃ atthi, Sn. 1076). It was the most desirable state to attain, and the highest aesthetic experience, although it was to be realised only by shedding our self-centred desires.

In contrast, what falls short of Nirvanic reality is, to that extent, afflicted with the evils of unhappiness or suffering, imperfection, ignorance and the bondage of finite self-centred existence. The degree to which those in conditioned forms of existence are affected by these evils varies with their level of existence and the extent of their moral and spiritual development.

So all sentient beings are subject to evil in its various forms until they attain Nirvana. The evil they are subject to may be external and physical (natural or man-made), such as floods, accidents, nuclear weapons, etc., or they may be experienced in one's body in the form of illness. They may be psychological, such as the experience of pain or mental anguish. The evil may be moral, such as the presence of undesirable traits in us, such as jealousy, hypocrisy, ingratitude, etc. Or the evil which affects and afflicts us may be social and political, such as the experience of poverty, injustice, inequality or the lack of freedom.

HELL

Yet, whatever evils we may be subject to in our finite self-centred conditioned existence, there is no form of existence in the universe which is intrinsically evil according to the Buddhist texts. Nothing could be more intrinsically evil than the sufferings of an everlasting hell, from which there is no escape for eternity, but there is no such place, according to the Buddhist conception of the universe.

In fact, the Buddhist conception of hell was both enlightened and rational. The Buddha denounced some of the superstitious popular beliefs about hell held by the people at the time. For instance, he says in one place: 'When the average ignorant person makes an assertion to the effect that there is a Hell (pātāla) under the ocean, he is making a statement which is false and without basis. The word "hell" is a term for painful bodily sensations' (S. IV. 306).

This does not mean that we create our heavens and hells only in this life, and that there is, in fact, no after-life, for elsewhere the Buddha speaks of the worlds that he could observe with his clairvoyant vision, in which everything one senses and experiences (including the thoughts that occur to one) are foul, repulsive aad ugly (S. IV. 126), while other worlds are quite the opposite.

These are the 'hells' of the Buddhist texts, apart from the experience of 'hell' in this life itself. We learn from history about the existence of cannibalistic tribes in the past, not to speak of life in the concentration camps set up not so long ago in the centres of twentieth-century civilisation. As such, we need not necessarily look to other planets for the presence of sub-human forms of existence which are 'foul, repulsive and ugly'. Yet none of these states are permanent, even though they exist.

PROBLEM OF EVIL

The Buddha squarely faces the existence of evil in the universe. He sees things 'as they are' (yathābhūtaṃ) and wants his disciples, too, to look at things in this way through the eyes of a realist. There is no escape into a world of make-believe, no undue pessimism nor facile optimism. The Buddha says: 'There are religious teachers who, because of their state of confusion, do not recognise the difference between night and day, but I would treat night as night and day as day' (M. I. 21). Buddhism, therefore, frankly accepts the existence of both good and evil in the world of conditioned existence.

Evil becomes a problem only for a theist, who maintains that the world was created by a perfect Being, omniscient, omnipotent and infinitely good. In such a situation, it would be possible to account for evil by denying the omniscience, omnipotence or goodness of God, but then one would be denying that the world was the creation of a perfect Being. So the problem is – *Si Deus bonus, unde malum?* If God is good, whence cometh evil?

In order to account for evil with these presuppositions, some have denied outright the fact of evil, others have stated that evil is a privation or illusion, that evil is necessary as a component in the best of all possible worlds, which God necessarily creates. This last solution has, on the whole, been favoured by modern theists, but even this does not satisfactorily account for the suffering of animals, of little children and innocent people within the framework of orthodox theistic beliefs.

What is the Buddhist solution? The problem does not exist in the above form for thc Buddhist since he does not start with the theistic presumption that the world was created by a perfect Being. Instead, he accepts the fact of evil and argues on its basis that the world with all its imperfections could not be the creation of a perfect Being.

The argument is briefly stated as follows: 'If God (Brahmā)

is lord of the whole world and creator of the multitude of beings, then why (1) has he ordained misfortune in the world without making the whole world happy, or (2) for what purpose has he made a world with injustice, deceit, falsehood and conceit, or (3) the lord of beings is evil in that he has ordained injustice where there could have been justice?' (J. VI. 208).

The Buddhist is under no compunction to deny or explain away the fact of evil. If we deny the existence of evil, there would be no reason nor even the possibility of getting rid of it. If we justify it, it would still be unnecessary to try and eliminate it. But evil is real for the Buddhist and must be removed as far as possible at all its levels of existence for the good and happiness of mankind, by examining its causal origins.

This does not mean that Buddhism holds that all existence is evil. The Buddha is often represented by Western scholars as having said this or assumed such a stand.

The *Encyclopaedia of Religion and Ethics* says that 'existence ... seemed to the Buddha to be evil' (see article on *Good and Evil*). Yet nowhere has the Buddha said that even finite conditioned existence is wholly evil. What he has often said is that such existence has its good side or pleasantness (assāda) as well as its evil consequences (ādīnava), and considering the possibility of transcending such finite conditioned existence without ceasing to exist or continuing to exist in a spatio-temporal sense, it was desirable to do so.

## PRIMACY OF THE GOOD

Nor does Buddhism hold that evil predominates in nature. It is possible to take up different positions regarding the presence or primary of good or evil.

We can say that (1) good predominates over evil although both exist, or that (2) good alone exists but not evil, or that (3) evil predominates over good although both exist, or that

(4) evil alone exists but not good or that (5) both good and evil exist with equal strength and vigour (dualism) and there is a perpetual battle in the universe between them, or that (6) neither good nor evil exist in any strict sense (e.g. relativism, amoralism, illusionism (māyāvāda)).

Buddhism seems to favour the first point of view. It accepts the reality of both good and evil and seems to uphold the view that good predominates over evil.

The presence of some forms of evil, such as suffering has, it is said, a tendency to awaken us from our lethargic state of existence and induce belief in moral and spiritual values (dukkhūpanisā saddhā) (S. II. 1).

We are attached to the world because of the joys and satisfactions it affords us by way of the gratification of our desires. But because of the disappointments, frustrations, anguish and suffering that we also experience in the process, we seek to understand and transcend our finite conditioned existence.

So some forms of evil, such as suffering, have a tendency to make us seek the good. But, in general, the problem of evil for the Buddhist is to recognise evil as such, to look for its verifiable causes and, by removing the cause, eliminate evil as far as possible at all its level of existence.

To look for the metaphysical causes of evil is deemed to be intellectually atultifying and morally fruitless. If we are struck with an arrow, our immediate task should be to remove it rather than investigate the credentials of the person who shot it. We may be in a better position to do so after we have been healed. The Dhamma, as the Buddha pointed out, was comparable to a raft which has to be thrown aside after we have attained Nirvana with its help and acquired a more comprehensive picture of the totality of things. In the meantime, the presence of evil is a challenge to us and our task should be to get rid of it: 'One should conquer evil with good' (asādhuṃ sadhunā jine).

The baseless charge has been brought against Buddhism

that it is pessimistic, but it is a curious fact that it has given a less pessimistic account of both man and nature than some forms of theism. We have already pointed out that there is no conception of an 'eternal hell' in nature according to Buddhist teachings. Even man has never been regarded as predominantly evil.

Man is fundamentally good by nature, and the evil in him is an extraneous outcome of his saṃsāric conditioning. The mind of man is compared in the Buddhist texts to gold ore, which is said to have the defilements of iron, copper, tin, lead and silver, but when these impurities are removed, then the gold shines with its natural lustre. So does the mind when the evil is got rid of.

The Buddha states that 'the mind is naturally resplendent, though it is corrupted by adventitious defilements' (pabhassaraṃ idaṃ cittaṃ taṃ ca kho āgantukehi upakkilesehi upakkiliṭṭhaṃ). Man, therefore, despite the fact that he has committed sin (pāpa) and is capable of sinning is not addressed as a 'sinner' but as a 'meritorious being' (e.g. Siṇhala, piṇvatnī) because of his potentiality for good.

Even the evil that he commits is not due to his basic depravity or wickedness but to his ignorance. This ignorance can be got rid of and man himself is capable of doing so. Buddhism does not agree with the theist who holds that man in his present condition is so degenerate by nature that he is incapable of saving himself without the grace of an external power. The future of man is in his own hands; he is master of his fate. In denying an eternal hell, in not regarding man as a sinner who is incapable of attaining salvation by his own efforts, Buddhism gives a less pessimistic account of man and nature than is to be found in some forms of theism.

Although, in this respect, it upholds the primacy of the good, Buddhism is not an easy-going optimism, which ignores the evil in man and nature. A realistic view of nature is partly pessimistic in that one has to take cognisance of the darker side of things as well.

Many people do not, out of fear, wish to contemplate the fact that we are all liable to suffer from decay, disease and death. The Buddha, on the contrary, holds (like Socrates and Plato) that 'the contemplation of death' (maraṇānussati) is of therapeutic value in making for mental stability and peace. To this extent, Buddhism recommends a partly 'pessimistic outlook' (asubhānupassiṃ viharantaṃ) (Dh. 8), in so far as it is realistic and is a factor necessary to promote and establish one's personal happiness on firm foundations.

### MĀRA

Buddhist realism, therefore, takes stock of all that is evil in man and nature, so that we may understand evil for what it is and overcome it at all its levels of existence in so far as this can be done.

Death (mṛtyuḥ) had been personified prior to Buddhism and the *Śathapatha-Brāhmaṇa* refers to the legendary figure of 'Death, the Evil One' (mṛtyuḥ pāpmā). This conception reappears in the Buddhist scriptures as Māro Pāpimā, i.e. 'Death, the Evil One', who signifies all the evil associated with or causally related to the phenomenon of death. Since all conditioned existence is subject to death, Māra is said to hold sway over the entire universe.

The term Māra is formed of mṛ, to kill (cf. Latin, *mors*), and means 'killer or death'. In the scholastic tradition, the term is said to have four meanings. It may signify physical death (maccu-māra), it may denote the constituents of one's personality, which are subject to change and therefore to 'death' in this wider sense (khandha-māra), it may mean 'moral evil' or the defilements which are the cause of repeated (birth and) death (kilesa-māra), or it may refer to the Evil One as a person (devaputta-māra) who tempts and obstructs people who seek emancipation from conditioned existence by means of a life of moral and spiritual development.

In this last sense, Māra symbolises all the opposition and obstruction that spiritual seekers have to contend with, whether this be internal (psychological) or external (physical, social). It is difficult to say that there is no such opposition towards those who seek to do good when we know that outstanding teachers in history who tried to preach or establish a new universal ethic had to face not only opposition but even death at the hands of their own people, which provoked the Shavian remark that 'it is dangerous to be too good'.

The question is often asked as to whether Buddhism recognises the existence of such an Evil One as a person (such as Satan or the Devil). The forces (senā) of Māra as depicted in the Buddhist texts constitute merely the symbolic representation of evil in various forms. For example, the *Mahā Niddesa* speaks of the forces of Māra as consisting of 'lust (kāma), aversion (arati), hunger and thirst (khuppipāsā), desire (taṇhā), sloth and torpor (thīnamiddha), fear (bhīru), doubt regarding moral and spiritual truths and values (vicikicchā), hypocrisy (makkha), hardness of heart (thambha), the gain of praise, respect and fame obtained by false pretences (lābho siloko sakkāro micchāladdho ca yo yaso) as well as boasting about oneself while despising others (yo c'attānaṃ samukkaṃse pare ca avajānati)' (*Mahā Niddesa*, I. 96).

There are, however, situations in the Canon where Māra appears in person and criticises some of the teachings of the Buddha or propounds doctrines which are opposed to them. Does this not prove the personal existence of Māra? Even prior to Buddhism we find that the *Kaṭha Upaniṣad* employed the figure of Death or Mṛtyuḥ to impart an Ātman-doctrine. The entire teaching of the *Kaṭha Upaniṣad* is said to have been 'declared by Death' (mṛtyu-proktāṃ) (*Kaṭha*, 6.18), who does not appear in a derogatory role, probably because the functions of death, control and creation are in the hands of the Supreme Being. It would, therefore, not be surprising if the legendary figure of Māra is utilised as a literary device by the compilers of the Canon to indicate the Buddha's comments and criticisms of doctrines, belief in which was likely to prolong one's conditioned existence. On the other hand, we cannot rule out the possibility of higher intelligences in the cosmos, who believe profoundly in and like to propagate some of the views attributed to Māra.

However, it is quite evident that the figure of Māra is often introduced in the Canon for purely didactic purposes and no personal manifestation of evil is meant. In the *Nivāpa Sutta* (M. I. 151–60) it is said that a sower sows crops for the deer to come and eat. The first herd eat indulgently and fall an easy prey to the sower. The second herd, observing this, avoid the crops and repair to the forest close by, but, weakened by hunger, are forced to come and eat the crops and do so with avidity and thereby fall a prey to the sower. The third herd, observing what happened to the first two, partake of the crops without being infatuated and repair to a lair close by, which, however, is easily discovered by the sower, who is able to catch them. The fourth herd, observing the mistakes committed by the first three, repair to a lair to which the sower has no access and thereby escape.

Here, the sower is said to be Māra, the evil One, and crops constitute indulgence in the pleasures of the senses. The four herds constitute four types of religious sects. The first finds nothing wrong in free indulgence in the pleasures of sense and become an easy victim of Māra. The second resorts to asceticism but eventually returns to indulgence, the need for it being heightened by their repressions. The third exercises restraint in the enjoyment of sense-pleasures but their dogmatic beliefs about man and the world keep them within the realm and dominance of Māra. It is only the fourth, who follow a Buddhist way of life, who are successful in going beyond the clutches of Māra. There is nothing to suggest that Māra, in actual fact, operates as a personal entity here. The parable of the crops merely shows that ultimate salvation cannot be found within the realm of conditioned existence.

DESTRUCTION OF EVIL

The passage quoted from the *Niddesa* above, where various evils were figuratively referred to as 'the forces of Māra', ends by saying that 'It is only by conquering the forces of Māra that one attains happiness' (jetvā ca labhate sukhaṃ). The Buddha and the arahants, it is said, have conquered Māra and therefore can recognise him and do not fall a victim to his wiles. The *Dhammapada* recommends that we 'should fight Māra with the weapon of wisdom' (yodhetha Māraṃ paññāvudhena) (Dh. 40).

So the Buddhist attitude to evil is not to deny its presence or try to reconcile its existence with the creation of the world by a good God, but to observe its presence and, by studying its nature and causes, to eliminate it.

As far as one's personal evolution is concerned, one must develop the awareness and 'the will to prevent the arising of evil states of mind not arisen, the will to eliminate evil states of mind which have arisen, the will to make arise good states of mind which have not arisen and the will to preserve. develop, refine and perfect good states of mind which have arisen' (S. V. 268).

It is the same with social and political forms of evil. According to the Buddhist social contract theory of government, the people are ultimately responsible for the good government of the country. If the country is not properly governed, it is up to the people to ensure such a government in order to promote the material and spiritual welfare of the people by the promotion of the good and the elimination of evil in the body politic.

PIRIT

We have so far dealt with realistic forms of evil. But some of our fears (which are themselves evil) are based on irrational foundations, such as the fear of the unknown. At the time of the Buddha, such fears were allayed by magical and ritualistic means with the help of the chants and incantations of the *Atharva Veda* or the resort to demonological practices. Where the people were not mentally equipped to give up these beliefs and practices, what the Buddha did was to substitute Buddhist chants (paritta, safeguard) of a more meaningful character, which developed into the institution of pirit.

Instead of chanting in an unintelligible language, the Buddha used the language of the people. In doing so, he used it as a vehicle of instruction as well. For example, the *Maṇgala Sutta* (chanted as pirit) is an attempt to answer the question, 'What are the auspicious things?' The word mangala could also be ranslated as 'superstitious observance', and in one place the tBuddha, referring to the lay people at the time, says that they were 'superstitious' (gihī maṅgalikā) (Vin. II. 140). Now the list of 'auspicious things or observances' given in the *Maṅgala Sutta*, far from being superstitious, were factors or practices which contributed to the social and personal advancement of people. To take but one stanza, the Buddha says: 'a good education (bāhusaccaṃ) acquiring a technical skill (sippaṃ), a well-cultivated sense of discipline (vinayo ca susikkhito) and cultured speech (subhāsitā ca yā vācā) – these are the auspicious things' (S. 261). The practices recommended are of relevance to any civilised society.

So while the people derived a psychological satisfaction and a sense of security, by listening to this chant, they also received an education in the Dhamma. Those who listened with rapt attention, appreciated what was said and tried to live in accordance with the teachings, would also have the protection of the Dhamma, for it is said that 'the Dhamma protects him who lives in accordance with the Dhamma' (Dhammo have rakkhati Dhamma-cāriṃ).

# Index of Names


Ajita Kesakembali 27
Ālāra Kālāma 14
Ānanda 28, 107
Anaximander 90
Anukramani 59
Anuruddha 75, 100
Apollonius 92
Aristarchus 92
Augustine 18
Ayer, A. J. 161, 177

Baker, Anne 188
Barnett, S. A. 157
Basham, A. L. 67
Baynes, Norman H. 113
Bebbington, John 190
Beloff, John 158
Bernstein, M. 82
Bonnor, W. 95, 97
Brain, Lord 156
Bridey Murphy 189
Broad, C. D. 149, 150
Buddhaghosa 209, 220
Burt, Cyril 158

Cayce, Edward 195
Cerminara, Gina 195
Chang 169
Confucius 18, 19, 20
Conze, E. 113
Copernicus 92

Dahlke, Paul 204
Democritus 90
Ducasse, C. J. 162, 163, 189, 190

Eccles, John 158
Eng 169
Eysenck, H. J. 175, 176

Flew, A. 108, 109
Flournoy, Theodore 178, 186
Freud, S. 34, 172

Galileo 92
Geldarad, Frank A. 81
Giordano, Bruno 173, 174

Hart, Howell 155, 159
Hebb, H. O. 156
Herschel 92
Hick, John 111
Hilgard, Ernest R. 223
Hitler, Adolf 113

Imad Elewar 191, 192

Jacobi 203
Jayatilleke, K. N. 9
Jayatilleke, Pat 9
Johansson, Rune 118
Johnson, Raymond C. 194

Karunadasa, Y. 76
Keith, A. B. 67
Kern 204
Klebanoff 156

Lamont, C. 162, 163
Lao Tse 18
Leucippus 90

Lovell, A. C. B. 95

McDougall, William 187
McTaggart 149, 150, 154
Maeterlick, Maurice 142
Mahavira 12, 28, 44
Makkali Gosala 11, 105, 106, 107
Malalasekara 9, 247
Manu 56
Marcuse, F. L. 177
Martin, A. R. 178, 182
Miranda, H. C. 180

Newman, H. H. 169
Nyanatiloka 204, 205, 220

Opik, Ernst J. 94

Pakudha Kaccāyana 12, 27
Penfield, Wilder 155, 157
Philolaus 92
Pischel 203
Plato 18
Plotinus 18
Poussin, de la V. 51
Ptolemy 92
Purāṇa Kassapa 12
Pythagoras 17

Radhakrishnan, S. 56
Rashdall, Hastings 244, 245
Rodney, J. 82, 188

Sangarāva 99
Sañjaya Belaṭṭhiputta 12, 13
Śankara 22
Sāriputta 13
Schayer 203
Shapley, H. 94
Singer 156
Smart, J. J. C. 132
Smythies, J. R. 132
Stevenson, Ian 62, 191, 192, 193
Subha 56
Subhadda 29

Thiel, Rudolf 96, 101
Tigh, Virginia 189, 190
Towers, Geraldine 9

Uddaka Rāmaputta 14

Walpola Rahula 248
Walter, Grey 157
Wells, H. G. 18
White, W. C. 194
Widgery, Allan S. 142
Wilensky 156
Wiltshire, Martin 9
Woodward 101

Zoroaster 18
Zürcher, E. 19